BUSINESS CYCLE THEORY

for Tanja

[Y]*ou think I am attacking them for talking nonsense? Not a bit! I like them to talk nonsense. That's man's only privilege over all creation.*

Dmitri Prokofitch Razumihin in Fyodor Dostoyevsky's *Crime and Punishment*

BUSINESS CYCLE THEORY

Lutz G. Arnold

OXFORD
UNIVERSITY PRESS

OXFORD
UNIVERSITY PRESS

Great Clarendon Street, Oxford OX2 6DP

Oxford University Press is a department of the University of Oxford.
It furthers the University's objective of excellence in research, scholarship,
and education by publishing worldwide in

Oxford New York

Auckland Bangkok Buenos Aires Cape Town Chennai
Dar es Salaam Delhi Hong Kong Istanbul Karachi Kolkata
Kuala Lumpur Madrid Melbourne Mexico City Mumbai Nairobi
São Paulo Shanghai Taipei Tokyo Toronto

with an associated company in Berlin

Oxford is a registered trade mark of Oxford University Press
in the UK and in certain other countries

Published in the United States
by Oxford University Press Inc., New York

British Library Cataloguing in Publication Data

Data available

Library of Congress Cataloging-in-Publication Data

Arnold, Lutz G.
Business cycle theory/Lutz G. Arnold.
p. cm.
Includes bibliographical references.
1. Business cycles–History   2. Business cycles–Mathematical models.
3. Keynesian economics–Mathematical models.
4. Neoclassical school of economics–Mathematical models. I. Title.

HB3714.A76 2002   338.5'42–dc21   2002067191

ISBN 0-19-925681-0 (hbk.)
ISBN 0-19-925682-9 (pbk.)

10 9 8 7 6 5 4 3 2 1

Typeset by Newgen Imaging Systems (P) Ltd, Chennai, India
Printed in Great Britain
on acid-free paper by
T.J. International Ltd., Padstow, Cornwall

PREFACE

Business cycle theory is a broad and disparate field. Different schools of thought offer alternative explanations for cycles, often using different mathematical methods. This book provides a compact exposition of business cycle theory since Keynes. It puts the main theories—Keynesian economics, monetarism, new classical economics, the real business cycles theory, and new Keynesian economics—in a historical perspective by presenting them in the chronological order of their appearance and highlighting their differences and commonalities. It minimizes the necessary mathematical prerequisites by using a unifying mathematical approach: stochastic second-order difference equations, which are explained in detail in the book. Throughout the book, the international dimension of business cycles is acknowledged. The theoretical results obtained are compared to the empirical facts in separate boxes. A set of exercises at the end of each chapter can be used to deepen the understanding of the theories presented and to access related material.

Business cycle theory is concerned with why economies do not grow smoothly, but show recurrent fluctuations. Like its object of study, this book has undergone a sort of damped oscillation. It grew to about 300 pages as my Habilitationsschrift, then contracted by half, before I added some new material, and so on. My greatest thanks are due to my academic teacher Heinz Holländer. The first versions of the book developed in the stimulating climate at his chair for macroeconomics at the economics faculty of the University of Dortmund. Later on, his insightful comments helped shorten it. He also read the revised version and was, again, responsible for major improvements. In particular, the novel models presented in Sections 3.2, 6.2, and 6.3 were very much improved following his sometimes critical but always helpful suggestions. The book would look different without Heinz Holländer's major influence. Three anonymous Referees have also helped considerably to improve the book by pointing to the parts where additional material was required or the exposition was biased. I am indebted for helpful discussions, advice on selected parts of the book, and proofreading to Volker Arnold, Thomas Beissinger, Brian Browne, Peter Flaschel, Douglas Gale, Christoph Knoppik, Jürgen Meckl, Ulrich Teichmann, Uwe Walz, and Victor Zarnowitz, to conference and seminar participants at various places, and to many students

v

at the University of Dortmund, the Technical University of Dresden, and the University of Regensburg.

I will try to give answers to open questions in the book brought to my attention on my web page: http://www.uni-regensburg.de/Fakultaeten/WiWi/arnold/. Comments are welcome.

L.A.

CONTENTS

Contents

4   New Classical Economics

5   Real Business Cycles

Contents

Appendix 3

1
•••

INTRODUCTION

1.1 History of Business Cycle Theory

Aggregate production fluctuates markedly in capitalist economies. It has a strong positive trend, but far from growing smoothly, it fluctuates about this trend with sizeable amplitude. These fluctuations are called *business cycles*. Classical economists did not perceive output movements as cycles (i.e. as 'a sequence of events that is constantly repeated in the same order', Hansen 1964: 6). In their view, the supply of the factors of production, which grew relatively smoothly, determined aggregate production in normal times. At irregular intervals, the relatively smooth growth path was interrupted by sharp commercial crises. According to Hansen (1964: 216), the term 'commercial cycle' was first used in 1833 by the English journalist John Wade. Loyd (later Lord Overstone) coined the term 'cyclical' in relation to output movements in 1837: 'The history of what we are in the habit of calling the "state of trade" is [...] subject to various conditions which are periodically returning; it revolves apparently in an established cycle. First we find it in a state of quiescence, – next improvement, – growing confidence, – prosperity, – excitement, – overtrading, – convulsion, – pressure, – stagnation, – distress, – ending again in quiescence' (quoted from Persons 1927: 98). In 1860, Juglar published the first large-scale work devoted exclusively to business cycles. In the late nineteenth and early twentieth centuries, eminent economists were concerned with the theoretical explanation of business cycles; Cassel, Hawtrey, Hayek, Robertson, Schumpeter, Spiethoff, and Wicksell were a few among them (Haberler (1937/1941) provides a brilliant survey of their theoretical achievements). In the first half of the twentieth century, the US National Bureau of Economic Research (NBER) initiated a systematic investigation of the statistical regularities of observed business cycles (see Burns and Mitchell

1946). Keynes's (1936/1973) *General Theory of Employment, Interest and Money* shifted the problem of fluctuations in aggregate output to the centre of economic interest. Soon after the publication of the *General Theory*, the first mathematical business cycle models were developed by Hicks, Kalecki, Metzler, Samuelson, and others. Ever since, the explanation of business cycles has been at the centre of economic theorizing. This book gives an overview of the developments in mathematical business cycle theory since the *General Theory*.

1.2 Five Schools of Macroeconomic Thought

The exposition of the alternative theories is organized chronologically. Following Phelps (1990), the theories are classified as five *schools of macroeconomic thought*. However, the classification chosen differs somewhat from Phelps's; we distinguish between Keynesian economics, monetarism, new classical economics, the real business cycle (RBC) theory, and new Keynesian economics.

The development of *Keynesian economics* began in 1936 with the publication of the *General Theory*, which challenged the classical presumption that aggregate output is determined, in normal times, by the supply of the factors of production. Keynesian economics emphasizes the role aggregate demand plays in the determination of aggregate production and the role the government can play in creating additional demand in circumstances of low output due to lack of aggregate demand. Pioneering work was performed by Samuelson. Keynesian economics became the predominant school of macroeconomic thought and remained in this position until the late 1960s.

In the 1960s, growing discomfort with the Keynesian neglect of supply-side factors arose. M. Friedman initiated the *monetarist* counter-revolution, which brought the supply side back to the fore. The monetarist critique of Keynesian economics gave rise to a widely shared macroeconomic consensus in the late 1960s: the average rate of aggregate production is determined by supply-side factors. The interplay between aggregate supply (a monetarist Phillips curve) and aggregate demand (the Keynesian IS–LM system) causes fluctuations in aggregate production around the average level. This macroeconomic consensus assigns to the government a much less important role than does the original Keynesian theory.

In the early 1970s, under the lead of Lucas, *new classical economics* appeared on the scene. New classical economics popularized the use of rational expectations in macroeconomics. It shows that the effectiveness of government policies is strongly dependent on the way in which expectations are formed. The new classical policy ineffectiveness proposition asserts that only unanticipated demand policies affect aggregate economic activity.

In the early 1980s, Prescott and others initiated the development of the RBC theory. The RBC approach to business cycles readopts the classical view that output determination is a supply-side phenomenon. It demonstrates that, given exogenous variations in total factor productivity, calibrated versions of pure supply-side models without any market imperfections are capable of generating output movements and co-movements of other macro variables that resemble closely the observed time series. The RBC theory thus interprets observed output fluctuations as the optimal outcome of firms' and households' optimizing behaviour under rational expectations, given exogenous variations in total factor productivity and, therefore, denies the need for any kind of effort to stabilize the economy. The position of the RBC theory in economics is somewhat ambiguous. The RBC theory became the dominant approach to business cycles in professional journals. Most economics textbooks, by contrast, continued to rely on the older Keynesian-monetarist consensus or on new Keynesian explanations of business cycles.

Our fifth school of macroeconomic thought, *new Keynesian economics*, encompasses a heterogeneous set of models developed since the 1970s. Broadly speaking, new Keynesian economics is concerned with deriving Keynesian-style propositions from RBC-style models with rational expectations and optimizing behaviour. Attention is focused on the explanation of nominal and real rigidities, on the role of firms' balance sheets in business cycles, and on the impact of extrinsic uncertainty on economic activity. Leading proponents of the new Keynesian approach are Bernanke, Blanchard, Mankiw, and Stiglitz.

1.3 Modelling Business Cycles

The cycle is not a phenomenon regulated by a mathematical law.
        Hansen (1964: 281) about Tugan–Baranowsky's view of the business cycle

Describing business cycles

Traditionally, following Lord Overstone and Juglar, business cycles have been regarded as somewhat disturbed sine-like waves. This view is inherent, for instance, in Keynes's (1936/1973: 313–14) description of a cycle: 'By a cyclical movement we mean that as the system progresses in, e.g. the upward direction, the forces propelling it upward at first gather force and have a cumulative effect on one another but gradually lose their strength until at a certain point they tend to be replaced by forces operating in the opposite direction; which in turn gather force for a time and accentuate one another, until they too, having reached their maximum development, wane and give place to their opposite'. The view of business cycles as disturbed sine waves is also consistent with the NBER studies, which are concerned with characterizing the lengths, amplitudes, and turning points of observed cycles (see Box 1.1). According to the NBER studies, postwar US business cycles are characterized by an average duration of roughly five years from trough-to-trough, which can be split into a long expansion and a short contraction phase. In other countries, the average duration of full cycles tends to be longer, but a similar pattern with long expansions and short contractions arises. A crucial observation is that investment is much more volatile than aggregate production. This had been stressed before the NBER studies by Cassel, Spiethoff, Tugan–Baranowsky, Wicksell, and many others. Cassel (1932: 552) went so far as to assert that 'the alternation between boom and slump is fundamentally a variation in the production of fixed capital, but has no direct connection with the rest of production.' Koopmans criticized the NBER studies as 'measurement without theory'.

....

Box 1.1 Characterizing business cycles

Zarnowitz (1992a) presents a recent update of the NBER business cycles chronology. In the period 1857–1990, the US experienced thirty full trough-to-trough cycles. The average duration of a full cycle was 53 months. Expansions (from trough-to-peak) lasted 35 months, contractions (from peak-to-trough) 18 months on average. In the postwar period 1945–90, nine full cycles with an average duration of 61 months were observed, expansions lasted 50 months, contractions 11 months. Thus, while the duration of full cycles was roughly constant, expansions have become longer and contractions shorter. (Including the unusually long 1991–2001 cycle, the average duration rises to 56 months for 1857–2001 and to 67 months for the postwar period.) In other countries, business cycle durations tend to be longer, but a similar pattern with long upswings and short contractions arises. Fluctuations tend to have become less severe in the postwar period. For instance, the maximum peak-to-trough decline in quarterly real GNP was −4.9 per cent in the 1973–75 recession, as opposed to −32.6 per cent during the Great Depression 1929–33. Romer (1986) highlights, however, that if one takes account of poor data quality before the First World War, the moderation of business fluctuations compared to the pre-First World War period is not as pronounced as it appears at first glance. One of the most striking observations about business cycles is that investment and the production of durable consumer goods are much more volatile than aggregate production: 'business cycles, which developed in the age of industrialization, still affect most strongly industries producing goods, especially durables' (Zarnowitz 1992a: 49).

....

More recently, it has become customary to characterize business cycles by means of the statistical properties of observed time series for detrended and deseasonalized real GNP. Viewed from this angle, there are three important characteristics of business cycles (see Box 1.2). First, even after eliminating trend and season, there remains some variability in real GNP. The standard deviation of detrended quarterly real GNP equals about 2 per cent if the Hodrick–Prescott detrending procedure, which attributes some of the variability in observed GNP to the trend, is chosen. With linear detrending, the standard deviation of quarterly real GNP rises to about 5 per cent. Second, real GNP movements are persistent. That is, the correlation between quarterly real GNP at nearby dates is positive and great in absolute value. Third, the autocorrelation with lags of 5–8 quarters is negative. That is, there is reversion: if output is high today, it is likely to be low two years later, and vice versa. Also, these studies confirm that the fluctuations in investment and consumer durables are much more severe than those in aggregate production: the standard deviation of investment and consumer durables is about three times as great as the standard deviation of aggregate production.

In the financial press, the variable cited most frequently in order to characterize the economy's position in the business cycle is annual real GNP growth. A popular definition of a recession is two successive quarters of shrinking (deseasonalized) quarterly GNP.

Modelling business cycles

Throughout this book, following Frisch's (1933) suggestion, *business cycles are modelled by means of stochastic second-order difference equations*. Why is this a useful approach? Because the solution to a stochastic second-order difference equation can be viewed either as a disturbed sine wave or as a time series with variability, persistence, and reversion, as explained in the remainder of this section. It is, thus, compatible both with the traditional characterization and with the time series characterization of observed business cycles. We do not claim that the approach chosen is superior to alternative methods of modelling business cycles. But we hold that it is *one* useful way to model cycles.

A stochastic second-order difference equation relates a variable y (in discrete time) to two lagged values of the variable y itself and to a random variable ϵ. We will focus our attention on linear equations where the random variable is white noise:

$$y_t + a_1 y_{t-1} + a_2 y_{t-2} = \epsilon_t, \tag{1.1}$$

where a_1 and a_2 are constants and ϵ is distributed independently and identically with mean zero.

....

Box 1.2 Characterizing business cycles by means of the statistical properties of observed time series for GNP

Table 1.1 Data on US quarterly detrended and deseasonalized GNP y_t over the period 1950–79

$\hat{\sigma}$	$\hat{\rho}_1$	$\hat{\rho}_2$	$\hat{\rho}_3$	$\hat{\rho}_4$	$\hat{\rho}_5$	$\hat{\rho}_6$	$\hat{\rho}_7$	$\hat{\rho}_8$
1.80%	0.84	0.57	0.27	−0.01	−0.20	−0.30	−0.38	−0.44

Source: Robert Hodrick and Edward Prescott (1997). Postwar U.S. Business Cycles: An Empirical Investigation. *Journal of Money Credit and Banking* **29**(1), 5. Copyright © 1997 by The Ohio State University Press. All Rights Reserved. Table reprinted with permission.

Table 1.1 reports data about the US quarterly detrended and deseasonalized GNP y_t over the period 1950–79. The detrending is performed using the Hodrick–Prescott filter: the logarithm of deseasonalized quarterly GNP x_t ($t = 1, \dots, T+1$) is split into trend z_t and cycle y_t. The cyclical component of GNP y_t is determined as the solution to

$$\min_{\{y_t\}_{t=1}^T} : \sum_{t=1}^T y_t^2 + 1600 \sum_{t=2}^T (\Delta z_{t+1} - \Delta z_t)^2, \quad z_t = x_t - y_t$$

(Δ is the difference operator: $\Delta y_t \equiv y_t - y_{t-1}$). y_t is approximately equal to the percentage deviation of GNP from trend. The variance of detrended GNP is defined as $\hat{\sigma}^2 \equiv (1/T) \sum_{t=1}^T y_t^2$ (the mean of y_t is zero because of detrending). The correlation with lag j is $\hat{\rho}_j \equiv (1/T) \sum_{t=j+1}^T (y_t y_{t-j})/\hat{\sigma}^2$. Three facts are noteworthy. First, even after detrending and deseasonalizing aggregate output, there remains some variability: on average, aggregate output deviates by 1.80 per cent from the trend. The amplitude of y_t is about 4 per cent. Second, output fluctuations are persistent: the autocorrelation with low lag values is positive and large; $\hat{\rho}_1$ is close to one. Third, output fluctuations show reversion: the autocorrelation with longer lags is negative. For instance, $\hat{\rho}_8 = -0.44$. Hence, if aggregate output is high today, the economy is likely to be in a recession in eight quarters. Moreover, Hodrick and Prescott (1997: 8) report that the standard deviations of fixed investment and consumer durables (also detrended using the Hodrick–Prescott filter) equal 5.1 and 5.6 per cent, respectively. That is, investment is about three times as volatile as aggregate production. Similar figures are found for different countries.

Different detrending methods yield different figures for the cyclical component of GNP (see, e.g. Canova 1998). With linear detrending, the standard deviation of y_t equals about 4 per cent and the amplitude 7 per cent. With first-order differencing, one obtains quarterly growth rates, which display standard deviation and amplitude equal to 1 and 2.5 per cent, respectively. An attractive property of the Hodrick–Prescott filter is that the implied dates of the turning points are roughly coincident with the dates identified in the NBER chronologies. With linear detrending, on the other hand, the cycles are longer. With first-order differencing, a very irregular series (i.e. very short cycles) is obtained.

....

There is (unless $1 + a_1 + a_2 = 0$) a unique y^* such that y is constant ($y_t = y_{t-1} = y_{t-2}$) in the absence of shocks ($\epsilon = 0$), namely $y^* = 0$. Suppose for a moment that for a given time span no shocks occur: $\epsilon_t = 0$ and

$y_t + a_1 y_{t-1} + a_2 y_{t-2} = 0$, for $t = 0,\ 1,\ 2,\ \ldots$. It can be shown (see Appendix 1) that if

$$a_1^2 < 4a_2,$$

the solution to the non-stochastic equation $y_t + a_1 y_{t-1} + a_2 y_{t-2} = 0$ obeys

$$y_t = A\sqrt{a_2}^{\,t} \cos(\omega t - e),$$

where $A\,(\neq 0), \omega$, and e are constants emerging in the derivation of the formula. y_t then displays an oscillatory movement. If, in addition,

$$a_2 < 1,$$

then these oscillations are damped, and y converges to its steady state $y^* = 0$. Suppose the conditions for the emergence of damped cycles in the absence of shocks are satisfied. Suppose further that $y_{-2} = y_{-1} = 0$. Then, a shock $\epsilon_0 \neq 0$ occurs, followed by a series of $\epsilon_t = 0$ realizations ($t = 1, 2, \ldots$). The shock moves y away from the steady state: $y_0 = \epsilon_0$. Afterwards, the deterministic dynamics described above apply and y converges to zero in damped oscillations. Thus, a one-off shock $\epsilon \neq 0$ causes a damped sine-like movement of y; the impulse response is damped cyclical (see Fig. 1.1a). The behaviour of the solution to the stochastic difference equation (1.1) in the presence of recurrent shocks can, thus, be regarded as a series of superimposed damped oscillations. This is Frisch's (1933) central insight. We will repeat this impulse-response exercise at various places in the analysis in order to grasp the economic mechanisms responsible for the occurrence of business cycles. Notice that $a_2 > 0$ is a necessary condition for an oscillatory solution ($a_2 > a_1^2/4$). Linear first-order equations ($a_2 = 0$) cannot have an oscillatory solution; if, e.g. $-1 < a, < 0$, the impulse-response function is monotonic (see Fig. 1.1b). One strand of the business cycle literature focuses on endogenous cycles which emerge in *nonlinear* first-order equations. These models often give rise to chaos, that is, non-periodic and non-convergent dynamics, as well. We do not consider such models in this book and mention them in the suggestions for further reading.

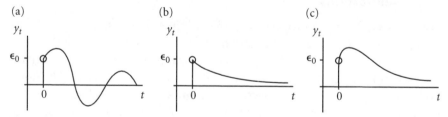

Fig. 1.1 Impulse-response functions.

Alternatively, the solution y_t of (1.1) can be described by means of its stochastic properties. Taking expectations in (1.1) yields $Ey_t = 0$; y_t is stationary. Let $\sigma^2 \equiv Ey_t^2$ denote the variance of y_t, and $\rho_j \equiv E(y_t y_{t-j})/\sigma^2$ the autocorrelation with lag j. The variance of ϵ_t is denoted by σ_ϵ^2. Evidently, y_t shows variability in the presence of recurrent shocks ($\sigma_\epsilon^2 > 0$): The variance of y_t is proportional to the variance of ϵ_t (see Appendix 1):

$$\sigma^2 = \frac{1 + a_2}{(1 - a_2)\left[(1 + a_2)^2 - a_1^2\right]}\sigma_\epsilon^2.$$

It can be shown (see Appendix 1) that the autocorrelation function, ρ_j, obeys

$$\rho_1 = -\frac{a_1}{1 + a_2}, \qquad \rho_2 = \frac{a_1^2}{1 + a_2} - a_2$$

and

$$\rho_j + a_1 \rho_{j-1} + a_2 \rho_{j-2} = 0, \tag{1.2}$$

for all $j > 2$. Assume that the conditions $a_1^2 < 4a_2$ and $a_2 < 1$ for damped oscillations, in the absence of shocks, are satisfied. Then, since $a_2 > 0$, if

$$a_1 < 0,$$

there is positive autocorrelation (persistence): $\rho_1 > 0$. Moreover, given ρ_1 and ρ_2, the second-order difference equation (1.2) determines ρ_j for all $j > 2$. The coefficients of ρ_{j-1} and ρ_{j-2} in this equation are the same as those of y_{t-1} and y_{t-2}, respectively, in (1.1). Therefore, like the solution y_t to (1.1) with $\epsilon_t = 0$, ρ_j displays damped oscillations. The period of the oscillations y_t displays in the absence of shocks is $2\pi/\omega$. That is, in the absence of shocks, if y is high, it will become low π/ω periods later and high again $2\pi/\omega$ periods later. In the presence of shocks, the autocorrelation with lag $2\pi/\omega$ is great. Hence, if y is high, it is likely to become low π/ω periods later and high again $2\pi/\omega$ periods later: the solution displays reversion.

Two qualifications

We have seen that for appropriate parameter values the solution to a stochastic second-order difference equation can be described as a disturbed sine wave or as a time series with variability, persistence, and reversion. So, it is compatible with both the traditional and the modern way of characterizing business cycles. One could raise the objection that our so-called 'modern' notion of business cycles is too deeply rooted in the tradition of viewing cycles as disturbed sine-like waves. In fact, while finding oscillatory dynamics was the main task of the early writers in mathematical business cycle theory, model builders today often do not aim at such oscillatory behaviour. Some argue that the noteworthy features of business cycles are variability and persistence. For instance, Blinder and Fischer (1981: 277) define business cycles as 'serially correlated deviations of output from trend'. On this view, the reversion property is inessential, and business cycles can be modelled by means of stochastic first-order difference equations with $a_1 > 0$ (i.e. $\rho_1 = -a_1 > 0$). Others, notably proponents of the RBC approach, emphasize that the wave-like movement stressed by the traditional view is not necessary for the presence of turning points. A turning point also arises if the response of GNP to a one-off shock is a hump-shaped function, that is, if GNP rises for some periods and then converges monotonically to its trend (see Fig. 1.1c). This hump-shaped impulse-response function is what many macroeconometric models predict (see Box 1.3). The most direct way to obtain a hump-shaped impulse-response function is to assume that y_t depends not only on the current realization, but also on lagged values of a random disturbance term. For instance, let $y_t + a_1 y_{t-1} + a_2 y_{t-2} = \epsilon_t + b\epsilon_{t-1}$. Suppose y_t converges monotonically (i.e. without oscillations) in the absence of shocks and consider a one-off shock $\epsilon_0 > 0$. Then, $y_0 = \epsilon_0$ and $y_1 = (b - a_1)\epsilon_0$. If $b - a_1 > 1$, the impulse-response function is hump shaped: first, y_t rises, but then it converges to zero.

....

Box 1.3   Hump shapes and unit roots in GNP movements

According to Blanchard and Fischer (1989: 9), cyclical US GNP y_t from 1973 to 1987 is related to two lagged values of itself and to the current and two lagged values of a disturbance term ϵ_t with $\sigma_\epsilon = 1$ per cent as follows:

$$y_t - 1.31y_{t-1} + 0.42y_{t-2} = \epsilon_t - 0.06\epsilon_{t-1} + 0.25\epsilon_{t-2}.$$

Alternatively, the growth rate of (undetrended) GNP Δy_t can be described by (Blanchard and Fischer 1989: 10)

$$\Delta y_t - 0.2\Delta y_{t-1} = c + \epsilon_t + 0.08\epsilon_{t-1} + 0.24\epsilon_{t-2},$$

where $\sigma_\epsilon = 1$ per cent and $c/0.8$ is the average growth rate. The first equation has a hump-shaped impulse-response function: y_t rises for three quarters (to $y_2 = 1.47\epsilon_0$) and then falls monotonically to zero. The second equation is a stationary process for the growth rate of GNP. Since the coefficient on lagged GNP growth is relatively small in absolute value, GNP growth is close to a random walk with drift. In fact, Nelson and Plosser (1982) and many subsequent authors demonstrate that standard unit-root tests fail to reject the hypothesis that GNP has a unit root.

....

A second objection relates to the fact that we have taken it for granted that business cycle movements are stationary fluctuations about a given trend. Nelson and Plosser (1982) have objected that this distinction between trend and cycle is artificial. They hold that the dynamic forces that yield trend growth and variability are in fact one and the same, so that separating trend and cycle is economically meaningless. Rather, one should regard GNP *growth* as generated by a stationary stochastic difference equation with a positive mean. This process, then, explains both growth (since the mean is positive) and fluctuations (since there is noise). As mentioned in Box 1.2, there is little persistence in GNP growth movements. So GNP growth, $\Delta y_t \equiv y_t - y_{t-1}$, can be modelled as $\Delta y_t = \gamma + \epsilon_t$, where γ is the average growth rate. That is, GNP movements follow a random walk with drift.

Bearing these objections in mind, we will model business cycles by means of stochastic second-order difference equations for the level of GNP in what follows. Consistent with the way Keynesian and monetarist economists analysed business cycles, we spend much effort on finding oscillatory dynamics in Chapters 2 and 3 and say that GNP 'displays business cycles' if it shows variability, persistence, and reversion. As new classical and new Keynesian authors deemphasize the reversion property, we focus on the first-order special case of second-order difference equations in Chapters 4 and 6. In Chapter 5 on the RBC theory, we come back briefly to non-oscillatory equations with hump-shaped impulse-response functions.

Co-movements

Many economists agree that the most notable regularities of observed business cycles concern not output movements themselves but the co-movements of other macroeconomic variables over the business cycle. Lucas (1977: 218) writes that 'with respect to the qualitative behavior of co-movements among series, *business cycles are all alike*'. We have seen already that the components of GNP display procyclical co-movements, with investment and spending on consumer durables being much more volatile than aggregate output (see Boxes 1.1 and 1.2). Box 1.4 summarizes some further stylized facts about the co-movements of other macro variables, which give some first hints at the working of business cycles. For instance, different sectors of the macroeconomy tend to move together, which justifies the use of aggregative models. Variations in hours worked are primarily due to variations in employment, which suggests that involuntary unemployment is an important part of the picture. Procyclical factor costs might help explain turning points. The high volatility of corporate profits and the strongly procyclical character of

Box 1.4 Co-movements

Over the business cycle, different sectors of the economy move closely together. Inventory investment is procyclical and especially volatile. Though it contributes no more than roughly half a per cent to GNP on average, decreases in inventory investment accounted for an astonishing 68 per cent of the decreases in aggregate production in the US postwar recessions till 1982 (Blinder and Holtz-Eakin 1986: 185). As for the labour market, hours worked are procyclical, most of the variation in hours worked is due to movements into and out of the labour force, rather than variations in hours worked per capita, and the real wage rate is procyclical, but shows little variability (details in Section 5.4). Short-term interest rates are procyclical. Money and GNP are strongly positively correlated (details in Section 3.2). The same holds true for credit and GNP, as stressed by B. Friedman (1983: 163): 'the relationship between economic activity and the public's outstanding credit liabilities exhibits the same degree of regularity and stability as does the relationship between economic activity and the public's holdings of money balances'. Corporate profits are procyclical and extremely volatile: the standard deviation of profits is 10.49 per cent, more than five times that of GNP (Boldrin and Horvath 1995: 974). Inventory investment, profits, and money are leading indicators. Further, procyclical leading indicators include hours per capita, the yield spread (the difference between long-term and short-term interest rates), new orders, new building permits, new business incorporations, and business confidence. Liabilities of business failures and the *Economist's* 'R-word index' (the number of articles in a specified set of newspapers which includes the word 'recession') are countercyclical leading indicators.

credit suggests that firms' balance sheets play a major role in business cycle movements. Of special interest for forecasting are leading indicators, whose co-movements with GNP are characterized by significant leads. Box 1.4 lists some of the most prominent leading indicators.

1.4 Summary

1. Business cycles came to be regarded as such in the nineteenth century.
2. There are five schools of thought which provide alternative explanations for business cycles: Keynesian economics, monetarism, new classical economics, the RBC theory, and new Keynesian economics.
3. Business cycles can be viewed as disturbed sine wave-like movements in aggregate production. Alternatively, business cycles can be characterized with the statistical properties of observed time series for aggregate output: aggregate production displays variability, persistence, and reversion.

4. As suggested by Frisch, business cycles can be modelled by means of stochastic second-order difference equations. The solution to a stochastic second-order difference equation can be viewed as a disturbed sine wave. For appropriate parameter values, it features variability, persistence, and reversion.
5. The co-movements of many macroeconomic variables show a high degree of conformity with GNP.

Further Reading

Hansen (1964: Part III) provides a brilliant survey of the history of business cycles since the eighteenth century. A lucid discussion of the theoretical achievements can be found in Haberler (1937/1941). Zarnowitz (1992a, b) presents recent versions of the NBER business cycles chronology. An informative survey of the literature about the statistical characterization of observed GNP series is to be found in Canova (1998). Any textbook on economic dynamics, e.g. Gandolfo (1996), can be consulted for a treatment of non-stochastic second-order difference equations. On stochastic second-order difference equations, see Pindyck and Rubinfield (1991). For an introduction to endogenous cycles and chaos in nonlinear first-order systems, see Goodwin and Pacini (1992).

References

Blanchard, O. J. and Fischer, S. (1989). *Lectures on Macroeconomics*. Cambridge, MA: MIT Press.

Blinder, A. S. and Fischer, S. (1981). 'Inventories, Rational Expectations, and the Business Cycle'. *Journal of Monetary Economics*, 8: 277–304.

—— and Holtz-Eakin, D. (1986). 'Inventory Fluctuations in the United States since 1929', in R. J. Gordon (ed.), *The American Business Cycle—Continuity and Change*. Chicago: University of Chicago Press, pp. 183–236.

Boldrin, M. and Horvath, M. (1995). 'Labor Contracts and Business Cycles'. *Journal of Political Economy*, 103: 972–1004.

Burns, A. F. and Mitchell, W. C. (1946). *Measuring Business Cycles*. New York: NBER.

Canova, F. (1998). 'Detrending and Business Cycle Facts'. *Journal of Monetary Economics*, 41: 475–512.

Cassel, G. (1932). *Theory of Social Economy*, vol. II. New York: Harcourt, Brace & Co.

Friedman, B. M. (1983). 'The Roles of Money and Credit in Macroeconomic Analysis', in J. Tobin (ed.), *Macroeconomics, Prices and Quantities, Essays in Memory of Arthur Okun*. Oxford: Basil Blackwell, pp. 161–89.

Frisch, R. (1933). 'Propagation Problems and Impulse Problems in Dynamic Economics', in *Economic Essays in Honor of Gustav Cassel*. London: George Allen and Unwin, pp. 171–205.

Gandolfo, G. (1996). *Economic Dynamics*, 3rd edn. Berlin: Springer.

Goodwin, R. M. and Pacini, P. M. (1992). 'Nonlinear Economic Dynamics and Chaos: An Introduction', in A. Vercelli and N. Dimitri (eds), *Macroeconomics: A Survey of Research Strategies*. Oxford: Oxford University Press.

Haberler, G. (1st edn 1937/cited edn 1941). *Prosperity and Depression*. Geneva: League of Nations.

Hansen, A. H. (1964). *Business Cycles and National Income*, expanded edn. New York: W. W. Norton.

Hodrick, R. J. and Prescott, E. C. (1997). 'Postwar U.S. Business Cycles: An Empirical Investigation'. *Journal of Money, Credit and Banking*, 29: 1–16.

Keynes, J. M. (1st edn 1936/ cited edn 1973). *The General Theory of Employment, Interest and Money*. London: Macmillan.

Lucas, R. E., Jr. (1977). 'Understanding Business Cycles', in K. Brunner and A. Meltzer (eds), *Stabilization of the Domestic and International Economy*. Amsterdam: North-Holland, pp. 7–29.

Nelson, C. R. and Plosser, C. I. (1982). 'Trends and Random Walks in Macroeconomic Time Series: Some Evidence and Implications'. *Journal of Monetary Economics*, 10: 139–62.

Persons, W. M. (1927). 'Theories of Business Fluctuations: I. A Classification of the Theories'. *Quarterly Journal of Economics*, 41: 94–128.

Phelps, E. S. (1990). *Seven Schools of Macroeconomic Thought*. Oxford: Clarendon Press.

Pindyck, R. S. and Rubinfield, D. L. (1991). *Econometric Models and Economic Forecasts*, 3rd edn. New York: McGraw-Hill.

Romer, C. (1986). 'Is the Stabilization of the Postwar Economy a Figment of the Data?' *American Economic Review*, 76: 314–34.

Zarnowitz, V. (1992*a*). 'What Is a Business Cycle?', in M. T. Belongia and M. R. Garfinkel (eds), *The Business Cycle: Theories and Evidence. Proceedings of the Sixteenth Annual Economic Policy Conference of the Federal Reserve Bank of St. Louis*. Boston: Kluwer Academic Publishers, pp. 4–72.

—— (1992*b*). *Business Cycles: Theory, History, Indicators, and Forecasting*. Chicago: Chicago University Press.

KEYNESIAN ECONOMICS

2.1 Introduction

The central Keynesian proposition is [. . .] the principle of effective demand.

Tobin (1993: 46)

In classical economics, aggregate production is determined (except in times of severe crises) on the economy's supply side: factor supplies and technology jointly determine how much an economy produces. Say's law explains why aggregate demand (AD) is not a matter of concern: the level of aggregate income generated in the production process is equal to the value of aggregate production, and income not spent on consumption is channelled to investors in the capital market. So the sum of consumption and investment (AD) is equal to aggregate income and the value of aggregate production—supply creates its own demand. Keynes's (1936/1973) *General Theory of Employment, Interest and Money* revolutionized economic theory because, turning the classical view upside-down, Keynes put AD at the centre of the determination of aggregate production. We use the label 'Keynesian economics' for theories in which the demand side has a role to play in the determination of equilibrium aggregate production.

This chapter reviews some of the most important developments in Keynesian economics: the Keynesian income expenditure analysis (Section 2.2), the multiplier accelerator model (Section 2.3), the Hicks–Fleming–Mundell model (Section 2.4) and aggregate supply–aggregate demand (AS–AD) analysis (Section 2.5). Section 2.6 summarizes the main results.

2.2 Income Expenditure Analysis

I myself believe the broad significance of the *General Theory* to be in the fact that it provides a relatively realistic, complete system for analyzing the level of effective demand and its fluctuations. [...] With respect to the level of total purchasing power and employment, Keynes denies that there is an *Invisible Hand* channeling the self centered action of each individual to the social optimum. This is the sum and substance of his heresy.

Samuelson (1946: 192)

Model

Suppose aggregate production is characterized by the continuously differentiable production function, $Y = F(L)$, which relates aggregate output Y to aggregate employment L and satisfies the standard requirements $F(0) = 0$ and $F'(L) > 0 > F''(L)$. Suppose further that the supply of labour $\bar{L}$ (>0) is inelastic. Then, full employment production, $\bar{Y} \equiv F(\bar{L})$, is likewise exogenous. In the classical view, equilibrium aggregate production is $\bar{Y}$. Can equilibrium aggregate production fall short of $\bar{Y}$?

Keynes's answer to this question is yes, because of insufficient AD. Income expenditure analysis represents the simplest way to understand the reasoning behind Keynes's answer. The AD for goods Y^d is made up of four components: consumption C, investment I, government expenditure G, and net exports X ($X = 0$ in a closed economy). Assume consumption is a linear function of disposable income $Y - T$, where T denotes taxes: $C = A + c(Y - T)$, with $A > 0$ and $0 < c < 1$. All other demand components, including investment, are assumed to be exogenous and non-negative:

$$Y^d = A + c(Y - T) + I + G + X.$$

The goods market is in equilibrium. Aggregate production Y is equal to AD Y^d:

$$Y = Y^d.$$

Equilibrium

Only one level of aggregate production Y^* yields an equilibrium in the goods market (see Fig. 2.1):

$$Y^* = \frac{A + I + G + X - cT}{1 - c}. \qquad (2.1)$$

The sum of the autonomous expenditure components is multiplied by the factor $1/(1 - c)$, the Keynesian multiplier. In general equilibrium, aggregate production Y cannot exceed Y^*. For firms correctly anticipate that they would be unable to sell the total of the goods produced ($Y > Y^d$, for all $Y > Y^*$). Assume $Y^* < \bar{Y}$ (as in Fig. 2.1). Then Y^* gives equilibrium aggregate production. Labour demand equals $L^* = F^{-1}(Y^*) < \bar{L}$ (see Fig. 2.1). There is unemployment due to lack of AD. In Keynes's (1936/1973: 27) own words (government expenditure G and net exports X are ignored): 'to justify any given amount of employment there must be an amount of current investment sufficient to absorb the excess of total output over what the community chooses to consume when employment is at the given level'. If the amount of current investment is lower, unemployment prevails. Why does Say's law fail to hold? For $Y = Y^*$, we have $Y = Y^d$. When production and income rise above Y^*, the increase in income is split into additional consumption and additional saving. But, since investment is exogenous, the additional funds saved are not channelled to investors. Hence, the increase in the sum of

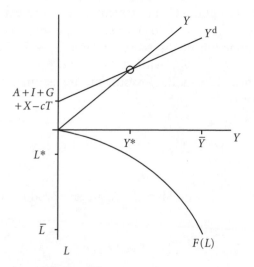

Fig. 2.1 The income expenditure model.

consumption and investment is smaller than the increase in aggregate income and production—supply does not create its own demand.

Both increases in government expenditure and tax cuts raise aggregate output. A debt-financed increase in government expenditure has multiplier effects, equilibrium aggregate production rising by a multiple of the fiscal stimulus: $\partial Y^*/\partial G = 1/(1 - c) > 1$. By contrast, 'money does not matter'. The supply of money does not have a role to play in the determination of aggregate output.

2.3   The Multiplier Accelerator Model

Maybe the most famous second-order difference equation in economics is the one associated with Samuelson's multiplier accelerator model.

Sargent (1979: 184)

Model

Shortly after the invention of Keynesian economics, Samuelson (1939) dis-covered that a simple dynamic extension to the income expenditure model is capable of generating business cycles. In this section, we develop a variant of Samuelson's model. The model introduced in the preceding section is mod-ified in one respect: investment now obeys the principle of acceleration; it equals $I + v\Delta Y_{t-1} + \epsilon_t$, where I and v are positive constants, and ϵ is white noise. The larger the increase in aggregate production one period earlier, the higher the level of investment is. The greater the value of v, the stronger this dependence is. The basic idea underlying the principle of acceleration is that an upswing makes the buildup of additional capacities necessary, and vice versa. Alternatively, it can be argued that rising income raises business optimism and, therefore, stimulates investment. Fluctuations in ϵ_t reflect autonomous variations in firms' inducement to invest, the importance of which is emphasized by Keynes (1936/1973: 143–4): it 'is important to under-stand the dependence of the marginal efficiency of a given stock of capital [the investment function] on changes in expectation, because it is chiefly this dependence which renders the marginal efficiency of capital [the invest-ment function] subject to the somewhat violent fluctuations which are the explanation of the trade cycle'.

17

2 Keynesian Economics

Equilibrium

The condition for an equilibrium in the market for goods becomes

$$Y_t = A + c(Y_t - T) + I + v\Delta Y_{t-1} + G + X + \epsilon_t.$$

Steady-state output (set $\Delta Y_{t-1} = 0$) is given by the multiplier formula:

$$Y^* = \frac{A + I + G + X - cT}{1 - c}.$$

Letting $\tilde{Y}_t \equiv Y_t - Y^*$ denote the deviation of aggregate production Y_t from its steady-state level Y^*, the condition for an equilibrium in the goods market can be rewritten as:

$$\tilde{Y}_t - \frac{v}{1-c}\tilde{Y}_{t-1} + \frac{v}{1-c}\tilde{Y}_{t-2} = \frac{1}{1-c}\epsilon_t.$$

Applying the results stated in Section 1.3, it can be seen that in the absence of shocks, oscillations occur if $v < 4(1 - c)$ and that these cycles are damped if $v < 1 - c$. Recurrent shocks give rise to business cycles in Frisch's sense. y_t displays variability, persistence, and reversion.

Assume these conditions are satisfied. What economic mechanisms, then, are at work driving the cycles? Suppose the economy is at its steady state ($\tilde{Y} = 0$). Then, a positive investment shock $\epsilon_0 > 0$ occurs, and $\epsilon_t = 0$ for some t's thereafter ($t = 1, 2, \ldots$). In response to the shock, aggregate production starts to rise ($\Delta \tilde{Y} > 0$). However, $\Delta \tilde{Y}$ cannot rise forever. And when output *growth* $\Delta \tilde{Y}$ starts to fall ($\Delta^2 \tilde{Y} < 0$), one period later the *level* of investment declines ($\Delta I_t = v\Delta^2 \tilde{Y}_{t-1} < 0$). This decline in investment activity is responsible for the upper turning point. By continuity, $\Delta^2 \tilde{Y} < 0$ during the initial stages of the downswing. That is, $\Delta \tilde{Y}$ is negative and becomes greater in absolute value; the downturn gains momentum. Therefore, the economy does not settle down at $\tilde{Y} = 0$, but overshoots into the region $\tilde{Y} < 0$. $\tilde{Y}$ does not fall without bound. So sooner or later, $\Delta \tilde{Y}$, though still negative, must increase ($\Delta^2 \tilde{Y} > 0$). This increase in production *growth* brings about an increase in the *level* of investment one period later ($\Delta I_t = v\Delta^2 \tilde{Y}_{t-1} > 0$), which is responsible for the lower turning point. Since, by continuity, $\Delta^2 \tilde{Y} > 0$ in the wake of the turning point, a cumulative upswing takes its course. The economy does not settle down at $\tilde{Y} = 0$, but overshoots into the $\tilde{Y} > 0$ region. This process repeats with declining amplitudes.

Metzler (1941) has shown that business cycles can also be explained in a model with inventory investment instead of investment in physical capital (see Exercise 2.6).

The multiplier accelerator model was the standard textbook explanation for business cycles in the 1950s and 1960s (see, e.g. Matthews 1964 and Allen 1968). A related approach to the explanation of business cycles is the *over-investment theory*, the dominant pre-Keynesian explanation for business cycles. The over-investment theory, briefly summarized in Appendix 2, provides additional explanations for the emergence of the turning points of aggregate economic activity.

2.4 The Hicks–Fleming–Mundell Model

We are all Keynesians now.

Nixon

The income expenditure model of Section 2.2 and the multiplier accelerator model of the previous section are pure goods market models: equilibrium aggregate production is determined by the condition for an equilibrium in the market for goods alone (under the proviso that it is smaller than aggregate production at full employment). These Keynesian models can, therefore, be criticized on the grounds that other markets appear to also play a role in the determination of equilibrium aggregate production. The present section is concerned with the most prominent Keynesian models that address this criticism: Hicks's (1937) IS–LM model for the closed economy and Fleming (1962) and Nobel Laureate Mundell's (1961, 1963) classic open economy version of the IS–LM model. These models are concerned with the determination of equilibrium aggregate production and the equilibrium interest rate at a given point in time in the presence of sticky goods prices.

Model

Some additional notation is required. Let i, M, P, P^*, S, and i^* denote the nominal interest rate, the supply of money, the price level, the foreign price level, the spot exchange rate (the spot price of foreign currency in terms of domestic currency), and the foreign nominal interest rate, respectively. Furthermore, let y, g, m, p, p^*, and s denote the logarithms of Y, G, M, P, P^*, and S, respectively. Then, the Hicks–Fleming–Mundell model can be described by

2 Keynesian Economics

the following equations:

$$y = \delta(s + p^* - p) - \sigma i + \mu g, \tag{2.2}$$

$$m - p = \phi y - i/\lambda, \tag{2.3}$$

$$\delta = 0 \quad \text{or} \quad \delta > 0, \quad i = i^*,$$

where $\delta, \sigma, \mu, \phi$, and λ are non-negative constants. $\delta = 0$ yields Hicks's IS–LM model. With $\delta > 0$ and $i = i^*$, one obtains the Fleming–Mundell model. Equation (2.2) is the condition for an equilibrium in the goods market. Assume that investment $I(i)$ depends negatively on the interest rate and net exports $X(SP^*/P)$ depend positively on the real exchange rate SP^*/P (the relative price of foreign versus domestic goods). Then, ignoring taxes for simplicity, the condition for an equilibrium in the goods market (2.1) becomes $Y = [A + I(i) + G + X(SP^*/P)]/(1 - c)$. Equation (2.2) is a log-linear approximation to this equation (see Exercise 2.7). In Fig. 2.2, the relationship is labelled the IS curve. Equation (2.3) is the condition for an equilibrium in the market for money. Assume the demand for real money balances $L(Y, i)$, depends positively on income Y and negatively on the interest rate i. Then, $M/P = L(Y, i)$ in a money market equilibrium. Equation (2.3) is a log-linear approximation to this equation, depicted as the LM curve in Fig. 2.2 (again see Exercise 2.7). In the Hicks–Fleming–Mundell model, the supply of money m and prices p are exogenous. m is fixed by the central bank, the exogeneity of p reflects price stickiness. The assumed log-linearity is inessential for the results derived below.

In the closed economy model, net exports are zero ($\delta = 0$) and the interest rate is determined in the home country. As for the open economy model ($\delta > 0$), three assumptions are made. First, the focus is on a *small open economy*, which has no impact on p^* and i^*. Second, the exchange rate is flexible, so that s is an endogenous variable. (For fixed exchange rates, see Exercise 2.11.)

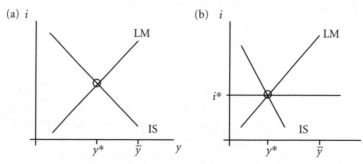

Fig. 2.2 The Hicks–Fleming–Mundell model.

Box 2.1 PPP and interest rate parity

The theoretical arguments in favour of PPP and interest parity rest on arbitrage. If domestic prices are above the level compatible with PPP, arbitrageurs buy goods abroad and sell them at home at a profit, thereby driving up the exchange rate until PPP holds, and vice versa. If the domestic interest rate is higher than the world interest rate, arbitrageurs borrow funds abroad and invest them at home, thereby driving down the domestic interest rate until interest parity holds, and vice versa. Why is it not assumed that PPP holds? Because it fails to hold empirically. In order for PPP to be valid ($SP^* = P$), the relative nominal price of domestic goods P/P^* must be equal to the spot exchange rate S. That this is not true in practice follows from the simple observation that 'relative nominal prices are far less volatile than exchange rates' (Rogoff 1996: 652). The exchange rate shows a tendency to slowly converge towards its PPP level (see Rogoff 1996), but the failure of PPP to hold in the short term is striking. Why is it assumed that interest parity holds? Because there are strong a priori reasons to believe that arbitrage does work in financial markets. World financial markets have been deregulated drastically since the mid-1970s and are now characterized by low transaction costs, great transparency, and extremely high turnover. In 1975, cross-border transactions in bonds and equities equalled less than 5 per cent of GDP in the major industrialized countries. In 1998, they amounted to a multiple of GDP: 230 per cent in the US, 334 per cent in Germany, 640 per cent in Italy (Bank for International Settlements 1999: 132). So, professional investors are likely to exploit any profitable arbitrage opportunities. (A direct test of the validity of interest parity would be to inspect if interest rates are equalized internationally. The reason why this is not a sound test is examined in the next chapter: possible exchange rate changes have to be taken into account when comparing expected rates of return on holding securities denominated in different currencies.)

Notice that since s is endogenous while p and p^* are exogenous, purchasing power parity (PPP) (i.e. $SP^* = P$, $s + p^* = p$) is generally violated. Third, financial capital is perfectly mobile and domestic and foreign securities are perfect substitutes (Exercise 2.10 considers the case of imperfect capital mobility). As a consequence, domestic securities pay the same interest as foreign ones: $i = i^*$. Box 2.1 provides the motivation behind the assumptions that PPP does not hold, but interest parity does.

Equilibrium

In the closed economy model, the IS and LM equations (2.2) and (2.3) can be solved for the equilibrium interest rate and for equilibrium aggregate production y^*:

$$y = \frac{m - p + \mu g/(\sigma\lambda)}{\phi + 1/(\sigma\lambda)} \equiv y^*. \tag{2.4}$$

In terms of Fig. 2.2, the general equilibrium is found at the point of inter-section of IS and LM. The income expenditure model is the special case with $\sigma = 0$, which implies that the IS curve is vertical. As to the open economy specification, (2.3) can be solved for equilibrium aggregate output:

$$y = \frac{m - p + i^*/\lambda}{\phi} \equiv y^*. \tag{2.5}$$

Equation (2.2), then, yields the equilibrium exchange rate. In terms of Fig. 2.2, the LM curve together with the requirement $i = i^*$ determines y^*, and s adjusts such that IS intersects LM at i^*. Assume that $y^* < \bar{y} (\equiv \log \bar{Y})$. Then, as in Section 2.2, equilibrium aggregate production is determined by AD. Firms are unable to sell the full employment level of aggregate production. Production and employment are restricted to the levels compatible with an equilibrium in the goods market. There is equilibrium unemployment due to lack of AD. Say's law fails to hold because at the interest rate which equilibrates the money market at full employment output, investment is below the level needed for full employment.

The Hicks–Fleming–Mundell model has important implications as to the efficacy of fiscal policy (changes in g) and monetary policy (changes in m) in the open economy as compared with the closed economy. Fiscal policy is effective in the closed economy ($\partial y^*/\partial g = \mu/(1 + \sigma\lambda\phi)$). In the open econ-omy, fiscal policy is less effective than in the closed economy ($\partial y^*/\partial g = 0$). This is because the rise in the interest rate that tends to be associated with expansionary fiscal policy leads to an increase in the demand for domestic securities and, hence, to an appreciation of the domestic currency. Given sticky prices, this means a loss in competitiveness and, therefore, lower AD. In our model with perfect capital mobility, only one level of aggre-gate income is compatible with equilibrium in the money market and in the world financial market, so that fiscal policy is completely ineffective. If we had assumed imperfect capital mobility instead, fiscal policy would be effective, though less so than in the closed economy. Monetary policy, on the other hand, is more effective in the open economy ($\partial y^*/\partial m = 1/\phi$) than in the closed economy ($\partial y^*/\partial m = 1/[\phi + 1/(\sigma\lambda)]$). Falling interest rates decrease financial asset holders' demand for the domestic currency, a depreciation increases competitiveness, and AD rises. Under perfect capital mobility, the interest rate does not fall and investment does not eventually rise. As, nonetheless, aggregate output does rise, this increase is solely due to higher net exports (a classic beggar-my-neighbour policy). Under imper-fect capital mobility, the interest rate falls and, in addition to net exports, investment soars. These results notwithstanding, the mainstream Keynesian view in the 1950s and 1960s was that, to a first approximation, 'money does not matter'. For one thing, this is because the interest elasticity of investment was considered small ($\partial y^*/\partial m$ goes to zero as σ goes to zero in the closed economy). For another, the exchange rates between the major currencies were fixed under the Bretton Woods system, so that the stance of monetary policies was dictated by the requirement of external equilibrium. Moreover, the significance of international capital flows was quite limited until the mid-1970s (see Box 2.1). So the expansionary effect of monetary policy on net exports through capital outflows and devaluation was weak when exchange rates changed.

Keynesian macroeconomics without the LM curve

The equations of the Fleming–Mundell model can be attached another interpretation. Consider a closed economy. The central bank does not have a monetary target. Rather, it aims at an exogenous interest rate target i^* and tolerates the variations in the money supply needed to achieve i^*. Formally, $\delta = 0, i = i^*$, and m is endogenous. The model becomes even simpler than the Hicks model, because the new assumptions eliminate any simultaneity: from (2.2), output obeys $y^* = -\sigma i^* + \mu g$. The supply of money adjusts such that $m = p + \phi y^* - i^*/\lambda$. In terms of Fig. 2.2b, y^* is obtained by evaluating the IS curve at $i = i^*$, and m adjusts such that LM intersects IS at y^*. Romer (2000) points out that this model is not only even simpler than IS–LM but also more realistic if monetary policymakers have an interest rate target and are willing to tolerate the required variations in the supply of money, an issue we will come back to in Chapter 4.

2.5 The AS–AD model

Keynes (1936/1973) did not stress the stickiness of goods prices, but put heavy emphasis on the rigidity of nominal wages. In particular, he contended that nominal wages show considerable downward rigidity because wage setting is staggered and no group of employees is likely to accept a decrease in its wage rate relative to other groups. In this section, it is assumed that goods prices are flexible, but nominal wages are fixed. The resulting model is called the AS–AD model.

Model

Denote the logarithm of the nominal wage rate as w. The AS–AD model is given by the following set of equations:

$$y = \delta(s + p^* - p) - \sigma i + \mu g, \tag{2.6}$$

$$m - p = \phi y - i/\lambda, \tag{2.7}$$

$$\gamma y = -(w - p), \tag{2.8}$$

$$\delta = 0 \quad \text{or} \quad \delta > 0, \quad i = i^*.$$

Equations (2.6) and (2.7) are the IS and LM curves already encountered in the previous section. However, the price level p is now an endogenous variable. Equation (2.8) is the aggregate supply (AS) function. It relates the quantity of goods supplied y inversely to the real wage rate $w - p$ (γ is a positive constant). This is because firms aim to equate the marginal product of labour to the real wage rate: the higher the wage rate, the higher the marginal product of labour, the lower employment. The smaller γ, the stronger the impact of real wages on AS. The nominal wage rate w is exogenous. With $\delta = 0$ and i endogenous, one obtains a closed economy model. The assumptions $\delta > 0$, $i = i^*$, and s endogenous lead us to a small open economy with a flexible exchange rate and perfect capital mobility.

Equilibrium

In the closed economy ($\delta = 0$), equation (2.4) holds and gives a demand-side relationship between output y and prices p, depicted as the AD curve in Fig. 2.3. The AS curve (2.8) is a second relationship between y and p. Solving

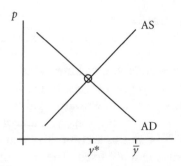

Fig. 2.3 The AS–AD model.

(2.4) and (2.8) for y gives equilibrium aggregate output:

$$y^* = \frac{m - w + \mu g/(\sigma \lambda)}{\phi + \gamma + 1/(\sigma \lambda)}.$$

Under the assumption $\sigma = 0$ made in the income expenditure model in Section 2.2, the AD curve is vertical. In the open economy, equation (2.5) gives the AD curve. Solving (2.5) and (2.8) for equilibrium aggregate production yields:

$$y^* = \frac{m - w + i^*/\lambda}{\phi + \gamma}.$$

Assume $y^* < \bar{y}$ (as in Fig. 2.3). Then the equilibrium level of aggregate production determined simultaneously by AS and AD falls short of full employment aggregate production.

With regard to fiscal and monetary policies, much the same as has already been said with regard to the Hicks–Fleming–Mundell model applies. Fiscal policy is ineffective in the open economy because of the appreciation it precipitates. Under imperfect capital mobility, fiscal policy is effective, though less effective than in the closed economy. Monetary policy, on the other hand, is more effective in the open economy ($\partial y^*/\partial m = 1/(\phi + \gamma)$) than in the closed economy ($\partial y^*/\partial m = 1/[\phi + \gamma + 1/(\sigma \lambda)]$) because it leads to a depreciation and higher net exports. Box 2.2 gives an appraisal of the efficacy of monetary and fiscal policies in practice.

In contrast to the Hicks–Fleming–Mundell model, successful stabilization policies have inflationary effects in the AS–AD model: whenever a rightward

....

Box 2.2   Fiscal and monetary policies in practice

Inspired by the seminal efforts of Nobel Laureate Tinbergen in the 1930s, empirical economists began to construct large-scale macroeconometric models (some consisting of more than 1000 equations) and estimate the parameter values in order to forecast macroeconomic variables and to make numerical predictions of the effects of fiscal and monetary policies on these variables. (Pioneering work was done at the Cowles Commission in the 1940s and 1950s.) The basic structure of many of these models is similar to the AS–AD extension to the Hicks–Fleming–Mundell model. In a prominent research project, the Brookings Institution asked twelve of the most influential modelling groups to prepare identically specified simulations of fiscal and monetary policies in the US (see Bryant *et al.* 1988). It was found that with debt finance the fiscal policy multiplier equals 1.2 on average. A 4 per cent increase in the quantity of money raises output *ceteris paribus* by 1.2 percentage points. Both measures are subject to considerable lags: the effects of fiscal and monetary policies peak about two years after their implementation.

....

shift of the AD curve increases equilibrium aggregate output y^*, it also raises the equilibrium price level ($p^* = w + \gamma y^*$). Let p_{-1} denote the price level in the previous period. For the sake of convenience, assume that the wage rate w is equal to the lagged price level: $w = p_{-1}$ (we will be more specific about the wage setting process in the next chapter). Then, from the AS equation (2.8), $\gamma y = \Delta p$. There is a positive relation between output and inflation and, therefore, a tradeoff between high output and low unemployment, on the one hand, and price stability, on the other hand. The existence of an inverse relationship between unemployment and inflation, called the *Phillips curve*, was also found empirically. Samuelson and Solow (1960: 193) expressed the view that the Phillips curve is a 'menu that relates obtainable price and unemployment behaviour' from which the policymaker can choose his most preferred (least disliked) combination of the two.

One major problem with the AS–AD approach to income determination is that it predicts countercyclical real wages $w - p^* = -\gamma y^*$, as do the income expenditure model and the Hicks–Fleming–Mundell model if it is assumed that labour is rewarded according to its marginal product so that equation (2.8) holds (see Box 2.3).

Keynesian economics, as expounded in this chapter, gave rise to the so-called Neoclassical synthesis. Left on its own, the economy is subject to severe fluctuations. But the government has the power to stabilize the economy with appropriate monetary and, in particular, fiscal policies. Once macroeconomic stability is thus established, the price system brings about an efficient microeconomic allocation of the economy's resources to their most productive uses. In 1955, this view was 'accepted in its broad outlines by all but about

....

Box 2.3   The Dunlop–Tarshis critique

One disturbing property of the AS–AD model expounded here, and of many other Keynesian models as well, is that it predicts countercyclical real wages. Business fluctuations are the consequence of shifts in the AD curve along the AS curve. Hence, prices are positively correlated and, due to sticky nominal wages, real wages are negatively related with aggregate production. Only two years after the publication of the *General Theory*, Dunlop (1938), considering UK data for the period 1860–1937, pointed out that the implied countercyclicality of the real wage rate is at odds with the facts: 'statistically, real wage rates [...] rise during a first period after the peak, and then fall under the pressure of severe wage reductions' (Dunlop 1938: 434). Similarly, Tarshis (1939), using monthly US data for the period 1932–38, finds that real wages are positively correlated with weekly wages, which are procyclical. In the postwar US data, the correlation between GNP and real wages is about 0.4 (see, e.g. Cho and Cooley 1995). The Dunlop–Tarshis critique of the behaviour of real wages in Keynesian models is one of the most forceful challenges of Keynesian economics.

....

5 per cent of extreme left wing and right wing writers', according to Samuelson (1955: 212).

In Appendix 3, a Goodwinian model that is concerned with the role of changes in the income distribution over the cycle is examined. The model is similar in some respects to the Keynesian models introduced in the present chapter. It is not, however, a demand-side model. Since it is the characteristic feature of Keynesian economics that the demand side matters in the determination of aggregate production, we have chosen not to present the model in the main text, but to delegate it to an appendix.

2.6 Summary

1. Income expenditure analysis demonstrates that if investment is exogenous, the economy may fail to reach a full employment equilibrium due to lack of AD. Fiscal policy helps raise output and employment, monetary policy does not.
2. The interaction of the Keynesian multiplier and the principle of acceleration suffices to explain business cycles. Investment is the crucial variable in the multiplier accelerator model. Autonomous fluctuations in investment keep the cycles from ebbing away and induced investment is the variable that initiates the turning points in aggregate economic activity.
3. If prices are sticky, lack of AD may prevent the achievement of full employment even though investment is interest elastic. In the closed economy, both fiscal and monetary policies are effective. In the small open economy with flexible exchange rates, fiscal policy is less effective than in the closed economy, while monetary policy is more effective than in a closed economy. Under perfect capital mobility, fiscal policy is ineffective.
4. With nominal wage stickiness instead of price stickiness, expansionary demand-side policies raise both equilibrium aggregate production and the equilibrium price level. Hence, there exists an inverse relation between inflation and unemployment. This Phillips curve represents a menu from which policymakers can choose their most preferred inflation-unemployment combination.
5. Keynesian economics gave rise to the so-called Neoclassical synthesis: the free market economy left on its own is subject to potentially severe fluctuations, but the government has ample power to stabilize

the macroeconomy. Once this task is accomplished, the price system brings about microeconomic efficiency.

Further Reading

The starting point of Keynesian economics is Keynes's (1936/1973) *General Theory*. For more on multiplier accelerator type models, see Allen (1968: chs 17–19). A collection of nonlinear models in the tradition of Goodwin is in Velupillai (1990). A detailed exposition of the role of capital mobility for the efficacy of fiscal and monetary policies under flexible and fixed exchange rates is in Caves *et al.* (1999: part IV), for instance.

References

Allen, R. G. D. (1968). *Macro-Economic Theory*. London: Macmillan.

Bank for International Settlements (1999). *69th Annual Report*. Basle: Bank for International Settlements.

Bryant, R. C., Henderson, D. W., Holtham, G., Hooper, P., and Symansky, S. A. (eds) (1988). *Empirical Macroeconomics for Interdependent Economies*. Washington: The Brookings Institution.

Caves, R. E., Frankel, J. A., and Jones, R. W. (1999). *World Trade and Payments*, 8th edn. New York: Harper Collins College Publishers.

Cho, J.-O. and Cooley, T. F. (1995). 'The Business Cycle with Nominal Contracts'. *Economic Theory*, 6: 13–33.

Dunlop, J. T. (1938). 'The Movement of Real and Money Wage Rates'. *Economic Journal*, 48: 413–34.

Fleming, J. M. (1962). 'Domestic Financial Policies under Fixed and under Floating Exchange Rates'. *IMF Staff Papers*, 9: 369–9.

Hicks, J. R. (1937). 'Mr. Keynes and the Classics: A Suggested Interpretation'. *Econometrica*, 5: 147–59.

Keynes, J. M. (1st edn 1936/cited edn 1973). *The General Theory of Employment, Interest and Money*. London: Macmillan.

Matthews, R. C. O. (1964). *The Trade Cycle*. Cambridge: Cambridge University Press.

Metzler, L. A. (1941). 'The Nature and Stability of Inventory Cycles'. *Review of Economics and Statistics*, 23: 113–29.

Mundell, R. (1961). 'The International Disequilibrium System'. *Kyklos*, 14: 154–227.

—— (1963). 'Capital Mobility and Stabilization Policy under Fixed and Flexible Exchange Rates'. *Canadian Journal of Economics and Political Science*, 29: 475–85.

Poole, W. (1970). 'Optimal Choice of Monetary Policy Instruments in a Simple Stochastic Macro Model'. *Quarterly Journal of Economics*, 84: 197–216.

Rogoff, K. (1996). 'The Purchasing Power Parity Puzzle'. *Journal of Economic Literature*, 34: 647–68.

Romer, D. (2000). 'Keynesian Macroeconomics without the LM Curve'. *Journal of Economic Perspectives*, 14: 149–69.

Samuelson, P. A. (1939). 'Interactions Between the Multiplier Analysis and the Principle of Acceleration'. *Review of Economics and Statistics*, 21: 75–8.

—— (1946). 'Lord Keynes and the General Theory'. *Econometrica*, 14: 187–200.

—— (1955). *Economics*, 3rd edn. New York: McGraw-Hill.

—— and Solow, R. M. (1960). 'Analytical Aspects of Anti-Inflation Policy'. *American Economic Review*, 50: 177–94.

Sargent, T. J. (1979). *Macroeconomic Theory*. New York: Academic Press.

Tarshis, L. (1939). 'Changes in Real and Money Wages'. *Economic Journal*, 49: 150–4.

Tobin, J. (1993). 'Price Flexibility and Output Stability: An Old Keynesian View'. *Journal of Economic Perspectives*, 7: 45–65.

Velupillai, K. (ed.) (1990). *Nonlinear and Multisectoral Macrodynamics: Essays in Honour of Richard Goodwin*. London: Macmillan Press.

Exercises

2.1 The Haavelmo Theorem. Show: In the income expenditure model of Section 2.2, a tax financed increase in government expenditure raises output one-to-one.

2.2 Analyse the income expenditure model by plotting savings $S \equiv Y - C$ and investment as functions of real income Y (ignore government expenditure and net exports). Discuss the non-validity of Say's law using this diagram.

2.3 Show: In the multiplier accelerator model, fiscal policy has a positive impact on the average level of production Y^*.

2.4 In the multiplier accelerator model of Section 2.3, let $c = 0.8$ and $v = 0.18$. Assume $\tilde{Y}_{-1} = \tilde{Y}_{-2} = 0$. Then, a one-off investment shock $\epsilon_0 = 1$ occurs. Compute $\tilde{Y}_t$ for $t = 0, \ldots, 20$.

2.5 The original Samuelson (1939) model. Assume consumption depends on lagged income: $C_t = A + cY_{t-1}$. Assume further that investment $I + v\Delta C_t + \epsilon_t$ depends on the current change in the demand for consumption. Ignore government expenditure and net exports. Show:

$$\tilde{Y}_t - c(1 + v)\tilde{Y}_{t-1} + cv\tilde{Y}_{t-2} = \epsilon_t,$$

where $\tilde{Y}_t \equiv Y_t - Y^*$ and $Y^* = (A + I)/(1 - c)$. Characterize the range of parameters that give rise to business cycles.

2 Keynesian Economics

2.6 Metzler's (1941) inventory cycle model. Let Q_t denote the firms' inventories. Suppose aggregate output Y_t is equal to the sum of expected consumption C_t^e, expected investment I_t^e, and desired inventory investment $Q_t^d - Q_{t-1}$: $Y_t = C_t^e + I_t^e + Q_t^d - Q_{t-1}$. Once production has taken place, firms service the demand for consumption C_t and investment I_t and accept the resulting change in inventories: $Y_t = C_t + I_t + Q_t - Q_{t-1}$. Investment equals ϵ_t, which is white noise. Consumption equals $C_t = cY_t$. The level of investment is correctly anticipated: $I_t^e = \epsilon_t$. Expected consumption, by contrast, is given by lagged consumption: $C_t^e = C_{t-1}$. Desired inventories rise with lagged consumption: $Q_t^d = kC_{t-1}(k > 0)$. Show that aggregate production obeys

$$Y_t - (2 + k)cY_{t-1} + (1 + k)cY_{t-2} = \epsilon_t$$

and that business cycles occur if

$$c < \frac{1}{1 + k}.$$

2.7 The IS curve (2.2) is interpreted as a log-linear approximation to the Keynesian multiplier formula $Y = (A + I + G + X - cT)/(1 - c)$. That is, $\delta \equiv d\log Y/d\log(SP^*/P)$, $\sigma \equiv d\log Y/di$, and $\mu \equiv d\log Y/d\log G$, all evaluated at the equilibrium. Show:

$$\delta \equiv \frac{d\log Y}{d\log(SP^*/P)} = \frac{1}{1 - c} \frac{X}{Y} \frac{dX/d(SP^*/P)}{X/(SP^*/P)}.$$

Compute the corresponding expressions for σ and μ. Discuss the factors which determine the responsiveness of output to exchange rate movements, interest rate movements, and changes in government expenditure.

2.8 Money supply targets versus interest rate targets (Poole 1970). Suppose the location of either the IS curve or the LM curve varies. The government wants to stabilize aggregate production with an appropriate monetary policy. Argue the following using the Hicksian IS–LM model: If the LM curve is unstable due to money demand shocks and the IS curve fixed, an interest rate target is preferable to a money supply target. If the IS curve is unstable and the LM curve stable, a money supply target is preferable to an interest rate target.

2.9 Liquidity trap. In the Hicks model, assume the demand for money becomes infinitely interest elastic ($\lambda \to 0$). Explain in economic terms why monetary policy becomes ineffective ($\partial y^*/\partial m \to 0$).

2.10 Monetary and fiscal policies under fixed exchange rates. Consider the Fleming–Mundell model with a fixed exchange rate: s is exogenous. Argue the following algebraically and with the help of an IS–LM diagram. First, the IS equation and the interest parity condition jointly determine aggregate output. Second, autonomous monetary policy is not feasible; the monetary authority has to set

$$m = p + \phi[\delta(s + p^* - p) - \sigma i^* + \mu g] - i^*/\lambda.$$

Third, fiscal policy is more effective than in the closed economy. Compare this model with the macroeconomics-without-the-LM-curve model.

2.11 Imperfect capital mobility. Return to the assumption of a flexible exchange rate. When capital mobility is not perfect, equilibrium in the market for foreign exchange requires that net exports (which increase with $s + p^* - p$) equal net capital exports (which increase with the interest rate differential $i^* - i$). Write this as $s + p^* - p = -v(i - i^*)$, where v is a positive constant. The Fleming–Mundell model with imperfect capital mobility is made up of this equation, (2.2), and (2.3). Use the condition for an equilibrium in the foreign exchange market to eliminate $s + p^* - p$ from the IS equation. Argue: international capital movements make y more interest elastic. Show: equilibrium aggregate output is

$$y^* = \frac{[1 + \sigma/(\delta v)]\lambda(m - p) + i^* + \mu g/(\delta v)}{1/(\delta v) + \lambda\phi[1 + \sigma/(\delta v)]}.$$

Discuss the effectiveness of monetary and fiscal policies and the limiting case with $v \to \infty$.

2.12 In Hicks's IS–LM model, suppose investment depends on the real interest rate r, which is the nominal interest rate minus expected inflation. Does expansionary monetary policy necessarily bring about higher AD and production if it leads to the expectation of future disinflation?

2.13 Does the AS–AD model, as expounded in Section 2.5, lend support to the view that increases in nominal wages raise equilibrium aggregate production? Does this result hinge upon the assumption that AD is unaffected by the wage rate?

3
...

MONETARISM

Money is a fascinating subject of study because it is so full of mystery and paradox. The piece of green paper with printing on it is little different, as paper, from a piece of the same size torn from a newspaper or magazine, yet the one will enable its bearer to command some measure of food, drink, clothing, and the remaining goods of life; the other is fit only to light the fire.

Friedman and Schwartz (1963: 695–6)

3.1 Introduction

The Keynesian models expounded in Chapter 2 put much emphasis on aggregate demand. They predict that insufficient aggregate demand can bear the responsibility for protracted periods of less than full employment. At the same time, the Keynesian models assign to the government an important role in the stabilization of the macroeconomy via fiscal and monetary policies, the relevant options being described by the Phillips curve. What is more, they predict that a permanent increase in equilibrium aggregate production can be accomplished by means of fiscal and monetary policies that permanently raise aggregate demand. Discomfort with these propositions—the need for, and efficacy of, activist demand management both in the short run and in the long run—led to the development of monetarism as a counterposition to Keynesian economics in the 1960s. Monetarists, including their leading proponent, Nobel Laureate Friedman, believe that the self-correcting forces of the economy work sufficiently fast such that there is no need for demand management. At any rate, fiscal and monetary policies are regarded as ineffective means of stabilizing the economy. In the long run, demand management is deemed to be futile because supply-side factors, which were, by and large, ignored by the Keynesians, determine the natural rates of aggregate output and employment—there is no permanent unemployment-inflation trade-off. In the short run, activist policy is likely to add to, rather than reduce, the volatility of the economic system because of long and variable data lags, recognition lags, legislative lags, implementation lags, and effectiveness lags (see Box 2.3 and Mishkin 1998: 680).

Section 3.2 introduces a stylized monetarist model of business cycles. Some extensions are in Section 3.3. Section 3.4 summarizes the main results.

3.2 A Basic Monetarist Model

I think it is part of the common core of macroeconomics that the trend movement is predominantly driven by the supply side of the economy [...] In my picture of the usable common core of macroeconomics, [...] fluctuations are predominantly driven by aggregate demand impulses.

Solow (1997: 230), in reply to the question: 'Is There a Core of Usable Macroeconomics We Should All Believe In?'

Model

Laidler (1976) presents a closed economy monetarist model which neatly summarizes the implications of the monetarist ideas for business cycles. In this section, we examine an extension of Laidler's model that applies to the open economy as well. In this model, irregular monetary shocks lead to cyclical output movements in R. Frisch's sense (Box 3.1 discusses the importance of monetary shocks for output movements). The model is made up of the following set of equations:

$$y_t = \delta(s_t + p_t^* - p_t) - \sigma r_t + \mu g_t, \tag{3.1}$$

$$m_t - p_t = \phi y_t - i_t/\lambda, \tag{3.2}$$

$$r_t = i_t - \Delta p_{t+1}|_t^e, \tag{3.3}$$

$$\Delta p_{t+1}|_t^e = \Delta p_t, \tag{3.4}$$

$$\delta = 0 \text{ or } \delta > 0, \ i_t = i_t^* + \Delta s_{t+1}|_t^e, \tag{3.5}$$

$$r^* = i_t^* - \Delta p_{t+1}^*|_t^e, \tag{3.6}$$

$$\bar{s}_t \equiv p_t - p_t^*, \tag{3.7}$$

33

....

Box 3.1 Money and aggregate production

Many pre-Keynesian economists regarded monetary disturbances as the main cause of aggregate output fluctuations. For instance, Hawtrey proposed a purely monetary theory of the cycle, and Robertson developed a monetary variant of the over-investment theory. The Keynesian theory shifted attention to real expenditure shocks and deemphasized monetary shocks. In the simplest Keynesian model, the income expenditure model, 'money does not matter' at all. Friedman and Schwartz (1963) brought money back to the fore with the publication of their *Monetary History of the U.S.* In this influential book, Friedman and Schwartz show that, as mentioned in Box 1.4, money and real aggregate production move together closely over the business cycle. This is confirmed by recent studies, which find a correlation between the stock of money and aggregate production of about two-thirds. It has been remarked, both by Keynesian economists and by proponents of the RBC approach, that correlation does not imply causation. But Friedman and Schwartz (1963) point out that in the monetary history of the US there are (in 1920, 1931, and 1937) instances of sharp recessions which followed evidently autonomous monetary policy actions that tightened already restrictive monetary policies. A similar episode is the Volcker disinflation of the early 1980s. The pattern of the US business cycles over the period 1948–91 provides further support for the view that money matters: during the economic expansions, inflation began to accelerate, which caused the Fed to raise interest rates, thereby bringing about the downturn. This recurrent pattern led Samuelson to speak of 'recessions made by the Fed'. Sims (1972) presents econometric evidence which supports the view that money causes output. Today most economists believe that monetary shocks have a strong impact on real economic activity.

....

$$\Delta(s_{t+1} - \bar{s}_{t+1})|_t^e = -\theta(s_t - \bar{s}_t), \tag{3.8}$$

$$\gamma y_t = -(w_t - p_t), \tag{3.9}$$

$$w_t = p_t|_{t-1}^e, \tag{3.10}$$

$$\Delta p_t|_{t-1}^e = \Delta p_{t-1}. \tag{3.11}$$

Equation (3.1) is the IS curve, the condition for an equilibrium in the goods market. r_t denotes the real interest rate, which is now explicitly distinguished from the nominal interest rate i_t. Since investment depends negatively on the real interest rate, aggregate production in a goods market equilibrium falls when the real interest rate rises. Equation (3.2) is the condition for an equilibrium in the market for money already encountered in Sections 2.4 and 2.5. According to Cagan (1987: 720), the 'roots of Monetarism lie in the quantity theory of money'. This suggests that we should set $\lambda = \infty$ so that (3.2) becomes the quantity equation, $m_t - p_t = \phi y_t$. However, in contrast to early monetarist evidence presented by Friedman, empirical studies have found a significantly negative interest elasticity of money demand (see Box 3.2), so that we allow for $\lambda < \infty$. For any variable x_t, the expression $x_{t+j}|_{t-k}^e$ denotes

---

Box 3.2 The interest elasticity of money demand

Friedman argued both theoretically and statistically for the validity of the quantity theory. He contended that interest rates on demand deposits are strongly positively correlated with interest rates on other assets. So, the opportunity cost of holding money is, by and large, constant and variations in interest rates do not affect the demand for money. A statistical test supported this conjecture (Friedman 1959). However, Laidler (1966) demonstrated that Friedman's test is fallacious and that standard regression analysis using annual observations for the US from 1892 to 1960 yields significantly negative estimates for the interest elasticity to an order of magnitude of $-1/6$. Many similar results are reported in the literature. Yet, Cooley and LeRoy (1982) raise two objections. First, 'it is next to impossible to say anything about the interest elasticity of money demand' (Cooley and LeRoy 1982: 836) because of serious identification problems. Second, reported values tend to be biased downward because of selective reporting of the results of specification search, which implies that the true value 'is in any case much closer to zero than is indicated in much of the reported literature' (Cooley and LeRoy 1982: 828).

---

the expected value of x in period $t + j$ as of period $t - k$. For example, $\Delta p_{t+1}|_t^e$ is expected inflation in period $t + 1$ as of period t. Equation (3.3) is the Fisher equation: nominal interest equals real interest plus expected inflation. Equation (3.4) states that agents form inflation expectations adaptively: the inflation rate in period $t + 1$ expected as of period t is equal to current inflation Δp_t. Thomas (1999: 133) presents survey evidence in favour of the adaptive inflation expectations assumption. In his study of survey measures of US inflation, he finds that 'the various forecasts [...] all tend to underestimate inflation in periods of rising inflation and to overestimate inflation when inflation is declining' and that 'the turning points in expected inflation consistently lag behind turning points in actual inflation. These regularities suggest a strong adaptive or backward-looking element in the formation of inflation expectations.'

Like the Hicks–Fleming–Mundell model of Section 2.4 and the AS–AD model of Section 2.5, this model comprises a closed economy variant and an open economy version (see equation (3.5)). The closed economy model is obtained by setting $\delta = 0$ so that net exports are zero. Equations (3.6)–(3.8) have no role to play in the closed economy. As for the open economy model, we assume (as in Chapter 2) that the economy is small, so that foreign interest rates and prices are taken as given. The exchange rate s_t (the spot price of foreign currency) is flexible. Finally, financial capital is perfectly mobile internationally and domestic and foreign securities are perfect substitutes. Therefore, domestic and foreign bonds pay the same expected return. In Chapter 2, this led us to assume $i = i^*$. However, this ignores potential exchange rate changes. Equality of expected returns requires that the domestic nominal interest rate i_t is equal to the foreign nominal interest rate i_t^* plus the expected rate of appreciation of the foreign currency $\Delta s_{t+1}|_t^e$. This uncovered interest rate parity condition is stated in equation (3.5). According to equation (3.6), the foreign real interest rate $r^* = i_t^* - \Delta p_{t+1}^*|_t^e$ is constant. Equation (3.7) defines the exchange rate $\bar{s}_t$ that implies purchasing power parity (PPP). Since PPP is an unreasonable assumption in the short run (see Box 2.1), we allow for deviations of the spot exchange rate s_t from $\bar{s}_t$. Following Caves *et al.* (1999: 553, S54–5), regressive exchange rate expectations are assumed: according to (3.8), the spot exchange rate s_t is expected to regress toward its PPP level $\bar{s}_t$ at rate $\theta(<1)$. This completes the description of the economy's demand side.

Equation (3.9) is the aggregate supply function already seen in the AS–AD model in Section 2.5. Notice that the Dunlop–Tarshis critique (Box 2.3) applies: equation (3.9) establishes a stable negative link between aggregate output and real wages. In Section 2.5, the wage rate w was assumed to be exogenous. Here, nominal wages w_t are set one period in advance, at $t - 1$, so that w_t is an endogenous, but predetermined variable. According to equation (3.10), wages are set equal to expected prices. The rate of output that obtains if expectations are fulfilled (i.e. if $p_t = p_t|_{t-1}^e$) is called the 'natural rate' of output. From equation (3.9), the natural rate is $y_t = 0$. Two interpretations of the wage-setting process are possible: either wage setters have a target real wage rate (which is normalized to zero here), or they set wages in order to achieve a target employment level (which is normalized to zero here). Friedman (1968: 8) identifies the natural rate of output as 'the level that would be ground out by the Walrasian system of general equilibrium equations, provided there is embedded in them the actual structural characteristics of the labour and commodity markets, including market imperfections, stochastic variability in demands and supplies, the cost of gathering information about job vacancies and labour availabilities, the costs of mobility, and so on'. That is, wages are set at the labour market-clearing level. In Section 3.3, we show that the model can readily be adapted to include structural unemployment due to union power. Equation (3.11) is (3.4) lagged once: wage setters have adaptive inflation expectations. Money growth Δm_t is assumed to follow a random walk, that is, $\Delta^2 m_t$ is white noise. Money-growth shocks are the only source of stochastic variability in the economy considered.

The model (though not the closed economy version) is novel. But, obviously, it is obtained by putting together standard building blocks.

Aggregate supply: the Phillips curve

Consider first the supply side of the model, described by equations (3.9)–(3.11). Substituting for w_t from (3.10) in (3.9) yields $\gamma y_t = p_t - p_t|_{t-1}^e$.

Aggregate output exceeds its natural rate ($y_t > 0$) if prices are higher than expected, and vice versa. From (3.11), $p_t - p_t|_{t-1}^e = \Delta^2 p_t$. Hence,

$$\gamma y_t = \Delta^2 p_t. \tag{3.12}$$

This equation, called the *accelerationist Phillips curve*, is valid both in the closed and in the open economy. It has far-reaching implications: 'there is always a temporary trade-off between inflation and unemployment; there is no permanent trade-off. The temporary trade-off comes not from inflation *per se*, but from unanticipated inflation, from a rising rate of inflation' (Friedman 1968: 11). This brings the supply side, pushed to the background by Keynesian economics, back to the fore: if inflation does not accelerate, aggregate output is equal to its natural rate, which is determined on the economy's supply side. The natural rate of output is, therefore, also called the *non-accelerating-inflation rate of output* (NAIRO). The Friedmanian Phillips curve is important empirically because the Keynesian view of the Phillips curve proved untenable in the 1970s (see Box 3.3). In what follows, we first examine Laidler's (1976) closed economy version of the model and then turn to the open economy.

....

Box 3.3   The breakdown of the Phillips curve in the 1970s

In the Keynesian view, the Phillips curve describes a stable, positive relationship between aggregate production and employment, on the one hand, and inflation, on the other hand. The inflation and employment experiences of many countries in the 1960s lent strong support to this view: as inflation soared in the 1960s, output grew strongly, and the unemployment rate came down. In the 1970s, however, the breakdown of the Phillips curve predicted by Friedman in 1967 happened, as sluggish output growth and rising unemployment were accompanied by rising inflation after the first oil price shock in 1973 ('stagflation'). The monetarist model helps explain this breakdown of the stable Phillips relation: expected inflation rose in the 1970s, thereby shifting the Phillips curve upward. Moreover, the stagflationary experience of the 1970s directed attention to supply shocks. In the Keynesian view, aggregate fluctuations are primarily due to fluctuations in aggregate demand. So, observed output-inflation pairs trace out the aggregate supply curve, an upward-sloping relation between output and inflation, as was observed in the 1960s. If, on the other hand, aggregate fluctuations are due to supply shocks, observed output-inflation pairs trace out the downward-sloping aggregate demand curve. This also contributes to the explanation for the observed inverse relation between output growth and inflation after the first oil price shock. The instability of the Phillips curve reduces its usefulness for forecasting and its importance as a 'policy menu'.

....

The closed economy: Laidler's model

Laidler (1976) focuses on the closed economy ($\delta = 0$) and assumes that the quantity theory is valid ($\lambda = \infty$, $m_t - p_t = \phi y_t$). Taking differences twice in the quantity equation gives:

$$\phi \Delta^2 y_t + \Delta^2 p_t = \Delta^2 m_t. \tag{3.13}$$

Inserting $\Delta^2 p_t = \gamma y_t$ (from (3.12)) and rearranging terms, one obtains the stochastic second-order difference equation:

$$y_t - \frac{2\phi}{\phi + \gamma} y_{t-1} + \frac{\phi}{\phi + \gamma} y_{t-2} = \frac{1}{\phi + \gamma} \Delta^2 m_t. \tag{3.14}$$

By assumption, $\Delta^2 m_t$ is white noise. So steady-state output is $y_t = 0$. Since money growth does not accelerate, inflation does not accelerate, and aggregate output is at its natural rate on average. The conditions for the occurrence of business cycles in R. Frisch's sense are satisfied:

$$4 \frac{\phi}{\phi + \gamma} > \left(\frac{2\phi}{\phi + \gamma} \right)^2 = 4 \frac{\phi}{\phi + \gamma} \frac{\phi}{\phi + \gamma}$$

and $\phi/(\phi + \gamma) < 1$.

In contrast to the multiplier accelerator model, business cycles here are the result of the interplay between aggregate supply (the Phillips curve) and aggregate demand (the quantity equation). In explaining these cyclical output dynamics, two pieces of information are essential. First, according to (3.12), inflation rises ($\Delta^2 p > 0$) whenever output is above its natural rate ($y > 0$), and vice versa. Second, according to the quantity equation (3.13), when no monetary shocks occur ($\Delta^2 m = 0$), output growth declines ($\Delta^2 y < 0$) whenever inflation rises ($\Delta^2 p > 0$), and vice versa. Consider the usual impulse-response thought experiment: Suppose that the economy is in its steady state at time $t = 0$. Then, a one-off positive money-growth shock ($\Delta m_0^2 > 0$) occurs and afterwards money growth is constant for a while ($\Delta^2 m_t = 0$, for $t = 1, 2, \dots$). The positive money-growth shock causes output to rise above the NAIRO: $y_0 > 0$. As a result, inflation starts to accelerate ($\Delta^2 p > 0$). This implies that output growth decelerates ($\Delta^2 y < 0$). It follows that sooner or later the economy reaches an upper turning point. In the initial phase of the downswing $\Delta y < 0$ and, since y is still above the natural rate, $\Delta^2 p > 0$ and $\Delta^2 y < 0$. The downward movement gains strength and output does not settle down at the natural rate, but overshoots into the $y < 0$ region. Once $y < 0$, the rate of inflation starts to fall ($\Delta^2 p < 0$). Hence, $\Delta^2 y > 0$: the pace of the downward movement decreases. This explains the lower turning point. An expansion takes its course ($\Delta y > 0$), at first gaining momentum ($\Delta^2 y > 0$). The economy then overshoots into the $y > 0$ region, where the expansion slows down. This process repeats itself with declining amplitudes. In the presence of recurrent monetary shocks, the economy displays business cycles in R. Frisch's sense.

Insofar as the money-growth shock is identified with a deliberate action of the monetary authority, the monetarist model predicts that monetary policy is effective. From equation (3.14), it follows that the initial response of aggregate output to the increase in money growth is the same as that of aggregate output to an increase in the money supply in the AS–AD model of Section 2.5: $y_0 = \Delta^2 m_0 / (\phi + \gamma)$, so $\partial y_0 / \partial \Delta^2 m_0 = 1/(\phi + \gamma)$. Moreover, if $\phi > \gamma$, the impact of the monetary shock on y_1 is even stronger than the impact on y_0: from equation (3.14), $y_1 = 2\phi y_0 / (\phi + \gamma)$. However, monetarists deny the potency of activist monetary policy because of the long and variable lags that elapse before monetary policies are implemented and become effective. Accordingly, the monetary shocks in the monetarist model are regarded as the unavoidable noise due to imperfect controllability of the money supply. Monetarists contend that the best the monetary authority can do is to enhance the stability and predictability of prices by minimizing the noise in the economy (the variance of the money-growth shocks). They recommend the use of a 'k-per cent money growth rule'. Moreover, the increase in inflation associated with an increase in the rate of money growth makes future disinflationary policies necessary. Since politicians are prompted to exploit the temporary output-inflation trade-off before elections, the government should credibly commit itself to a k-per cent rule by delegating the responsibility for monetary policy to an independent central bank. These monetarist prescriptions for the conduct of monetary policy are very influential and have had a strong impact on central banking, especially in the 1970s (see Box 3.4). Fiscal policy is ineffective in Laidler's model. This follows from the observation that the IS curve does not play a role in the determination of aggregate production (which is due to the assumption that $\lambda = \infty$). Additional government expenditure leads to an equal-sized crowding out of private expenditure. According to (3.1), this complete crowding out is brought about by an increase in the real interest rate r. Therefore, besides constant money growth, monetarists recommend non-activist fiscal policy. There is, thus, no scope for discretionary demand policy.

The open economy

Suppose $\lambda < \infty$ and $\delta > 0$. That the demand for money is interest elastic implies that equilibrium aggregate production can no longer be derived from aggregate supply and the LM equation (3.2) alone; the IS equation (3.1) is

....

Box 3.4   Central bank independence and inflation

Central banks differ in their degree of independence. Alesina and Summers (1993) rate
17 countries on a scale from 1 (lowest central bank independence) to 4 (highest central bank
independence). Germany and Switzerland are ranked 4, the US 3.5, France and the UK 2, and
Italy 1.75. As the theory predicts, one observes 'a near perfect negative correlation between
inflation and central bank independence' (Alesina and Summers 1993: 154), while unemployment is unrelated to central bank independence. The trend toward greater central bank
independence goes on. For instance, the European Central Bank (ECB), which has the control
of monetary policy in the European Monetary Union since the beginning of 1999, is, if anything, even more independent than the Bundesbank; in Britain too, several steps have been
taken in recent years to increase the Bank of England's independence. This reflects the 'benefits
of tying one's hands' by committing to price stability. Monetarism has been very influential in
this process.

....

needed in order to characterize the demand side of the economy. $\delta > 0$ implies
that net exports are one determinant of aggregate demand. Government
expenditure is ignored for simplicity: $g = 0$.

At first, it is shown that the main consequence of introducing international
capital flows is to make the IS curve more interest elastic (as in Exercise 2.11).
To see this, use $\Delta \bar{s}_{t+1}|_t^e = \Delta p_{t+1}|_t^e - \Delta p_{t+1}^*|_t^e$ (from (3.7)), $i_t - \Delta p_{t+1}|_t^e = r_t$
(from (3.3)), and $i_t^* - \Delta p_{t+1}^*|_t^e \equiv r^*$ (equation (3.6)) to rewrite the interest
parity condition in equation (3.5) as

$$\Delta(s_{t+1} - \bar{s}_{t+1})|_t^e = r_t - r^*. \tag{3.15}$$

This is uncovered interest parity in real terms: if the home country suffers a
depreciation in real terms (the real exchange rate $s_t - s_{t+1}$ is expected to rise),
domestic securities must pay a positive real interest rate differential. With
equations (3.7) and (3.8), it follows that $s_t + p_t^* - p_t = s_t - \bar{s}_t = -(r_t - r^*)/\theta$.
Plug this into the IS equation (3.1) to get

$$y_t = -\Gamma r_t + \delta r^*/\theta,$$

where $\Gamma \equiv \delta/\theta + \sigma$. The IS equation continues to give a relationship between
aggregate production y_t and the real interest rate r_t alone. The main effect
of the international interrelations is to increase the interest elasticity of the
IS curve: $\partial y_t/\partial r_t = \Gamma$, whereas $\partial y_t/\partial r_t = \sigma < \Gamma$ in the closed economy.
This is because in addition to the negative effect on investment captured by
the term $-\sigma r_t$ in the IS equation (3.1), an increase in the real interest rate
r_t has a negative impact on aggregate demand via net exports. According to
the uncovered interest parity condition in real terms (3.15), an increase in

the real interest rate r_t requires an increase in the expected rate of change of the real exchange rate $\Delta(s_{t+1} - \bar{s}_{t+1})|_t^e$. Because of regressive real exchange rate expectations (equation (3.8)), this implies a decrease in the current real exchange rate $s_t - \bar{s}_t = s_t + p_t^* - p_t$. This leads to a deterioration of competitiveness and a decline in net exports. Insert $r_t = i_t - \Delta p_t$ (from (3.3) and (3.4)) to obtain $y_t = -\Gamma(i_t - \Delta p_t) + \delta r^*/\theta$ and use the LM curve (3.2) to eliminate the interest rate i_t:

$$(1 + \Gamma\lambda\phi)y_t = \Gamma\lambda(m_t - p_t) + \Gamma\Delta p_t + \delta r^*/\theta.$$

This is the AD curve of the model: it relates income y_t in a simultaneous equilibrium in the markets for goods and money to the current price level p_t. The supply of money m_t, the lagged price level p_{t-1}, and the foreign real interest rate r^* are shift parameters of the aggregate demand curve. Notice that for the AD curve to fall, λ must be greater than one. Take differences twice to obtain:

$$(1 + \Gamma\lambda\phi)\Delta^2 y_t = \Gamma\lambda(\Delta^2 m_t - \Delta^2 p_t) + \Gamma\Delta^3 p_t. \tag{3.16}$$

This equation and the Phillips curve (3.12) jointly determine equilibrium aggregate output and inflation. Inserting $\Delta^2 p_t = \gamma y_t$ and $\Delta^3 p_t = \gamma\Delta y_t$ into the expression for aggregate demand and rearranging terms yields a stochastic second-order difference equation for aggregate production:

$$y_t - \frac{2 + \Gamma(2\lambda\phi - \gamma)}{1 + \Gamma[\lambda\phi + \gamma(\lambda - 1)]}y_{t-1} + \frac{1 + \Gamma\lambda\phi}{1 + \Gamma[\lambda\phi + \gamma(\lambda - 1)]}y_{t-2}$$

$$= \frac{\Gamma\lambda}{1 + \Gamma[\lambda\phi + \gamma(\lambda - 1)]}\Delta^2 m_t. \tag{3.17}$$

There is persistence if $\lambda > 1$ and $2+\Gamma(2\lambda\phi-\gamma) > 0$, which can be rewritten as

$$\lambda > \frac{1}{\phi}\left(\frac{\gamma}{2} - \frac{1}{\Gamma}\right). \tag{3.18}$$

The condition for the emergence of an oscillatory solution in the absence of monetary shocks can be written as

$$\frac{1 + \Gamma\lambda\phi}{1 + \Gamma[\lambda\phi + \gamma(\lambda - 1)]} > \left\{\frac{1 + \Gamma(\lambda\phi - \gamma/2)}{1 + \Gamma[\lambda\phi + \gamma(\lambda - 1)]}\right\}^2. \tag{3.19}$$

The stability condition is, then,

$$\frac{1 + \Gamma\lambda\phi}{1 + \Gamma[\lambda\phi + \gamma(\lambda - 1)]} < 1. \tag{3.20}$$

Given that (3.18) is satisfied, the latter two conditions are satisfied simultaneously if, and only if, $\lambda > 1$, that is, when the AD curve is downward sloping.

Evidently, the stability condition (3.20) is satisfied exactly if $\lambda > 1$. Moreover, the validity of (3.20) implies that the fraction on the left-hand side of (3.19) is less than one. Since the term in braces on the right-hand side of (3.19) is positive (due to (3.18)) and smaller than the term on the left-hand side, which is less than one, its square is smaller still. Thus, if the interest semi-elasticity of the demand for money $-1/\lambda$ is less than unity in absolute value and satisfies (3.18), business cycles occur.

Since the interest semi-elasticity $\partial m/\partial i$ equals $(\partial m/\partial \log i)(\partial \log i/\partial i) = (\partial m/\partial \log i)/i$, the condition $\lambda > 1$ amounts to the requirement that the interest elasticity of money demand is less than the interest rate: $\partial m/\partial \log i < i$ (recall that m is the the logged money supply). This condition is violated if the estimates for the interest elasticity of money demand in the order of magnitude of $-1/6$ (see Box 3.2) are correct. Recall, however, that the true value 'is in any case much closer to zero than is indicated in much of the reported literature' (Cooley and LeRoy 1982: 828). Moreover, for $\lambda < 1$, the condition (3.19) for cycles may still be satisfied, while the stability condition (3.20) is violated. So non-explosive cycles might occur if an additional stabilizing mechanism were added to the model.

The mechanisms leading to the occurrence of business cycles are analogous to the closed economy model. A one-off money-growth shock that hits the economy in its steady state causes output to rise above the natural rate $(y > 0)$. The Phillips curve (3.12) implies that inflation accelerates $(\Delta^2 p > 0)$. According to the AD expression (3.16), this tends to reduce output growth $(\Delta^2 y < 0)$, thereby bringing about the upper turning point. As inflation continues to accelerate during the early stages of the downswing $(\Delta^2 p = \gamma y > 0)$, the recession gains momentum. Aggregate output overshoots below the natural rate, where inflation falls, which, from the AD expression (3.16), tends to slow down the downward movement of aggregate production $(\Delta^2 y > 0)$ and brings about the lower turning point. The ensuing expansion first gains and later on loses momentum. This process repeats with declining amplitude. Recurrent monetary shocks cause Frischian cycles.

3.3 Further Developments in Monetarism

Structural unemployment

Monetarists usually identify the natural rate of output with the output level that obtains if the labour force, net of the frictionally unemployed, is fully employed ('the level that would be ground out by the Walrasian system of general equilibrium equations'). However, a simple extension to the model examined in the previous section allows for structural unemployment due to union power. The main results are unaffected: average output is determined on the economy's supply side alone, while output fluctuations are the result of the interplay between aggregate supply and aggregate demand. The model is important because—popularized by Layard et al. (1991: chs 1, 8, 9)—it has become a standard tool in the study of the macroeconomics of unemployment.

Consider the following closed economy:

$$m_t - p_t = \phi y_t, \tag{3.21}$$

$$\gamma y_t = -(w_t - p_t), \tag{3.22}$$

$$w_t = p_t|_{t-1}^e + \chi y_{t-1} - h, \tag{3.23}$$

$$\Delta p_t|_{t-1}^e = \Delta p_{t-1}, \tag{3.24}$$

Following Laidler (1976), it is assumed in equation (3.21) that the quantity equation holds. The aggregate supply equation (3.22) relates aggregate supply negatively to the real wage rate. Unions unilaterally set wages one period in advance. According to equation (3.23), unions charge a markup of wages over expected prices that decreases with the parameter h and increases with lagged income y_{t-1}. The higher the value of h, the lower the level of the unions' autonomous wage pressure. The higher the value of χ, the more sensitive the unions react to past employment performance. Equation (3.24) states that inflation expectations are adaptive. Money growth follows a random walk ($\Delta^2 m_t$ is white noise). Laidler's model is the special case with $h = \chi = 0$.

From equations (3.22)–(3.24), we have

$$\gamma y_t + \chi y_{t-1} = h + \Delta^2 p_t.$$

The NAIRO is determined by the parameters from the aggregate supply function (3.22) and the wage-setting equation (3.23) alone (set $\Delta^2 p_t = 0$ and $y_t = y_{t-1} \equiv y^*$):

$$y^* \equiv \frac{h}{\gamma + \chi}.$$

The NAIRO decreases when union wage pressure increases, the sensitivity of real wages to lagged employment levels increases, or the real wage elasticity of aggregate output decreases (i.e. when h falls, χ rises, or γ rises, respectively). The NAIRO is independent of the demand-side parameter ϕ. From equation (3.21), $\phi \Delta^2 y_t + \Delta^2 p_t = \Delta^2 m_t$. Substitute the expression above for $\Delta^2 p_t$, let $\tilde{y}_t \equiv y_t - y^*$ denote the deviation of aggregate output from the

NAIRO, and rearrange terms:

$$\tilde{y}_t - \frac{2\phi - \chi}{\phi + \gamma}\tilde{y}_{t-1} + \frac{\phi}{\phi + \gamma}\tilde{y}_{t-2} = \frac{1}{\phi + \gamma}\Delta^2 m_t.$$

Assume $2\phi > \chi$; otherwise, aggregate output would not display persistence. Since then,

$$4\frac{\phi}{\phi + \gamma} > 4\frac{\phi}{\phi + \gamma}\frac{\phi}{\phi + \gamma} = \left(\frac{2\phi}{\phi + \gamma}\right)^2 > \left(\frac{2\phi - \chi}{\phi + \gamma}\right)^2,$$

the model displays business cycles in R. Frisch's sense. The explanation for the occurrence of business cycles is analogous to the Laidler model. $\tilde{y}_t$ oscillates around zero and aggregate production y_t oscillates around the NAIRO. While the NAIRO is purely supply-determined, the fluctuations around the NAIRO are caused by the interplay between aggregate supply and aggregate demand.

Political business cycles

Nordhaus (1975) uses the monetarist model as the basis of his theory of political business cycles. In this theory, far-sighted politicians exploit the temporary unemployment-inflation trade-off implied by the accelerationist Phillips curve (3.12) with the goal of their re-election. Short-sighted households re-elect the government if unemployment is low when the election takes place. This gives rise to cyclical patterns in output and inflation. Before elections, the government increases output, at the cost of accelerating inflation. After having been re-elected because of low unemployment figures, they slowly bring down inflation, thereby causing a prolonged recession, which ends before the next election, when inflationary policy is used to boost output again.

The theory has been criticized on several grounds. First and most importantly, the empirical success of the theory of political business cycles is limited. Alesina (1988) points out that in the US in the postwar period, GNP growth has not been markedly higher in the years prior to elections than on average. Moreover, the prediction of short expansions and long recessions is the exact opposite of what is actually observed (see Box 1.1). Second, there are good reasons to mistrust the politico-economic explanation for cycles on theoretical grounds. For one thing, if monetary policy is conducted by an independent and inflation-averse central bank, the government has to rely on expansionary fiscal programmes before elections, and the central bank could counteract any inflationary impulses. For another, the model relies heavily on disappointed expectations. Not only do wage setters consistently underestimate inflation when it is rising and overestimate it when it is falling, the public's election behaviour is even more 'naive'. Governments are re-elected for their successes in fighting unemployment, even though disinflation and recession are sure to come. A more consistent way of forming expectations is the main topic of the next chapter.

A monetarist revolution?

Monetarism seemed, two decades ago, to provide a distinct approach to understanding the cycle. Nowadays it looks more like a particular version of the very orthodoxy to which it had one time been diametrically opposed.

Laidler (1992: 102)

Monetarism was drafted as a 'revolution' against the then orthodox Keynesian theory. In the early and mid-1960s, monetarism and Keynesian economics were regarded as distinct and probably unreconcilable explanations for business cycles. Provocative studies such as the Friedman–Meiselman (1963) test (see Box 3.5) contributed to the impression of disparity. Yet, the theoretical positions of the two schools of thought converged to a widely shared macroeconomic consensus in the early 1970s (see Johnson 1971 and Laidler 1992): the average output level is determined by supply-side factors, while the

....

Box 3.5   The Friedman–Meiselman test

Friedman emphasized the validity of the quantity theory of money (see Box 3.2), which implies that nominal GNP and nominal consumption (which is strongly procyclical) are closely correlated with money over the cycle. According to the Keynesian multiplier formula, there is a stable positive link between GNP and consumption, on the one hand, and the other expenditure components, on the other hand. Friedman and Meiselman (1963) proposed to compare the relative stability of these two relationships as a preliminary test of the validity of the monetarist versus the Keynesian explanation for business cycles (as noted in Box 3.1, the monetarists were aware of the caveat that correlation does not imply causation). With annual US data for the period 1897–1958, they found that the correlation between nominal consumption and money (0.985) is much larger than the correlation between nominal consumption and the other expenditure components (0.756) (Friedman and Meiselman 1963: table II-1, 190). In a regression of nominal consumption on other expenditure and money, the former is insignificant, while the coefficient of the latter is large (1.38) and highly significant (Friedman and Meiselman 1963: table II-2, 224). Friedman and Meiselman (1963: 213) conclude 'that the quantity-theory approach to income change is likely to be more fruitful than the income-expenditure approach; that the first corresponds to empirical relations that are far more stable over the course of business cycles than the second.' Subsequent studies failed to produce comparably clear-cut results, however. The postsample performance of the regressions is very sensitive to the choice of monetary and autonomous expenditure variables (see Poole and Kornblith 1973).

....

demand side is an important determinant of the fluctuations of aggregate production about the average level; this can be explained with a model (as the one expounded above) in which aggregate demand is determined in a Hicksian IS–LM sector and aggregate supply is given by a Friedmanian accelerationist Phillips curve. Both fiscal policy and monetary policy exert a strong influence on equilibrium aggregate production. Accurate timing is difficult to achieve, however, so an important goal of fiscal and monetary policies is to establish a stable and predictable economic environment.

3.4 Summary

1. Monetarism emerged as a separate school of thought in business cycle theory from Friedman's work on monetary economics in the 1950s and 1960s. The major accomplishment of monetarism is to bring the economy's supply side, which had been pushed to the background by Keynesian economics, back to the fore.
2. Monetarism is much more sceptical than Keynesian economics with regard to the need for, and efficacy of, stabilization policies. In order not to distort price signals, the government should make the supply of money stable and predictable. An independent central bank is helpful in achieving this goal.
3. Laidler's model shows that the interplay between a Friedmanian accelerationist Phillips curve and the quantity equation is sufficient to generate business cycles in R. Frisch's sense.
4. Much the same mechanisms potentially give rise to business cycles in the open economy with international trade in commodities and in securities.
5. Incorporating structural unemployment into the monetarist model does not affect the main results. The supply side determines average aggregate output (the NAIRO) and the interplay between supply and demand determines the fluctuations around this average level.
6. In the late 1960s and early 1970s, the Keynesian and monetarist positions jointly converged to a widely shared macroeconomic consensus. The main impact of the monetarist 'revolution' was to bring the supply side, pushed to the background by Keynesian economics, back to the fore: while aggregate demand plays an important role in the determination of the cyclical component of GNP, average aggregate output is determined on the supply side.

Further Reading

The classic article on the monetarist view of the economy is Friedman's 1967 Presidential Address to the American Economic Association (Friedman 1968). Santomero and Seater (1978) provide a brilliant discussion of the history of the Phillips curve. Dornbusch (1976) is the seminal paper on income determination in dynamic open economies with capital mobility and price stickiness. Layard *et al.* (1991: chs 1, 8, 9) provide an extensive discussion of the macroeconomics of unemployment. The theory of political business cycles originates from Nordhaus (1975) and is reviewed in Nordhaus (1989).

References

Alesina, A. (1988). 'Macroeconomics and Politics', in S. Fischer (ed.), *NBER Macroeconomics Annual.* Cambridge, MA: MIT Press.

—— and Summers, L. H. (1993). 'Central Bank Independence and Macroeconomic Performance: Some Comparative Evidence'. *Journal of Money, Credit and Banking*, 25: 147–62.

Cagan, P. (1987). 'Monetarism', in J. Eatwell *et al.* (eds), *The New Palgrave, A Dictionary of Economics.* London: Macmillan Press, pp. 719–24.

Caves, R. E., Frankel, J. A., and Jones, R. W. (1999). *World Trade and Payments*, 8th edn. New York: Harper Collins College Publishers.

Cooley, T. F. and LeRoy, S. F. (1982). 'Identification and Estimation of Money Demand'. *American Economic Review*, 72: 825–44.

Dornbusch, R. (1976). 'Expectations and Exchange Rate Dynamics'. *Journal of Political Economy*, 84: 1161–76.

Friedman, M. (1959). 'The Demand for Money: Some Theoretical and Empirical Results'. *Journal of Political Economy*, 67: 327–51.

—— (1968). 'The Role of Monetary Policy'. *American Economic Review*, 58: 1–17.

—— and Meiselman, D. (1963). 'The Relative Stability of Monetary Velocity and the Investment Multiplier in the United States, 1897–1958', in E. C. Brown, R. M. Solow, A. Ando, and J. Kareken (eds), *Stabilization Policies.* Englewood Cliffs, NJ: Prentice-Hall, pp. 165–268.

—— and Schwartz, A. J. (1963). *A Monetary History of the U.S.* Princeton: Princeton University Press.

Frisch, H. and Hof, F. (1981). 'A "Textbook"-Model of Inflation and Unemployment'. *Kredit und Kapital*, 14: 159–76.

Johnson, H. G. (1971). 'The Keynesian Revolution and the Monetarist Counter-Revolution'. *American Economic Review*, 61: 1–14.

Laidler, D. E. W. (1966). 'The Rate of Interest and the Demand for Money—Some Empirical Evidence'. *Journal of Political Economy*, 74: 543–55.

—— (1976). 'An Elementary Monetarist Model of Simultaneous Fluctuations in Prices and Output', in H. Frisch (ed.), *Inflation in Small Countries.* Berlin: Springer, pp. 75–89.

Laidler, D. E. W. (1992). 'The Cycle Before New-Classical Economics', in M. T. Belongia and M. R. Garfinkel (eds), *The Business Cycle: Theories and Evidence. Proceedings of the Sixteenth Annual Economic Policy Conference of the Federal Reserve Bank of St. Louis.* Boston: Kluwer Academic Publishers, pp. 85–112.

Layard, R., Nickell, S., and Jackman, R. (1991). *Unemployment, Macroeconomic Performance and the Labour Market.* Oxford: Oxford University Press.

Mishkin, F. S. (1998). *The Economics of Money, Banking, and Financial Markets,* 5th edn. Reading: Addison-Wesley.

Nordhaus, W. D. (1975). 'The Political Business Cycle'. *Review of Economic Studies,* 42: 169–90.

—— (1989). 'Alternative Approaches to the Political Business Cycle'. *Brookings Papers on Economic Activity,* 2: 1–68.

Poole, W. and Kornblith, E. (1973). 'The Friedman–Meiselman CMC Paper: New Evidence on an Old Controversy'. *American Economic Review,* 63: 908–17.

Santomero, A. M. and Seater, J. J. (1978). 'The Inflation-Unemployment Trade-off: A Critique of the Literature'. *Journal of Economic Literature,* 16: 499–544.

Sims, C. (1972). 'Money, Income and Causality'. *American Economic Review,* 62: 540–52.

Solow, R. M. (1997). 'Is There a Core of Usable Macroeconomics We Should All Believe In?' *American Economic Review,* 87: 230–2.

Thomas, L. B., Jr (1999). 'Survey Measures of U.S. Inflation'. *Journal of Economic Perspectives,* 13: 125–44.

Wicksell, K. (1905). *Lectures on Political Economy,* vol. 2. London: Macmillan & Co., Ltd.

Exercises

3.1 Phillips loops. In the Laidler model, figure out what business cycles set in motion by a one-off money-growth shock look like in a diagram with aggregate production on the horizontal axis and inflation on the vertical axis.

3.2 In the Laidler model, let $\phi = 1$ and $\gamma = 0.25$. Calculate the response of aggregate output y_t for $t = 0, \ldots, 20$ to a one-off money-growth shock $\Delta^2 m_0 = 5$.

3.3 Argue: The more favourable the short-run Phillips trade-off is for the policymaker who wants to decrease unemployment before an election, the more costly disinflation will be.

3.4 In the Laidler model, let inflation expectations obey $\Delta p_t|_{t-1}^e = \mu \Delta p_{t-1} + (1-\mu)\Delta p_{t-1}|_{t-2}^e$ (in the main text, we have implicitly assumed $\mu = 1$). Show:

$$y_t - \frac{2\phi + (1-\mu)\gamma}{\gamma + \phi} y_{t-1} + \frac{\phi}{\gamma + \phi} y_{t-2} = \frac{1}{\gamma + \phi} \Delta^2 m_t.$$

Characterize the range of parameters that give rise to business cycles.

3.5 H. Frisch and Hof's (1981) 'textbook' monetarist model:

$$m_t - p_t = \phi y_t,$$

$$-v\Delta u_t = \Delta y_t - (\Delta y)^*,$$

$$\gamma u_t = w_t - p_t,$$

$$w_t = p_t|_{t-1}^e,$$

$$\Delta p_t|_{t-1}^e = \Delta p_{t-1}.$$

The quantity theory holds. Unemployment rises (falls) if output growth is below (above) the natural rate of output growth $(\Delta y)^*$, which is assumed exogenous and constant. This relationship is known as *Okun's law*. Unemployment is positively related to the real wage rate. Wages are set one period in advance, based on adaptive inflation expectations. Money growth follows a random walk. Show: Unemployment obeys

$$u_t - \frac{2v\phi}{\gamma + v\phi}u_{t-1} + \frac{v\phi}{\gamma + v\phi}u_{t-2} = -\frac{1}{\gamma + v\phi}\Delta^2 m_t$$

and business cycles occur.

3.6 Wicksell's (1905) cumulative process. Consider the closed economy monetarist model with interest-elastic money demand and assume that the monetary authority sets the money supply such that the nominal interest rate is fixed at the exogenously set level $\bar{i}$:

$$y_t = -\sigma\bar{i} + \sigma\Delta p_{t-1},$$

$$m_t - p_t = \phi y_t - \bar{i}/\lambda,$$

$$\gamma y_t = \Delta^2 p_t.$$

Argue: The IS and aggregate supply equations imply,

$$\Delta p_t - \bar{i} = (1 + \gamma\sigma)(\Delta p_{t-1} - \bar{i})$$

and the LM equation yields the money supply path necessary for interest rate pegging. Unless $\Delta p_{t-1} = \bar{i}$ initially, a cumulative inflationary process starts.

3.7 Replace the quantity equation (3.21) with the liquidity preference schedule (3.2) in the model with structural unemployment and derive the conditions under which business cycles occur.

4
•••

NEW CLASSICAL
ECONOMICS

4.1 Introduction

In Keynesian economics, exogenous shifts in investors' expectations are important because they affect aggregate output via the Keynesian multiplier formula. In the monetarist model, expectations about future inflation have an important effect on nominal wages and aggregate supply. In both models, aggregate production is affected by random shocks and is, therefore, itself a random variable. Accordingly, we have used the mathematical expectations operator and the derived concepts of variance and correlation in order to describe equilibrium aggregate output. In a way, that is curious: we have effectively assumed that the economic agents inhabiting the model we analyse form expectations differently than we do when we analyse the model. We could have done differently and assume that, like we as theorists do, the agents who inhabit the model form expectations about random variables by calculating the corresponding mathematical expectations. This is the assumption of *rational expectations* (in the absence of uncertainty, rational expectations means perfect foresight). Obviously, rational expectations is a very demanding assumption. For, like we as theorists do, the agents in the model must perform the whole equilibrium analysis for the model economy they live in in their heads in order to come up with rational forecasts for the endogenous variables of the model. The resulting advantage of the rational expectations hypothesis is its internal consistency.

The seminal contribution of new classical economics is to incorporate rational expectations into macroeconomic models. New classical economics points out that the rationality of expectations has profound implications for the way aggregate production is determined and, in particular, devastating consequences for the effectiveness of activist stabilization policies. The central theoretical contributions to the new classical literature stem from Nobel Laureate Lucas (1972, 1973).

Section 4.2 analyses the Lucas (1973) model, the 'down-to-earth' (Phelps 1990: 42) version of Lucas's (1972) pioneering article on *Expectations and the Neutrality of Money*. Section 4.3 discusses some subsequent developments in new classical economics. The main results are summarized in Section 4.4.

4.2 The Lucas Model

Model

The Lucas (1973) model does not make a distinction between workers and producers. Agents have a fixed time endowment which is allocated to leisure or production. It is assumed that there is a large number n of competitive markets indexed i. Agents produce goods which are sold in one market i and consume goods from all n markets. They are 'specialists in production and generalists in consumption'. The distribution of agents across markets is taken as given. The logarithm of output in market i is denoted by y_i (we suppress the time index in this section). Let p_i denote the logarithm of the price level in market i and $p \equiv (\sum_{i=1}^{n} p_i)/n$, the aggregate price index. It is assumed that the price level in market i is determined by the price index and a sector-specific shock ϵ_i:

$$p_i = p + \epsilon_i. \tag{4.1}$$

ϵ_i is distributed identically and independently over time and across markets with expectation zero and variance σ_ϵ^2. So, there are two possible reasons why prices p_i in market i may rise: a shift in the relative price level $p_i - p = \epsilon_i$ and an increase in the aggregate price level p. Since agents in market i are specialists in production and generalists in consumption, an increase in the relative $p_i - p$ makes production more attractive relative to leisure. If the aggregate price level p were known with certainty, agents in market i would reduce their leisure and expand production y_i whenever $p_i - p$ rises, but would not expand production when p_i and p rise by the same amount due to general inflation. However, information is imperfect in that agents observe the price in their market p_i, but do not observe the aggregate price level p. As a result, they have to disentangle changes in the observed price level p_i into relative price shifts and general inflation. This is where expectations come into play. The crucial assumption in the Lucas (1973) model is that expectations

51

are formed rationally. That is, the expectation an agent holds with respect to a given variable is the mathematical expectation implied by the structure of the model, given his personal information set. Since the information sets are different, as producers in different markets i observe different market prices p_i, they hold different expectations of the aggregate price level $E_i p$. Production y_i in market i is a function of the relative price $p_i - E_i p$ expected by the agents in market i:

$$gy_i = p_i - E_i p, \qquad (4.2)$$

where g is a positive constant. Let $y \equiv \left(\sum_{i=1}^{n} y_i \right) / n$ denote average output. Following monetarist tradition, it is assumed that the quantity theory is valid:

$$m - p = \phi y, \qquad (4.3)$$

where m is the log of the supply of money. The central bank has imperfect control of the money supply, so m_t has a random component η_t, which is white noise (with variance σ_η^2). The central bank ties the supply of money to past realizations of the money supply (m_{t-j}), output (y_{t-j}), and prices (p_{t-j}), according to the feedback money supply rule:

$$m_t = a + \sum_{j=1}^{\infty} b_j m_{t-j} + \sum_{j=1}^{\infty} c_j y_{t-j} + \sum_{j=1}^{\infty} d_j p_{t-j} + \eta_t. \qquad (4.4)$$

The constants a, b_j, c_j, and d_j are policy parameters.

Equilibrium

Two non-rational ways of forming expectations about the aggregate price level p are: assuming that p is equal to the price level actually observed in the own market p_i; or assuming that p is equal to the expectation Ep neglecting the information contained in the observation p_i. To begin with, suppose that $E_i p$ is a weighted mean of p_i and Ep:

$$E_i p = \theta p_i + (1 - \theta) Ep, \quad 0 < \theta < 1. \qquad (4.5)$$

For now, the respective weights θ and $1 - \theta$ are taken as given; below we show that θ can be chosen such that (4.5) implies rational expectations. Inserting this simple expectations formation rule into the supply function (4.2) yields $gy_i = (1 - \theta)(p_i - Ep)$. Taking the sum over all i, dividing by n, using $\left(\sum_{i=1}^{n} p_i \right) / n = p$ and $y \equiv \left(\sum_{i=1}^{n} y_i \right) / n$, and letting $\gamma \equiv g/(1 - \theta)$, it follows that

$$\gamma y = p - Ep. \qquad (4.6)$$

This is the so-called *Lucas supply function*. Expected aggregate production equals $Ey = 0$. On average, y cannot exceed this natural rate, no matter how high inflation is and how fast it rises. (Some economists refuse to call the NAIRO in the monetarist model of Section 3.2 a natural rate because $y > 0$ is feasible permanently there, if at the cost of accelerating inflation.) Aggregate output y is above the natural rate if the aggregate price level is higher than rationally expected, and vice versa. This is because producers in each market i misperceive a positive 'price surprise' as an increase in the relative price of their respective good and expand production at the cost of a reduction in leisure time. From the quantity equation (4.3) and $Ey = 0$, it follows that $p = m - \phi y$ and $Ep = Em$. So (4.6) can be rewritten as:

$$y = \frac{m - Em}{\phi + \gamma}.$$

Aggregate output is an increasing function of the 'money surprise' $m - Em$. Since agents make use of all available information, including past realizations of money shocks, output, and prices, only current monetary shocks η come as a surprise: from the money supply rule (4.4), we have $m - Em = \eta$. Hence,

$$y_t = \frac{\eta_t}{\phi + \gamma}. \tag{4.7}$$

Equilibrium aggregate production is independent of the monetary policy parameters $a, b_j, c_j,$ and d_j. Only the uncontrollable and, therefore, unanticipated component of the supply of money affects output. This is Sargent and Wallace's (1975) famous *policy ineffectiveness proposition*. This is because only unanticipated money causes unanticipated inflation, and according to (4.6), only unanticipated inflation raises output. Like the monetarist model, Lucas's (1973) new classical model thus calls for a stable and predictable supply of money.

A sensible specification for the weights θ and $1 - \theta$, which agents in market i attach to the observed own price p_i and to the expected aggregate price level Ep, respectively, in forming expectations $E_i p$ about the aggregate price level is:

$$\theta = \frac{\sigma_p^2}{\sigma_p^2 + \sigma_\epsilon^2}. \tag{4.8}$$

The lower the variance of the sector-specific shocks σ_ϵ^2, the greater the weight θ attached to the observed own price p_i. The lower the variance of the aggregate price level σ_p^2, the greater the weight $1 - \theta$ attached to Ep. Since σ_p^2 is an endogenous variable, so are $\theta = \sigma_p^2/(\sigma_p^2 + \sigma_\epsilon^2)$ and $\gamma \equiv g/(1 - \theta) = g(\sigma_p^2 + \sigma_\epsilon^2)/\sigma_\epsilon^2$. From equations (4.6) and (4.7), $p - Ep = \eta/(1 + \phi/\gamma)$.

Hence, $\sigma_p^2 = \sigma_\eta^2/(1 + \phi/\gamma)^2$ or

$$\sigma_p^2 = \frac{1}{\left[1 + (\phi/g)\,\sigma_\epsilon^2/\left(\sigma_\epsilon^2 + \sigma_p^2\right)\right]^2}\sigma_\eta^2. \tag{4.9}$$

This equation pins down σ_p^2 as a function of σ_η^2 and σ_ϵ^2. σ_p^2 then determines the size of the weights θ and $1 - \theta$ in equation (4.5) via (4.8). The right-hand side of equation (4.9) equals $\sigma_\eta^2/(1 + \phi/g)^2$ (>0), for $\sigma_p^2 = 0$, increases monotonically with σ_p^2 and converges to σ_η^2 as σ_p^2 grows large. Therefore, the equation has a positive solution.

Finally, we prove (following Sargent 1979: ch. X) that expectations formation according to equations (4.5) and (4.8) is rational. The agents in all the markets i are aware of the fact that their forecasts of the aggregate price level $E_i p$ will in general differ from the actual value p. Due to the imperfect predictability of the supply of money, forecast errors are unavoidable. Rationality of expectations requires that the magnitude of the forecast errors is minimized. Define the forecast error as the expected squared deviation of the forecast $E_i p$ from the actual price level p, that is, as $E(p - E_i p)^2$. $E_i p$ is considered as a linear function of observed demand p_i : $E_i p = \varphi + \theta p_i$. The parameters φ and θ are set such that $E[p - (\varphi + \theta p_i)]^2$ is minimized. To prove the rationality of (4.5) and (4.8), it has to be shown that the solution to this minimization problem entails

$$\varphi = (1 - \theta)Ep, \quad \theta = \frac{\sigma_p^2}{\sigma_p^2 + \sigma_\epsilon^2}. \tag{4.10}$$

The necessary optimality conditions are:

$$-2E[p - (\varphi + \theta p_i)] = 0,$$
$$-2E\{[p - (\varphi + \theta p_i)]p_i\} = 0. \tag{4.11}$$

The first condition yields $\varphi = Ep - \theta Ep_i$ or, using $Ep_i = Ep$ (from (4.1)), $\varphi = (1 - \theta)Ep$, as asserted with the first equality in (4.10). Turning to the second equality in (4.10), rewrite (4.11) as

$$E(pp_i) = \varphi Ep_i + \theta Ep_i^2. \tag{4.12}$$

Use will be made of the following three results. First,

$$E(pp_i) = E[p(p + \epsilon_i)] = E(p^2 + p\epsilon_i) = Ep^2,$$

where $E(p\epsilon_i) = 0$ since p and ϵ_i are independent. Second, observing $\varphi = (1 - \theta)Ep$ and $Ep_i = Ep$,

$$\varphi Ep_i = (1 - \theta)(Ep)^2.$$

Third,
$$Ep_i^2 = E(p + \epsilon_i)^2 = E(p^2 + 2p\epsilon_i + \epsilon_i^2) = Ep^2 + \sigma_\epsilon^2.$$

Substituting these three expressions into (4.12) gives $Ep^2 = (1 - \theta)(Ep)^2 + \theta(Ep^2 + \sigma_\epsilon^2)$. Solving for θ and using the definition of the variance ($\sigma_p^2 \equiv Ep^2 - (Ep)^2$) yields the second expression in (4.10).

....

4.3 Further Developments in New Classical Economics

....

Rational expectations monetarism

In the Lucas (1973) model, unanticipated money leads to unanticipated infla-tion, which producers rationally, but mistakenly perceive as an increase in the relative price of their respective output goods. This induces them to expand production, so that aggregate output rises. It is generally held that 'this mech-anism is not persuasive as a model of business cycles' (Chari 1998: 180). But the rational expectations assumption can be built into more standard models of business cycles. Consider, for instance, the following model:

$$m_t - p_t = \phi y_t, \tag{4.13}$$

$$\gamma y_t = -(w_t - p_t), \tag{4.14}$$

$$w_t = E_{t-1} p_t. \tag{4.15}$$

Equation (4.13) is the quantity equation (Exercise 4.2 considers the model with interest elastic money demand). Equation (4.14) is the standard aggre-gate supply curve. Wages are set one period in advance. The target real wage rate is $w_t - p_t = 0$ (or, equivalently, the target employment level is such that $y_t = 0$). $E_{t-1} p_t$ denotes the mathematical expectation of p_t as of time $t - 1$. According to (4.15), wage setters hold rational expectations. Notice that the expectations formation problem is somewhat different here than in the Lucas model. In the Lucas model, uncertainty concerns the sectoral price levels in the current period. Here, uncertainty concerns the aggregate price level in the following period. This forward-looking way of expectations is the most fruitful application of rational expectations in macroeconomics and will be emphasized in the remainder of this book. The model made up of equations (4.13)–(4.15) differs from Laidler's (1976) closed economy monetarist model expounded in Section 3.2 in only one respect: adaptive expectations are replaced with rational expectations in the wage-setting pro-cess. So it can be viewed as a monetarist model with rational expectations.

The money supply rule (4.4) is assumed to hold. Substituting for w_t from (4.15) in (4.14) yields:

$$\gamma y_t = p_t - E_{t-1} p_t.$$

Wage setting one period in advance under rational expectations thus provides an alternative justification for the Lucas supply function. As in the Lucas (1973) model, the Lucas supply function (aggregate supply) and the quantity equation (aggregate demand) jointly determine aggregate production. From the Lucas supply function, $E_{t-1} y_t = 0$. So the quantity equation (4.13) yields $p_t = m_t - \phi y_t$ and $E_{t-1} p_t = E_{t-1} m_t$. Together with the fact that $m_t - E_{t-1} m_t = y_t$ (from (4.4)), it follows that

$$y_t = \frac{\eta_t}{\phi + \gamma}.$$

As in the Lucas (1973) model, only unanticipated money matters. The Sargent and Wallace (1975) policy ineffectiveness proposition remains valid: the monetary policy parameters a, b_j, c_j, and d_j do not affect aggregate production.

The crucial testable implication of both Lucas's new classical model and the monetarist variant is that aggregate output is positively related to monetary surprises. Econometric tests are generally not supportive of this hypothesis, however (see Box 4.1). This can be due to failure of the rational expectations assumption or some other assumption of the new classical models. Box 4.2 argues that while there is strong evidence of rational expectations in financial markets, the rationality of expectations in other markets is more questionable.

Rules versus discretion in monetary policy: the Barro–Gordon model

Like the monetarist model of Chapter 3, the new classical model calls for a stable and predictable supply of money. In Chapter 3, it was argued that in order to ensure the stability and predictability of the supply of money, it is reasonable to conduct monetary policy by rule rather than by discretion. As pointed out by Barro and Gordon (1983a), an even stronger case for rules versus discretion in monetary policy can be made on the basis of the monetarist model with rational expectations introduced in the preceding paragraph (equations (4.13)–(4.15)). For the sake of simplicity, suppose that perfect control of the supply of money is feasible ($\sigma_\eta^2 = 0$), so that rational expectations (perfect foresight) imply that accurate forecasts of all variables can be made. In particular, this implies that price surprises do not occur ($E_{t-1} p_t = p_t$), so that, according to the Lucas supply function, output is at

Box 4.1 Tests of the new classical model

New classical economics asserts that only unanticipated money matters. Is this prediction supported by the facts? Early econometric studies conducted by Barro produced strong evidence in favour of the new classical theory. Barro (1978) first ran regressions for M1 growth using annual US data from 1941 to 1978. He identified the regression estimates with anticipated money growth and the regression residuals with unanticipated money growth. Then, he regressed real GNP on current and lagged values of unanticipated money growth (and military personnel and time). The current and two lagged values of money growth are highly significant. When a 1 per cent money surprise persists over a four-year period, real GNP in the fourth year rises by 3 per cent. If unanticipated money growth is replaced with anticipated money growth in the real GNP regression, the results are much less clear-cut. This supports the findings of the new classical model. However, subsequent articles report results that are much less favourable to new classical economics. In an influential study, Mishkin (1982) regresses real GNP on current and twenty lagged values of both anticipated and unanticipated money growth using quarterly US data over the period 1954–76. As for unanticipated money growth, he finds that only current unanticipated money growth is significant; all lagged values are insignificant. By contrast, the current and seven lagged values of anticipated money growth are significant, and the coefficients are much larger than those for unanticipated money growth. Mishkin (1982: 40) concludes that 'anticipated monetary policy does not appear to be less important than unanticipated monetary policy; rather the opposite seems to be the case'. Boschen and Grossman (1982) challenge the view that only unanticipated money matters from a different angle. Two new classical hypotheses are: first, quickly available preliminary money growth figures should not have informational content because there would not be a signal extraction problem if they did; second, firms should make use of the information contained in revisions of preliminary money growth figures. Using quarterly US data for the period 1953–78, Boschen and Grossman (1982) refute both hypotheses: preliminary money growth figures do have a statistically significant influence on real GNP, while money growth revisions are insignificant. Without doubt, expectations are an important determinant of the effectiveness of monetary policy, but 'unanticipatedness' does not appear to be a necessary condition for the efficacy of monetary policy.

its natural rate ($\gamma y_t = p_t - E_{t-1}p_t = 0$), no matter how monetary policy is conducted.

Suppose further that the government's preferences for high output and low inflation can be represented by the loss function:

$$\text{loss}_t \equiv -y_t + \beta(\Delta p_t)^2/2. \tag{4.16}$$

The higher the value of β, the stronger the government's aversion to inflation. Since $y_t = 0$, the loss function (4.16) is minimized by $\Delta p_t = 0$, which implies $\text{loss}_t = 0$. This outcome can be achieved with a monetary policy rule. The central bank commits itself to zero inflation: $\Delta p_t = 0$. From

....

Box 4.2 Are expectations rational?

Rationality of expectations does not require that expectations are always correct, but that expectations are correct on average and that forecast errors are not predictable. The field in which the theory of rational expectations is most widely used is financial economics, where it appears under the name 'efficient markets theory'. There is strong evidence that security prices are consistent with rational expectations. Over short periods, the prices of securities are well described by a random walk. That is, price changes are zero on average and unpredictable. (See Fama 1970; Mishkin 1998: ch. 27 discusses exceptions to this rule.) There is a good explanation for why security prices reflect rational expectations: if they deviated from their rational forecasts, agents with rational expectations could beat the market and become rich quickly. The evidence for rational expectations in other markets is much weaker. Especially important for our purposes is the question of whether inflation expectations are rational in the wage-setting process. According to Thomas (1999: 133), survey measures of US inflation 'tend to underestimate inflation in periods of rising inflation and to overestimate inflation when inflation is declining', and 'the turning points in expected inflation consistently lag behind turning points in actual inflation. These regularities suggest a strong adaptive or backward-looking element in the formation of inflation expectations.' This is consistent with the theory: unlike rational forecasts of stock prices in a non-rational stock market, rational inflation forecasts are unlikely to make you rich even if other people have non-rational inflation forecasts. The appeal of rational expectations in non-financial markets stems more from its formal elegance than from empirical observations.

....

the quantity equation (4.13) and $y_t = 0$, this requires zero money growth: $\Delta m_t = \Delta p_t = 0$.

By contrast, $loss_t = 0$ cannot be achieved with discretionary monetary policy. Suppose the government does not commit itself to a money supply rule. Then, it will choose Δm_t such that the ensuing rate of inflation Δp_t minimizes the loss function:

$$loss_t = -(\Delta p_t - E_{t-1}\Delta p_t)/\gamma + \beta(\Delta p_t)^2/2,$$

where $y_t = (p_t - E_{t-1}p_t)/\gamma = (\Delta p_t - E_{t-1}\Delta p_t)/\gamma$ is eliminated using the Lucas supply function. The optimal rate of inflation is $\Delta p_t = 1/(\beta\gamma)$. The weaker the government's aversion to inflation (the lower the value of β) and the greater the output gain from a given amount of unanticipated inflation (the lower the value of γ), the greater the optimal rate of inflation. Rational expectations imply $E_{t-1}\Delta p_t = 1/(\beta\gamma)$. Together with $y_t = 0$, we have $loss_t = 1/(2\beta\gamma^2)$. The reason why the minimal loss value, $loss_t = 0$, cannot be achieved by a discretionary monetary policymaker is that he faces a *time consistency problem*. The announcement that he will realize $\Delta m_t = 0$ in order to achieve his most preferred inflation rate, $\Delta p_t = 0$, would not be credible because he will be tempted to choose $\Delta m_t = \Delta p_t = 1/(\beta\gamma)$ unless he is barred from doing so by rule. Rational wage setters anticipate this and set $\Delta w_t = 1/(\beta\gamma)$. The government's optimal response is $\Delta m_t = \Delta p_t = 1/(\beta\gamma)$ and expectations are fulfilled.

The result that the rate of inflation is constant at $\Delta p_t = 0$ in the commitment solution does not carry over to more general specifications. If the monetary authority has the capability of reacting to current supply shocks and the government dislikes output variability, then the minimization of the loss function entails zero inflation on average, but also calls for a counter-cyclical conduct of monetary policy (see Exercise 4.4). The central finding of the Barro–Gordon model, the inferiority of discretion to rules because of a time consistency problem continues to be present, however: if inflation expectations and, hence, wage growth were constantly equal to zero, a discretionary monetary authority would be tempted to produce positive inflation on average, thus contradicting rational expectations.

Credibility: monetary policy games

The Barro–Gordon model can be interpreted as a three-stage sequential game between wage setters and the central bank: in stage one, the central bank announces its monetary policy, in stage two, wage setters form inflation expectations and set wages, in stage three, the central bank chooses the rate of inflation. The discretionary solution is the subgame-perfect equilibrium. The rules-based solution occurs if the central bank has the potential to commit to an inflation target in stage one. The Barro–Gordon model, as presented in the previous paragraph, is silent on whether or not the central bank is actually able to make this commitment. But the game theoretic interpretation of the model has given rise to a literature which examines the question of 'how to tie one's hands' by applying results from the theory of games.

The most direct way of making a commitment is to force central bankers to bring about the targeted rate of inflation by law. In the model above, this would simply require a clause which makes central bankers responsible for zero inflation. Problems with this approach arise when, because of aggregate supply shocks, the target rate of inflation is not constant and the supply shocks are unobservable. In this case a principal-agent problem arises: the government (the principal) is unable to specify explicitly the rate of inflation the central bank (the agent) has to bring about depending on the realized state of nature. And the question becomes of how to write an (incomplete) contract in such a way that the central bankers have incentives to produce the rate of inflation desired by the government. Clearly, the central bankers' salary should be a decreasing function of inflation. Walsh (1995) shows that, under certain special assumptions, the salary is simply a linear and decreasing function of inflation *alone* (see Exercise 4.5).

Rogoff (1985) points to a second way of committing to low inflation: appointing a 'conservative' central banker. Suppose there is an agent in the economy who is more inflation-averse than the government itself: this agent's personal loss function is $\text{loss}'_t = -y_t + \beta'(\Delta p_t)^2/2$ with $\beta' > \beta$. If this agent is declared responsible for monetary policy, the rate of inflation in the subgame-perfect equilibrium of the game with the wage setters is $\Delta p_t = 1/(\beta'\gamma)$. The more 'conservative' the central banker is (the higher β'), the closer is the rate of inflation to the commitment value. $\Delta p_t = 0$ can be achieved with an infinitely conservative central banker (i.e. $\beta' = \infty$).

A third strand of the literature emphasizes that a formal commitment may not be necessary so as to make the announcement of zero inflation credible when the central bank and the wage setters interact repeatedly (Barro and Gordon 1983*b*). Suppose the monetary policy game is repeated an infinite number of times. The government's intertemporal loss function:

$$\text{Loss}_t \equiv \sum_{\tau=t}^{\infty} \beta^{\tau-t}\text{loss}_\tau, \quad 0 < \beta < 1,$$

is the discounted value of the present and all future loss levels. Assume that wage setters expect zero inflation initially and then form inflation expectations according to the 'trigger strategy':

$$E_{t-1}\Delta p_t = \begin{cases} 0, & \Delta p_{t-1} = 0, \\ 1/(\beta\gamma), & \Delta p_{t-1} \neq 0. \end{cases} \tag{4.17}$$

That is, as long as the central bank has not deviated from the commitment solution, wage setters expect this to continue. But once the central bank deviates, wage setters expect that it will choose its preferred rate of inflation $\Delta p_t = 1/(\beta\gamma)$ forever.

In periods with $E_{t-1}\Delta p_t = 0$, the central bank realizes $\text{loss}_t = 0$ if it sticks to zero inflation. If it chooses its preferred rate of inflation $\Delta p_t = 1/(\beta\gamma)$, output is $y_t = 1/(\beta\gamma^2)$, and the loss function (4.16) takes on the smaller value $\text{loss}_t = -1/(2\beta\gamma^2)$. In periods with $E_{t-1}\Delta p_t = 1/(\beta\gamma)$, the loss level from the discretionary solution to the one-shot game prevails: $\text{loss}_t = 1/(2\beta\gamma^2)$. Therefore, if the central bank deviates from $\Delta p_t = 0$ at t,

$$\text{Loss}_t = -\frac{1}{2\beta\gamma^2} + \frac{1}{2\beta\gamma^2} \sum_{\tau=t+1}^{\infty} \beta^{\tau-t}. \tag{4.18}$$

If, on the other hand, the central does not deviate at time t, it will not choose to deviate later on either. This is because the future it faces remains unchanged as long as it does not deviate. In this case, the loss function equals $loss_t = 0$, for all t. It is thus apparent from (4.18) that in this repeated game, the central bank reaps the current gain from higher inflation at the cost of an increase in the loss levels in all future periods. The cost overweighs the gain, and the central bank sticks to zero inflation, at t if the expression for $Loss_t$ in (4.18) is positive. This is the case if $-1 + \sum_{\tau=t+1}^{\infty} \beta^{\tau-t} = -1 + \beta/(1-\beta) > 0$, that is, if $\beta > 1/2$. Expectation formation according to (4.17) is rational then: wage setters always expect zero inflation, and zero inflation always prevails. Thus, if the central bank's discount factor for future loss levels is not too high, its promise to keep inflation low is credible even if no formal commitment exists.

The repeated-game explanation for credibility has been criticized for two important reasons. First, we have seen that the realization of the commitment solution in each period constitutes *one* equilibrium. But given other expectations formation mechanisms than (4.17), other equilibria obtain. The 'folk theorem' of game theory says that this potential multiplicity of equilibria is severe: with sufficiently weak discounting (high β), any strategy combination constitutes an equilibrium of the infinitely often repeated game. Second, the usual backward-induction argument proves that the reasoning above does not work when central bankers have finite horizons. In the final period, say T, the central bank chooses $\Delta p_T = 1/(\beta\gamma)$ because there is no penalty in the form of higher future loss levels. Since $loss_T = 1/(2\beta\gamma^2)$ is predetermined in this way, the central bank has nothing to lose from producing inflation $\Delta p_{T-1} = 1/(\beta\gamma)$ in the next-to-last period. So, from the viewpoint of period $T - 2$, the future losses, $loss_{T-1} = loss_T = 1/(2\beta\gamma^2)$ are predetermined. There is no cost of inflation, and $\Delta p_{T-2} = 1/(\beta\gamma)$. And so on until stage one. In the unique subgame-perfect equilibrium of the finitely often repeated game, the discretionary solution is realized in each period.

Their respective shortcomings notwithstanding, these three mechanisms contribute to the explanation of low inflation rates in countries with independent central banks.

Persistence

The models expounded so far have been criticized on the grounds that since y_t is white noise, it lacks an important characteristic of observed output movements: persistence. In response to this criticism, New classical economists have incorporated several mechanisms that produce persistence into their models. In Lucas (1975), physical capital is the source of persistence in output movements: high output in this period offers opportunities for high investment, which implies that the capital stock and, hence, aggregate production next period are high. (Capital stock dynamics will be important in the subsequent chapter concerned with the RBC theory.) In Sargent (1979: ch. 16), gradual adjustment of employment due to employment adjustment costs leads to the presence of serial correlation in aggregate output. Blinder and Fischer (1981) point out that the inclusion of inventory investment quite naturally gives rise to persistence. Rising demand due to a positive price surprise leads to both rising production and the depletion of inventories. Thereafter, firms continue to produce in excess of the natural rate of output in order to replenish their inventories. So movements in aggregate production are persistent (see Exercise 4.6 at the end of this chapter). In view of the pronounced procyclical movements in inventories (see Box 1.4), this is a promising way of generating persistence in the new classical model. New classical economists do not aim at obtaining business cycles in Frisch's sense (recall from Chapter 1 Blinder and Fischer's (1981: 277) definition of business cycles as 'serially correlated deviations of output from trend').

Macroeconomics without the LM curve

Section 2.4 introduced Keynesian macroeconomics without the LM curve. The Laidler model of Section 3.2 as well as the new classical models expounded in this chapter so far are macroeconomics without the IS curve. Here is another model without the LM curve:

$$y_t = -\sigma(i_t - E_t \Delta p_{t+1}) + \epsilon_t, \tag{4.19}$$

$$i_t = (\Delta p)^* + c y_t + d[\Delta p_t - (\Delta p)^*], \tag{4.20}$$

$$\gamma y_t = -(w_t - p_t), \tag{4.21}$$

$$w_t = E_{t-1} p_t. \tag{4.22}$$

Equation (4.19) is the IS curve. The calculation of the real interest rate $r_t = i_t - E_t \Delta p_{t+1}$ is based on rational expectations. Government expenditure g is ignored and ϵ_t is white noise. As in Section 2.4, we assume that the central bank has an interest rate target and tolerates the ensuing variations in the money supply. Equation (4.20) is this interest rate rule. Here, $(\Delta p)^*$ is the central bank's target value for average inflation. The short-term interest rate i_t is the monetary policy instrument, and c and d are parameters which characterize the conduct of monetary policy. The interest rate rule (4.20) says that the central bank raises the short-run interest rate i_t when output rises (i.e. monetary policy is countercyclical) or inflation soars. Notice that the fact that y_t and Δp_t appear in the interest rate rule (4.20) implies that the central bank reacts to current expenditure shocks ϵ_t. Box 4.3 argues that a rule like (4.20) is a good description of what central banks actually do. Together

....

Box 4.3   Monetary targets versus interest rate targets and the Taylor rule

The model composed of equations (4.19)–(4.22) has become a standard model for analysing monetary policy. At first glance, it appears odd to drop the LM curve and re-introduce the IS curve in order to carry out monetary policy analysis. But, the appeal of the model stems precisely from the way it models the conduct of monetary policy. In practice, central banks do not seem to care very much about monetary measures. In response to the 'monetarist revolution', the Fed adopted monetary targets in 1970 and gave up interest rates as an operating target in 1979. The Bank of England introduced monetary targets in 1973, the Bundesbank in 1975. However, monetary measures continued to fluctuate with no less variability than before for two reasons. First, it proved extremely difficult to control monetary aggregates effectively (probably because of financial innovation). Second, the central banks' commitment to monetary stability was weak: overshooting of monetary measures did not regularly trigger the necessary counter-measures. So, beginning in the early 1980s, monetary measures were deemphasized again. The Fed has not been using any monetary targets since 1993, and the Bank of England dropped monetary targets in 1990. The Bundesbank announced money growth targets until it gave away its power over monetary policy to the ECB in 1999, but evidently did not take these targets very seriously (Bernanke and Mihov 1997). The ECB does not have a monetary target, though it announces a 'reference value' for M3 growth, which is compatible with the inflation target of 2 per cent (see Mishkin 1998: ch. 19 on all this). Taylor (1993) has pointed out that the way the Fed controls interest rates can be described quite accurately by a very simple interest rate rule of the type introduced in equation (4.20). Let y_t denote here the percentage deviation of aggregate output from potential output (which is, of course, not easy to determine) and Δp_t the average inflation rate over the past four quarters. Taylor takes the average inflation rate aimed at by the Fed to be 2 per cent and assumes that the average real interest rate is also 2 per cent, so that the average nominal interest rate is 4 per cent. He shows that the Fed's behaviour over the period 1987–92 is very well described by the rule:

$$i_t = 4\% + 0.5y_t + 0.5(\Delta p_t - 2\%).$$

That is, for each percentage point of output above potential output and for each percentage point of inflation above 2 per cent, the Fed raises the short-term interest rate i_t by half a percentage point over its average level of 4 per cent, and vice versa. This Taylor rule is the empirical counterpart of equation (4.20).

....

(4.19) and (4.20) describe the demand side. Equations (4.21) and (4.22) are the aggregate supply and wage-setting equations, respectively (cf. (4.14) and (4.15)). Equations (4.19)–(4.22) determine the time paths for y_t, p_t, w_t, and i_t, independently of the LM curve. The LM curve $m_t - p_t = \phi y_t - i_t/\lambda$ can be used to find the time path for the supply of money m_t needed to achieve the given interest rate target. This requires that the central bank has perfect control of the money supply. Popularized by McCallum (1999), this model has become a standard tool in monetary policy analysis.

For the sake of convenience, let $(\Delta p)^* = 0$. Then, equations (4.19) and (4.20) imply

$$(1 + \sigma c)y_t = \sigma(E_t \Delta p_{t+1} - d\Delta p_t) + \epsilon_t.$$

From (4.21) and (4.22), we get the Lucas supply function: $\gamma y_t = p_t - E_{t-1}p_t$ or

$$\gamma y_t = \Delta p_t - E_{t-1}\Delta p_t. \tag{4.23}$$

Hence,

$$(1 + \sigma c)(\Delta p_t - E_{t-1}\Delta p_t) = \sigma\gamma(E_t \Delta p_{t+1} - d\Delta p_t) + \gamma\epsilon_t. \tag{4.24}$$

Suppose $\Delta p_t = d\Delta p_{t-1} + \varepsilon_t$, where ε_t is white noise. Then, $\Delta p_t - E_{t-1}\Delta p_t = \varepsilon_t$ and $E_t \Delta p_{t+1} - d\Delta p_t = 0$. Inserting these two equations in (4.24) yields $\varepsilon_t = \gamma\epsilon_t/(1 + \sigma c)$. It follows that $\gamma y_t = \Delta p_t - E_{t-1}\Delta p_t = \gamma\epsilon_t/(1 + \sigma c)$. Hence,

$$y_t = \frac{\epsilon_t}{1 + \sigma c}.$$

Aggregate output is white noise. Since the central bank is able to react to current shocks, the policy ineffectiveness proposition is not valid: the countercyclical component of the monetary policy rule serves to dampen the fluctuations: increases in c reduce the variance of y_t.

The Lucas critique

Suppose an economic model with behavioural functions for broad aggregates of economic agents (a consumption function, a money demand equation, etc.) has been estimated econometrically and is then used in order to predict the effects of policy measures on aggregate economic activity. Are the predicted effects a reliable guide for economic policy? In his famous article *Econometric Policy Evaluation: A Critique*, Lucas (1976) points out that this is unlikely to be the case. This is because policy analysis implicitly holds the parameters that describe the agents' behaviour fixed at their estimated values, whereas the true parameters depend on expectations, and expectations change when policy changes. In other words, econometric estimates of the effects of policy measures implicitly hold expectations constant, which in fact, they are not. This is the so-called *Lucas critique*.

The Lucas (1973) model expounded in Section 4.2 can be used to illustrate this point. Suppose the central bank has estimated the relation between output and unanticipated money $y = \eta/(\phi + \gamma)$ and knows the true value of $\phi + \gamma$. It sees an opportunity to stabilize the supply of money (reduce the variance

σ_η^2 of the monetary shocks η) and is interested in the effect on the variance of aggregate output $\sigma_y^2 = \sigma_\eta^2/(\phi + \gamma)^2$. Based on the estimated relationship between y and η, the prediction is that a reduction in σ_η^2 will lead to a $1/(\phi + \gamma)^2$-fold reduction in σ_y^2. But this is wrong. Why? Because the way expectations are formed changes when the variability of the supply of money is altered. From equation (4.9), the reduction in the variability of the supply of money reduces the variance of the aggregate price level σ_p^2 (given that the equation has a unique solution). According to (4.8), this induces agents to put less weight on the observed price in their own market in forming expectations of the aggregate price level, that is, to reduce θ. As a consequence, $\gamma \equiv g/(1 - \theta)$ falls, so that the responsiveness of aggregate output $y = \eta/(\phi + \gamma)$ to monetary shocks η is increased. Hence, the reduction in the variance of aggregate output $\sigma_y^2 = \sigma_\eta^2/(\phi + \gamma)^2$ will be less than predicted by the econometric model.

....

Box 4.4   Small-scale macroeconometric models

The breakdown of the Phillips curve in the 1970s (see Box 3.3) posed a big challenge to the large-scale macroeconometric models. Sims (1980) argues that the whole endeavour was deemed to fail anyway. In constructing large-scale models, model builders estimate the important structural equations of the economy, such as the consumption function, the money demand equation, etc. This requires very strong identifying restrictions, which in effect rule out the interdependencies among the important macro variables to a large extent. This, Sims argues, is fatal in view of the omnipresent simultaneity in complex economies. The problem is aggravated further by the fact that the structural parameters are not even independent of economic policy, as pointed out by the Lucas critique. Accordingly, Sims's (1980) suggestion is to give up the attempt to estimate the structural equations and focus on the reduced form equations from the outset. Formally, a vector of macro variables is regressed on lagged values of itself, using vector autoregression (VAR) techniques and an appropriate set of identifying restrictions. While what happens on a structural level remains hidden in a 'black box', the obtained regression allows it to trace out the impact of monetary and fiscal shocks on the endogenous variables through time, which is most easily done by constructing impulse-response functions. Numerous studies follow this approach. According to Blanchard and Quah (1989), a prominent and representative example, demand shocks raise real GNP. The impact is maximal after one year and fades away only slowly. After another year, only 50 per cent of the maximum effect have vanished. Blanchard and Quah (1989) also consider supply shocks, which are assumed to have a permanent effect on GNP. It takes two years until a supply shock unfolds its maximum effect. Unemployment rises at first in response to increasing productivity, but decreases in the medium run, before it returns to the natural rate. The small-scale models have also become the object of much criticism. For instance, they have been criticized as 'measurement without theory'. Since VAR predictions are based merely on past experience, they are unsuited in times of fundamental changes of the economic environment, when predictions are needed the most.

....

The Lucas critique contributed to the already growing discomfort with Keynesian-style large-scale macroeconometric models (see Box 2.2). In response to the mounting criticisms of these models, Sims (1980) initiated the development of a new generation of small-scale macroeconometric models based on vector autoregressions, which avoid the serious problems damaging the large-scale models (see Box 4.4). The predicted impact of fiscal and monetary stimuli on the real economy is similar to the large-scale models. For instance, Blanchard and Quah (1989) find that expansionary demand shocks have a positive impact on real GNP, which peaks after about one year and is still at 50 per cent of its maximum level after two years.

4.4 Summary

1. New classical economics popularized the use of rational expectations in macroeconomics. The rational expectations hypothesis says that the inhabitants of a model form expectations in exactly the same way as the theorist analysing the model, namely by calculating mathematical expectations.
2. In Lucas's new classical model, output deviates from its natural rate if, and only if, the supply of money deviates from its rationally expected level. Only unanticipated money matters. Therefore, it is beneficial to have a stable and predictable money supply.
3. Lucas's explanation for the result that only unanticipated money matters is that producers (rationally) misperceive the price surprise brought about by a money surprise as a shift in relative demand, which induces them to substitute labour for leisure and expand production. But the result also holds true in a monetarist style model with rational expectations and nominal wage setting one period in advance.
4. Under rational expectations, deliberate monetary policy actions are anticipated. Since only unanticipated money matters for aggregate output, monetary policy is ineffective. This is the Sargent–Wallace policy ineffectiveness proposition.
5. New classical economics makes a strong case for central bank independence. Policymakers' incentives to accommodate wage pressure with loose monetary policy make the economy inflation-prone. This time consistency problem can be solved by conducting monetary policy by rule rather than by discretion. The commitment to price stability can be the result of reputation. Alternatively, it can be enforced by installing

a conservative central banker or by writing contracts which bring the central bankers' interests in line with the goal of price stability.

6. While output is white noise in the Lucas model, it is straightforward to build new classical models which incorporate mechanisms that yield persistence.

7. The Lucas critique warns that econometric policy evaluation, which assumes that the estimated parameters describing economic behaviour are stable, is fallacious when the true parameters depend on expectations. This and other criticisms of the large-scale macroeconometric models have led to the development of a new generation of small-scale macroeconometric models, which confirm the presence of long lags of fiscal and monetary policies.

8. In general, new classical economics highlights that the effectiveness of stabilization policies depends crucially on expectations.

Further Reading

The seminal papers in new classical economics are Lucas's (1972) and (1973) articles. The policy ineffectiveness proposition is originally due to Sargent and Wallace (1975). For a detailed exposition of a test of the new classical model, see Mishkin (1983). The classical paper on rules versus discretion is Barro and Gordon (1983a). For the game theoretic approach to central banking, see the extensive discussion in Cukierman (1992), the essays in Persson and Tabellini (1994), and the brief summary in Fischer (1995). Cukierman (1992) also summarizes some developments in the theory of political business cycles with rational expectations. Darnell and Evans (1990: ch. 7) provide a brilliant survey of the development of small-scale macroeconometric models. Sargent (1996) and Chari (1998) discuss the impact of new classical economics on modern macroeconomics. Also see Lucas's (1996) Nobel Lecture. A more critical stance is taken, for instance, by Blinder (1987).

References

Barro, R. J. (1978). 'Unanticipated Money, Output, and the Price Level in the United States'. *Journal of Political Economy*, 86: 549–80.

——— and Gordon, D. B. (1983a). 'A Positive Theory of Monetary Policy in a Natural Rate Model'. *Journal of Political Economy*, 91: 589–610.

Barro, R. J. and Gordon, D. B. (1983*b*). 'Rules, Discretion, and Reputation in a Model of Monetary Policy'. *Journal of Monetary Economics*, 12: 101–20.

Bernanke, B. S. and Mihov, I. (1997). 'What Does the Bundesbank Target?' *European Economic Review*, 41: 1025–54.

Blanchard, O. J. (1979). 'Speculative Bubbles, Crashes and Rational Expectations'. *Economics Letters*, 3: 387–9.

——and Quah, D. (1989). 'The Dynamic Effects of Aggregate Demand and Supply Disturbances'. *American Economic Review*, 79: 655–73.

Blinder, A. S. (1987). 'Keynes, Lucas, and Scientific Progress'. *American Economic Review*, 77: 130–6.

——and Fischer, S. (1981). 'Inventories, Rational Expectations, and the Business Cycle'. *Journal of Monetary Economics*, 8: 277–304.

Boschen, J. and Grossman, H. I. (1982). 'Tests of Equilibrium Macroeconomics Using Contemporaneous Monetary Data'. *Journal of Monetary Economics*, 10: 309–33.

Chari, V. V. (1998). 'Nobel Laureate Robert E. Lucas, Jr: Architect of Modern Macroeconomics'. *Journal of Economic Perspectives*, 12: 171–86.

Cukierman, A. (1992). *Central Bank Strategy, Credibility, and Independence: Theory and Evidence*. Cambridge, MA: MIT Press.

Darnell, A. C. and Evans, J. L. (1990). *The Limits of Econometrics*. Aldershot: Edward Elgar.

Fama, E. F. (1970). 'Efficient Capital Markets: A Review of Theory and Empirical Work'. *Journal of Finance*, 25: 383–416.

Fischer, S. (1995). 'Central-Bank Independence Revisited'. *American Economic Review*, 85: 201–6.

Laidler, D. E. W. (1976). 'An Elementary Monetarist Model of Simultaneous Fluctuations in Prices and Output', in H. Frisch (ed.), *Inflation in Small Countries*. Berlin: Springer, pp. 75–89.

Lucas, R. E., Jr (1972). 'Expectations and the Neutrality of Money'. *Journal of Economic Theory*, 4: 103–24.

——(1973). 'Some International Evidence on Output-Inflation Tradeoffs'. *American Economic Review*, 63: 326–34.

——(1975). 'An Equilibrium Model of the Business Cycle'. *Journal of Political Economy*, 83: 1113–41.

——(1976). 'Econometric Policy Evaluation: A Critique', in K. Brunner and A. Meltzer (eds), *The Phillips Curve and Labor Markets, Carnegie-Rochester Conference Series, vol. 1*. Amsterdam: North-Holland, pp. 19–46.

——(1996). 'Nobel Lecture: Monetary Neutrality'. *Journal of Political Economy*, 104: 661–82.

McCallum, B. T. (1999). 'Recent Developments in the Analysis of Monetary Policy Rules'. *Federal Reserve Bank of St. Louis Review*, 81: 3–11.

Mishkin, F. S. (1982). 'Does Anticipated Money Matter? An Econometric Investigation'. *Journal of Political Economy*, 90: 22–51.

——(1983). *A Rational Expectations Approach to Macroeconometrics. Testing Policy Ineffectiveness and Efficient-Markets Models*. Chicago: Chicago University Press.

——(1998). *The Economics of Money, Banking, and Financial Markets*, 5th edn. Reading: Addison-Wesley.

Mussa, M. (1976). 'The Exchange Rate, the Balance of Payments and Monetary and Fiscal Policy Under a Regime of Controlled Floating'. *Scandinavian Journal of Economics*, 78: 229–48.

Persson, T. and Tabellini, G. (eds) (1994). *Monetary and Fiscal Policy, vol. 1: Credibility*. Cambridge, MA: MIT Press.

Phelps, E. S. (1990). *Seven Schools of Macroeconomic Thought.* Oxford: Clarendon Press.

Rogoff, K. (1985). 'The Optimal Degree of Commitment to an Intermediate Monetary Target'. *Quarterly Journal of Economics*, 100: 1169–90.

Sargent, T. J. (1979). *Macroeconomic Theory.* New York: Academic Press.

——(1996). 'Expectations and the Nonneutrality of Lucas'. *Journal of Monetary Economics*, 37: 535–48.

—— and Wallace, N. (1975). ' "Rational" Expectations, the Optimal Monetary Instrument and the Optimal Money Supply Rule'. *Journal of Political Economy*, 83: 241–54.

Sims, C. (1980). 'Macroeconomics and Reality'. *Econometrica*, 48: 1–47.

Taylor, J. B. (1993). 'Discretion versus Policy in Practice'. *Carnegie-Rochester Series on Public Policy*, 39: 195–214.

Thomas, L. B., Jr (1999). 'Survey Measures of U.S. Inflation'. *Journal of Economic Perspectives*, 13: 125–44.

Walsh, C. E. (1995). 'Optimal Contracts for Central Bankers'. *American Economic Review*, 85: 150–67.

Exercises

4.1 Price level indeterminacy (Sargent and Wallace 1975). Consider the following variant of the rational expectations monetarist model with stochastic velocity v_t:

$$m_t - p_t + v_t = \phi y_t,$$
$$\gamma y_t = -(w_t - p_t),$$
$$w_t = E_{t-1} p_t.$$

Velocity follows the autoregressive process $v_t = \rho v_{t-1} + \nu_t$, with $0 < \rho < 1$ and ν white noise. The monetary authority observes v_t before it fixes the money supply at time t so that m_t can be conditioned on v_t. Show: Aggregate production obeys

$$y_t = \frac{m_t - E_{t-1} m_t + v_t}{\phi + \gamma}.$$

Suppose the monetary authority announces that it will stabilize aggregate production at $y_t = 0$ with a money supply rule that implies $m_t = E_{t-1} m_t - v_t$. Show that the equilibrium price level is given by $p_t = E_{t-1} m_t + \rho v_{t-1}$. Is the monetary authority's commitment to stabilize aggregate production sufficient to determine the supply of money and the price level?

4.2 The new classical model with interest elastic money demand (Sargent and Wallace 1975):

$$y_t = -\sigma(i_t - E_{t-1}\Delta p_{t+1}),$$
$$m_t - p_t = \phi y_t - i_t/\lambda,$$
$$\gamma y_t = -(w_t - p_t),$$
$$w_t = E_{t-1}p_t.$$

Show:

$$y_t = \frac{\sigma\lambda}{1 + \sigma\lambda(\phi + \gamma)}(m_t - E_{t-1}m_t).$$

4.3 The new classical model with steady full employment and interest elastic money demand:

$$y_t = -\sigma(i_t - E_t\Delta p_{t+1})$$

$$m_t - p_t = \phi y_t - i_t/\lambda$$

$$y_t = 0.$$

Show: The current price level depends on the expectations about the entire future money stock path:

$$p_t = \frac{\lambda}{1 + \lambda}\left[m_t + \frac{E_t m_{t+1}}{1 + \lambda} + \frac{E_t m_{t+2}}{(1 + \lambda)^2} + \cdots\right].$$

4.4 Monetary policy games with a quadratic loss function and productivity shocks. Suppose the loss function is

$$\text{loss}_t = (y_t - y^*)^2 + \beta(\Delta p_t)^2.$$

$y^* > 0$ is the target output level. The Lucas supply function includes productivity shocks θ_t (which are white noise):

$$\gamma y_t = \Delta p_t - E_{t-1}\Delta p_t + \theta_t.$$

The central bank determines Δp_t after observing the realization of the supply shock θ_t, so that inflation $\Delta p_t = \Delta p_{\theta_t}$ is a function of θ_t. Argue: Because of rational expectations, output y_t falls short of y^* on average. Show that under discretion, inflation is positive on average ($E_{t-1}\Delta p_{\theta_t} = y^*/(\beta\gamma)$), that monetary policy reacts countercyclically to supply shocks ($\Delta p_{\theta_t} - E_{t-1}\Delta p_{\theta_t} = -\theta_t/(1 + \beta\gamma^2)$), and that

$$y_t = \frac{\beta\gamma}{1 + \beta\gamma^2}\theta_t.$$

The commitment solution entails $E_{t-1}\Delta p_{\theta_t} = 0$. It solves

$$\min_{\Delta p_{\theta_t}} : E_{t-1}\left[\left(\frac{\Delta p_{\theta_t} + \theta_t}{\gamma} - y^*\right)^2 + \beta(\Delta p_{\theta_t})^2\right],$$

$$\text{s.t.: } E_{t-1}\Delta p_{\theta_t} = 0.$$

Show: y_t obeys the same process as under discretion.

4.5 Optimal contracts for central bankers (Walsh 1995): Suppose it is not possible to write contracts contingent on the realization of θ_t. Assume that inflation and the deviation of output from y^* enter the central banker's loss function quadratically and that his salary enters linearly. The salary $w - \kappa\Delta p_t$ is a decreasing function of inflation, so that his loss function becomes

$$\text{loss}_t = (y_t - y^*)^2 + \beta(\Delta p_t)^2 - (w - \kappa\Delta p_t).$$

Prove that the discretionary solution entails $E_{t-1}\Delta p_{\theta_t} = y^*/(\beta\gamma) - \kappa/(2\beta)$ and the same process for output y_t as the commitment solution from Exercise 4.4. How must κ be chosen so as to ensure that the commitment solution is replicated?

4.6 Inventories and Persistence (Blinder and Fischer 1981):

$$\gamma y_t = p_t - E_{t-1}p_t - vq_t,$$
$$\Delta q_{t+1} = -\theta q_t - \phi(p_t - E_{t-1}p_t),$$

where q_t is the stock of inventories and $\theta < 1$. Price surprises induce firms to raise production and run down their inventories. A low level of inventories induces firms to raise inventory investment Δq_{t+1} and production. Derive the Lucas supply function:

$$y_t = (1 - \theta)y_{t-1} + \frac{1}{\gamma}(p_t - E_{t-1}p_t) + \frac{v\phi - (1 - \theta)}{\gamma}(p_{t-1} - E_{t-2}p_{t-1}).$$

(Hint: Solve the former equation for q_t and substitute the result into the latter.) Explain economically why there is persistence.

4.7 The monetary approach to exchange rate determination (Mussa 1976). Consider a small open economy with interest-elastic money demand in which both uncovered interest parity and purchasing power parity hold and labour is always fully employed:

$$m_t - p_t = \phi y_t - i_t/\lambda,$$
$$i_t = i_t^* + E_t \Delta s_{t+1},$$
$$p_t = p_t^* + s_t,$$
$$y_t = 0.$$

Show: The exchange rate obeys

$$s_t = \frac{x_t + E_t s_{t+1}}{1 + \lambda},$$

where $x_t \equiv \lambda(m_t - p_t^*) - i_t^*$ is exogenous. Show that the current exchange rate depends on the expectations about the entire future time path for x_t:

$$s_t = \frac{1}{1 + \lambda}\left[x_t + \frac{E_t x_{t+1}}{1 + \lambda} + \frac{E_t x_{t+2}}{(1 + \lambda)^2} + \cdots\right].$$

How does the exchange rate react to an increase in the expectation of the domestic money stock ten periods later m_{t+10}? Explain this result.

4.8 Suppose risk neutral investors consider a consol which pays a fixed interest rate r and a stock that pays a constant dividend d as perfect substitutes, so that arbitrage equates the expected returns on the two assets:

$$r p_t = d + E_t(p_{t+1} - p_t),$$

where p_t is the stock price. Show: One solution to this arbitrage equation is $p_t = f_t$, where f_t is the present discounted value of the future dividend payments (i.e. f_t represents the market fundamentals):

$$f_t = \frac{d}{1 + r} + \frac{d}{(1 + r)^2} + \cdots = \frac{d}{r}.$$

4.9 Rational bubbles (Blanchard 1979). Demonstrate that the arbitrage equation in the preceding problem is also satisfied by the bubble b_t which obeys

$d = 0$ and

$$b_{t+1} = \begin{cases} (1+r)b_t/q + \epsilon_{t+1}, & \text{with probability } q, \\ \epsilon_{t+1}, & \text{with probability } 1-q, \end{cases}$$

where ϵ_t is white noise. Show that the arbitrage equation is satisfied by the fundamentals plus bubbles price $p_t = f_t + b_t$. Figure out what the price path $p_t = f_t + b_t$ looks like.

5
...

REAL BUSINESS CYCLES

5.1 Introduction

....

Monetarism and new classical economics emphasize the importance of the supply side in the determination of aggregate production and raise doubts about the need for, and effectiveness of, the activist demand policies recommended by Keynesian economics. The real business cycle (RBC) theory, originating from Kydland and Prescott's (1982) and Long and Plosser's (1983) seminal contributions, goes one step further in these respects (or two steps back to the classical view). It offers a *pure* supply-side explanation for business fluctuations. According to the RBC theory, exogenous fluctuations in the level of total factor productivity make steady reallocations of the factors of production necessary in order to maintain an efficient economic allocation. The RBC theory assumes that households maximize intertemporal utility and firms maximize profits under rational expectations and that there are no market imperfections. As a result, the market equilibrium is efficient and there is no need for government intervention. The view that observed business fluctuations are the variations necessary for the maintenance of full economic efficiency is supported by the fact that it can be demonstrated that many of the crucial regularities of observed business cycles can be reproduced not only qualitatively but also numerically in models with perfect markets, optimizing behaviour on everyone's part and rational expectations.

Section 5.2 presents a very simple RBC model. The more elaborate basic RBC model is introduced in Section 5.3. In Section 5.4, some extensions to the basic RBC model are discussed. Section 5.5 summarizes the main results.

5.2 Simplest Model

We begin our exposition of the RBC theory with a grossly simplified model based on the assumptions that the propensity to save and the supply of labour are fixed, that capital depreciates fully within one period, and that production is Cobb–Douglas. This model does not do justice to the RBC approach, since *ad hoc* decision rules are used instead of optimal planning under rational expectations, but it serves as a useful benchmark for the subsequent analysis.

Consider a closed economy inhabited by a fixed number of infinitely-lived households. The representative household is endowed with L (>0) units of labour, which it supplies inelastically in the labour market. Full employment is assumed, and the aggregate production function is Cobb–Douglas. Therefore,

$$Y_t = \Theta_t K_t^{1-\alpha} L^{\alpha}, \qquad 0 < \alpha < 1, \tag{5.1}$$

where K_t denotes the capital stock at time t and Θ_t denotes the random level of *total factor productivity* (TFP). Fluctuations in TFP Θ represent productivity shocks. The process for Θ_t is specified below. We turn to a general discussion of the role and nature of productivity shocks in the RBC theory later in this chapter. Capital K_t depreciates fully within one period and saving equals a fixed fraction s ($0 < s < 1$) of aggregate income. Hence, $K_t = sY_{t-1}$. Inserting this into the production function gives $Y_t = \Theta_t(sY_{t-1})^{1-\alpha}L^{\alpha}$ or, after taking logarithms,

$$y_t = (1-\alpha)\log s + \alpha \log L + (1-\alpha)y_{t-1} + \theta_t, \tag{5.2}$$

where $\theta_t \equiv \log \Theta_t$ is the logarithm of total factor productivity, which is assumed stationary: $E\theta_t = 0$. Then, average output is $Ey_t = (1-\alpha)\log s/\alpha + \log L$ and the deviations $\tilde{y}_t \equiv y_t - Ey_t$ of output y_t from Ey_t obey

$$\tilde{y}_t - (1-\alpha)\tilde{y}_{t-1} = \theta_t.$$

Suppose first that θ_t is white noise. Obviously, aggregate production fluctuates and there is persistence. The source of the persistence is capital stock dynamics: if GNP is high in one period, then savings and, hence, the capital stock and GNP are still high in the following period.

However, this simple RBC model has two disturbing properties. First, RBC theorists aim at explaining certain empirical regularities, such as the high persistence of quarterly GNP, not only qualitatively, but also numerically. A standard estimate of α is 2/3. Here we have $\rho_{\tilde{y}}^1 = 1/3$ when $\alpha = 2/3$.

So the degree of autocorrelation in GNP that arises with the capital stock as the only source of persistence is low. (With less than full depreciation of the capital stock, there is even less autocorrelation in aggregate production. This is because the impact of additional savings in periods when output is high on the capital stock becomes weaker.) Second, as mentioned in Section 1.3, macro-econometric models predict a hump-shaped impulse-response function as an important characteristic of output fluctuations and RBC theorists take this as one of the features of output movements their models should explain. Here, since y_t obeys a first-order equation, the impulse-response function is mono-tonic (oscillatory output dynamics cannot arise, but this is not essential in the RBC view). A natural way to solve the first problem (low persistence) is to assume that the shocks to TFP θ_t are persistent, so that there is a second source of persistence besides capital stock dynamics. It turns out that this also helps to solve the second problem (no hump in the impulse-response function). Let $\theta_t = \rho\theta_{t-1} + \vartheta_t$: the autocorrelation of the productivity disturbance is ρ $(0 < \rho < 1)$. Consider the response of GNP to a one-off shock $\vartheta_0 > 0$ at $t = 0$. Since $\tilde{y}_0 = \vartheta_0$ and $\tilde{y}_1 = (1 - \alpha + \rho)\vartheta_0$, we have $\tilde{y}_1 > \tilde{y}_0$ if $\rho > \alpha$. As θ_t goes back to zero, so does y_t. Thus, the introduction of sufficiently strong autocorrelation in TFP not only generates additional persistence in GNP, but also leads to the presence of turning points in GNP movements.

5.3 The Basic RBC Model

If business-cycle phenomena are present in the behavior of our model economy, they are perfectly consistent with ideal economic efficiency.

Long and Plosser (1983: 42)

The major goal of the RBC theory is to demonstrate that neoclassical models with perfect markets are capable of describing observed business cycles numerically. In this section, the basic RBC model is developed. Assume there is a continuum of mass one of identical, infinitely-lived agents. The representative agent's time endowment is normalized to equal unity. Let L_t denote the time spent working. Leisure then equals $1 - L_t$. At a given point in time, a worker obtains utility $u(C_t, 1 - L_t)$ from consumption C_t and leisure $1 - L_t$. The utility function u is concave and continuously differentiable with positive and decreasing marginal utilities ($\partial u/\partial x > 0 > \partial^2 u/\partial x^2$ for $x = C_t, 1 - L_t$). Intertemporal utility from time t on is given by the discounted sum of current utilities:

$$\sum_{\tau=t}^{\infty} \beta^{\tau-t} u(C_\tau, 1 - L_\tau), \tag{5.3}$$

where β $(0 < \beta < 1)$ is the discount factor. As in the simple model above, there is a single homogeneous output good Y which serves both for consumption and for investment. The production process is described by the neoclassical production function:

$$Y_t = \Theta_t F(K_t, L_t).$$

F is concave and continuously differentiable with positive, decreasing marginal productivities $(\partial F/\partial x > 0 > \partial^2 F/\partial x^2$ for $x = K_t, L_t)$ and constant returns to scale $(\lambda \Theta_t F(K_t, L_t) = \Theta_t F(\lambda K_t, \lambda L_t)$ for all $\lambda > 0)$. Capital K_t depreciates at rate δ $(0 \le \delta \le 1)$. That is, between periods t and $t + 1$ a fraction δ of the capital stock K_t wears out:

$$K_{t+1} = (1 - \delta)K_t + \Theta_t F(K_t, L_t) - C_t.$$

The current supply shock Θ_t is observed before decisions are made in period t. There are no 'productivity surprises'.

Efficiency

Given a sequence of exogenous productivity shocks $\{\Theta_\tau\}_{\tau=t}^{\infty}$, the time paths for all variables are determined once paths for consumption $\{C_\tau\}_{\tau=t}^{\infty}$ and labour $\{L_\tau\}_{\tau=t}^{\infty}$ are chosen. In the present paragraph, we investigate the utility maximizing choices of $\{C_\tau\}_{\tau=t}^{\infty}$ and $\{L_\tau\}_{\tau=t}^{\infty}$. C_t and L_t jointly determine the capital stock in the next period K_{t+1} with certainty. However, since Θ_{t+1}, as well as all subsequent productivity shocks, are unknown as of time t, this is an optimization problem under uncertainty. As in the previous chapter, let $E_t x_{t+\tau}$ denote the rational expectation of $x_{t+\tau}$ as of time t. Then the maximization problem becomes:

$$\max_{\{C_\tau, L_\tau\}_{\tau=t}^{\infty}} : E_t \left[\sum_{\tau=t}^{\infty} \beta^{\tau-t} u(C_\tau, 1 - L_\tau) \right],$$

$$\text{s.t.} : K_{t+1} = (1 - \delta)K_t + \Theta_t F(K_t, L_t) - C_t. \tag{5.4}$$

We focus on an interior solution with $C_t > 0$ and $0 < L_t < 1$ for all t. Sufficient conditions for an interior solution to arise are $\partial F/\partial x = \infty$ for $x = 0$ $(x = K_t, L_t)$, $\partial u/\partial x = \infty$ for $x = 0$ $(x = C_t, 1-L_t)$, and $\partial u(C_t, 1)/\partial(1-L_t)$ small. The problem is solved via dynamic programming. (The solution is

self-contained. No prior knowledge of dynamic programming is required.)
The *principle of optimality* states that in order for a programme $\{C_\tau, L_\tau\}_{\tau=t}^\infty$
to be optimal, it must be true that from each date $t' > t$, the remainder
$\{C_\tau, L_\tau\}_{\tau=t'}^\infty$ of the programme maximizes expected utility over the remainder of the planning horizon $(t', t'+1, t'+2, \dots)$. If this were not the case,
then intertemporal utility could be increased by switching at t' to the programme $\{C_\tau, L_\tau\}_{\tau=t'}^\infty$ which maximizes utility from time t' onwards. (Notice
the analogy to backward induction in finitely often repeated games. See Sec-
tion 4.3.) The level of intertemporal utility attainable over the remainder of
the planning period depends on how much capital is available. Let $V(K_t)$
denote the present value of the programme from time t onwards. That is,
$V(K_t) \equiv \sum_{\tau=t}^\infty \beta^{\tau-t} u(C_\tau, 1 - L_\tau)$ with $\{C_\tau, L_\tau\}_{\tau=t}^\infty$ denoting the optimal
programme. Then,

$$V(K_t) \equiv \max_{C_t, L_t} \{u(C_t, 1 - L_t) + \beta E_t[V(K_{t+1})]\},$$

subject to (5.4). This equation is known as the *Bellman equation* for the maximization problem at hand. It states that the optimal decision today (C_t, L_t)
maximizes the sum of current utility $u(C_t, 1-L_t)$ and the expected discounted
value of all future utilities $\beta E_t[V(K_{t+1})]$, given that the latter is itself max-
imized. This follows from the principle of optimality. The maximization in
the Bellman equation yields the necessary optimality conditions:

$$\frac{\partial u}{\partial C_t} = \beta E_t[V'(K_{t+1})], \tag{5.5}$$

$$\frac{\partial u}{\partial (1 - L_t)} = \beta \Theta_t \frac{\partial F}{\partial L_t} E_t[V'(K_{t+1})]. \tag{5.6}$$

Use has been made of the fact that $\Theta_t \partial F / \partial L_t$ is known with certainty at time t.
Differentiating the Bellman equation with respect to K_t yields

$$V'(K_t) = \beta \left(1 - \delta + \Theta_t \frac{\partial F}{\partial K_t}\right) E_t[V'(K_{t+1})], \tag{5.7}$$

where use is made of the fact that $1 - \delta + \Theta_t \partial F / \partial K_t$ is known with certainty at time t. This equation says that the increase in intertemporal utility
$V'(K_t)$ due to the availability of one additional unit of capital is the discounted product of, first, the increase in the number of goods available
one period later if the additional capital is saved $(1 - \delta + \Theta_t \partial F / \partial K_t)$ and,
second, the expected increase in intertemporal utility due to the availability
of an additional unit of capital $(E_t[V'(K_{t+1})])$. That there are no indirect
effects in addition to this follows from the envelope theorem: the indirect

effects $(\partial V/\partial C_t)(\partial C_t/\partial K_t)$ and $(\partial V/\partial L_t)(\partial L_t/\partial K_t)$ vanish because C_t and L_t maximize $V(K_t)$ (i.e. $\partial V/\partial C_t = \partial V/\partial L_t = 0$).

If the value function $V(K_t)$ were known, then one could substitute for K_{t+1} from (5.4) into (5.5) and (5.6) and would obtain two equations relating C_t and L_t to the current capital stock K_t. Thus, C_t and L_t could be determined as functions of K_t. Inserting these functions into (5.3) would give a difference equation in the capital stock K_t alone. This difference equation would determine the evolution of the capital stock and, hence, of consumption C_t and work hours L_t. But the value function $V(K_t)$ is not known a priori. There is one additional equation, however, that is not used in the argument above: the envelope relation (5.7). Finding a solution to the maximization problem under consideration consists of finding a value function $V(K_t)$ and sequences for consumption C_t, hours worked L_t, and capital K_t which simultaneously satisfy (5.4)–(5.6), and the envelope relation (5.7). This is a difficult problem in general. A closed-form solution exists only under very special restrictions on u, F, and δ. We derive the closed-form solution for two special cases below. Before that, it is shown that the market equilibrium is efficient irrespective of the specific functional forms chosen.

Market equilibrium

Suppose there are perfect goods, labour, and capital markets, and let the final good be the numeraire. Assume households own the capital stock K_t directly and rent it to firms period-by-period in exchange for interest payment r_t. The (real) wage rate is denoted W_t. Because of constant returns to scale, the scale of each firm operating is indeterminate, and the production sector can be represented by a single price-taking firm, which maximizes profit $\Theta_t F(K_t, L_t) - W_t L_t - r_t K_t$ with an appropriate choice of capital K_t and labour L_t. Both factors are hired up to the point where their respective marginal products equal their prices, and equilibrium profit is zero:

$$W_t = \Theta_t \frac{\partial F}{\partial L_t}, \quad r_t = \Theta_t \frac{\partial F}{\partial K_t}, \quad Y_t = r_t K_t + W_t L_t. \tag{5.8}$$

(The last equality is obtained by differentiating $\lambda \Theta_t F(K_t, L_t) = \Theta_t F(\lambda K_t, \lambda L_t)$ with respect to λ, setting $\lambda = 1$, and inserting the former two equations.) Each agent earns capital income $r_t K_t$ and labour income $W_t L_t$. So the household budget constraint reads $K_{t+1} = (1 - \delta)K_t + W_t L_t + r_t K_t - C_t$.

5 Real Business Cycles

The individuals solve the following maximization problem:

$$\max_{\{C_\tau, L_\tau\}_{\tau=t}^\infty} : E_t \left[\sum_{\tau=t}^\infty \beta^{\tau-t} u(C_\tau, 1 - L_\tau) \right],$$

$$\text{s.t.} : K_{t+1} = (1 - \delta)K_t + W_t L_t + r_t K_t - C_t. \tag{5.9}$$

The solution to this problem is found by means of dynamic programming. The Bellman equation is:

$$V(K_t) = \max_{C_t, L_t} \{ u(C_t, 1 - L_t) + \beta E_t [V(K_{t+1})] \},$$

subject to (5.9). The necessary optimality conditions are:

$$\frac{\partial u}{\partial C_t} = \beta E_t [V'(K_{t+1})], \tag{5.10}$$

$$\frac{\partial u}{\partial (1 - L_t)} = \beta W_t E_t [V'(K_{t+1})]. \tag{5.11}$$

Differentiating the Bellman equation, using the fact that there are no indirect effects of K_t on $V(K_t)$ through C_t or L_t, yields:

$$V'(K_t) = \beta(1 - \delta + r_t) E_t [V'(K_{t+1})]. \tag{5.12}$$

Using the factor-price equations in (5.8), equations (5.9)–(5.12) can be rewritten as:

$$K_{t+1} = (1 - \delta)K_t + \Theta_t F(K_t, L_t) - C_t,$$

$$\frac{\partial u}{\partial C_t} = \beta E_t [V'(K_{t+1})],$$

$$\frac{\partial u}{\partial (1 - L_t)} = \beta \Theta_t \frac{\partial F}{\partial L_t} E_t [V'(K_{t+1})],$$

$$V'(K_t) = \beta \left(1 - \delta + \Theta_t \frac{\partial F}{\partial K_t} \right) E_t [V'(K_{t+1})].$$

These four equations are identical to equations (5.3)–(5.7), which determine the optimal path. Since the equilibrium path and the optimal path are thus determined by the same set of equations, it follows that *the market equilibrium is efficient*. This proposition is the RBC analogue of the First Welfare Theorem. (It holds under much more general conditions than the ones assumed here, see Lucas and Prescott (1971). So the market equilibrium is often analysed by examining the social planning problem in RBC models.)

Closed-form solutions

We now turn to two special cases for which a closed-form solution exists. In the first example, F has the Cobb–Douglas form in (5.1), capital depreciates fully at the end of each period ($\delta = 1$), and utility is logarithmic:

$$u(C_t, 1 - L_t) = \log C_t + v \log (1 - L_t), \qquad v \geq 0.$$

Equations (5.5)–(5.7) become

$$\frac{1}{C_t} = \beta E_t[V'(K_{t+1})], \tag{5.13}$$

$$\frac{v}{1 - L_t} = \beta \frac{\alpha Y_t}{L_t} E_t[V'(K_{t+1})], \tag{5.14}$$

$$V'(K_t) = \beta \frac{(1 - \alpha) Y_t}{K_t} E_t[V'(K_{t+1})]. \tag{5.15}$$

Eliminating $E_t[V'(K_{t+1})]$ from (5.13) and (5.15) yields

$$V'(K_t) = \frac{1}{C_t} \frac{(1 - \alpha) Y_t}{K_t}.$$

Consequently,

$$E_t[V'(K_{t+1})] = E_t \left[\frac{1}{C_{t+1}} \frac{(1 - \alpha) Y_{t+1}}{K_{t+1}} \right].$$

Inserting this into (5.13) gives an alternative expression for an optimal consumption profile:

$$\frac{1}{C_t} = \beta E_t \left[\frac{1}{C_{t+1}} \frac{(1 - \alpha) Y_{t+1}}{K_{t+1}} \right].$$

Suppose there exists a constant saving quota s such that $C_t = (1 - s) Y_t$ satisfies this condition for an optimal consumption profile. There are two possible consequences of using this postulate in the equations derived above. Either the equations produce a contradiction—then saving a constant fraction of income cannot be optimal—or else the equations help us to pin down the level of the savings quota s in terms of the parameters of the model, which will indeed be the case. From constancy of s and (5.3) with $\delta = 1$, it follows that $K_{t+1} = sY_t$. Inserting $C_{t+1} = (1 - s) Y_{t+1}$, $K_{t+1} = sY_t$, and $(1 - s) Y_t = C_t$

into the equation above gives

$$\frac{1}{C_t} = \beta E_t \left[\frac{1}{(1-s)Y_{t+1}} \frac{(1-\alpha)Y_{t+1}}{sY_t} \right] = \frac{\beta(1-\alpha)}{sC_t}.$$

Hence,

$$s = \beta(1-\alpha).$$

Given the constant propensity to save $s = \beta(1-\alpha)$, $C_t = (1-s)Y_t$ indeed represents an optimal consumption decision. Turning to the optimal labour supply L_t, eliminate $E_t[V'(K_{t+1})]$ from (5.13) and (5.14):

$$\frac{v/(1-L_t)}{1/C_t} = \frac{\alpha Y_t}{L_t}.$$

This is the usual static optimality condition saying that the marginal rate of substitution between leisure and consumption (left-hand side) is equal to the real wage rate (right-hand side), which, according to (5.8), equals $W_t = \alpha Y_t/L_t$ in the Cobb–Douglas special case. Substituting $C_t = [1 - \beta(1-\alpha)]Y_t$ and solving for L_t shows that the number of hours worked are constant through time:

$$L_t = \frac{\alpha}{\alpha + v[1 - \beta(1-\alpha)]}.$$

Here it becomes apparent why the simple model presented in Section 5.2 with a fixed propensity to save s and inelastic labour supply L is a useful benchmark: if capital depreciates fully in each period, production is Cobb–Douglas, and utility is logarithmic, then a constant savings quota and inelastic labour supply are the outcome of intertemporal maximization under rational expectations. This also means that the problems encountered in Section 5.2 carry over to the model with microfoundations.

In the second example, the utility function is $u(C_t, 1 - L_t) = C_t$. Since leisure does not enter the utility function, the supply of labour is inelastic: $L_t = L$. As in the first example, full depreciation of the capital stock at the end of each period is assumed ($\delta = 1$). Finally, it is assumed that Θ_t is distributed independently and identically through time with mean $E\Theta = 1$. Equations (5.5) and (5.7) become

$$1 = \beta E_t[V'(K_{t+1})], \tag{5.16}$$

$$V'(K_t) = \beta \Theta_t \frac{\partial F}{\partial K_t} E_t[V'(K_{t+1})].$$

Therefore,

$$V'(K_t) = \Theta_t \frac{\partial F(K_t, L)}{\partial K_t}.$$

Applying this equation to time $t + 1$, taking expectations as of time t, and making use of the fact that $\partial F/\partial K_{t+1}$ is known with certainty as of time t and that $E\Theta = 1$, we have $E_t[V'(K_{t+1})] = \partial F/\partial K_{t+1}$. From equation (5.16), it follows that

$$\frac{\partial F(K_{t+1}, L)}{\partial K_{t+1}} = \frac{1}{\beta}.$$

The equilibrium capital stock $K_t = K^*$ is constant through time: $\partial F(K^*, L)/\partial K_t = 1/\beta$. Aggregate production fluctuates randomly: $Y_t = \Theta_t F(K^*, L)$. (Assuming an interior solution amounts, here, to assuming that K^* can be reached in one period. If not, we get a corner solution. For instance, if K_t is too low initially, we have $C_t = 0$ until K^* is reached.)

Calibrating the RBC model

The goal of the RBC theory is not to generate cyclical fluctuations in Frisch's sense but to demonstrate that in the presence of productivity shocks, perfect markets models are capable of explaining some of the most important features of observed business cycles not only qualitatively but also numerically. To show this, RBC models are calibrated. That is, numerical values obtained from microeconomic and macroeconomic evidence are inserted for the model parameters and a process for the productivity shocks is specified. Then simulations of the calibrated model are performed and the statistical moments of the simulated series are compared with their empirical counterparts. Attention is focused on the second moments of the simulated and the observed time series: standard deviations, autocorrelations, and cross-correlations. For instance, in order to match the data, the autocorrelation of aggregate output with short lags should be positive and large (persistence), investment should be procyclical and 2–3 times as volatile as aggregate output, etc. (see Box 1.2). Box 5.1 describes the calibration results of the influential study of King et al.'s (1988). In this as well as in other studies, '[T]he match between theory and observation is excellent' (Prescott 1986: 21). Thus, the RBC theory is successful at describing observed business cycles numerically. Two objections can be raised. First, as the simple model in Section 5.2 indicates, an indispensable ingredient of a successful calibration is a strongly autocorrelated and relatively volatile process for TFP. Hence, the variability and autocorrelation in aggregate output and other important variables are to a large extent explained by an exogenous random variable: 'output dynamics are essentially the same as

---

Box 5.1   The RBC model at work

King *et al.* (1988) calibrate a baseline RBC model in order to demonstrate that (and check under what conditions) it is capable of describing observed business cycle data not only qualitatively but also numerically. The data they aim at are selected second moments of deseasonalized and detrended quarterly US time series for output, consumption, investment (denoted y, c, i, respectively), and hours worked L over the period 1948–86. For instance, $\hat{\sigma}_y = 5.62\%$ (which is large because linear detrending is performed, see Box 1.2), $\hat{\sigma}_c = 3.86\%, \hat{\sigma}_i = 7.61\%, \hat{\sigma}_L = 2.97\%$, and $\hat{\rho}_y^1 = 0.96$. The RBC model employed by King *et al.* (1988) differs from the basic RBC model presented here in only one respect: there is labour-augmenting technical progress, so that the (Cobb–Douglas) production function becomes $Y = \Theta K^{1-\alpha}(XL)^{\alpha}$, where X grows at an exogenously given rate $(X_t - X_{t-1})/X_{t-1} = \gamma$. King *et al.* (1988) set $\alpha = 0.58$ and $\gamma = 0.004$ in the production function. They use the logarithmic utility function. ν is chosen such that $L = 0.2$ on average, which corresponds to 33.6 work hours per week. They notice that the implied wage elasticity of labour supply is 4 (King *et al.* 1988: 215). The discount factor β equals 0.988 and the rate of depreciation is $\delta = 2.5\%$. King *et al.* (1988) show that the ratios $y \equiv Y/X, c \equiv C/X$, and $i \equiv I/X$ are constant on average (a well-known result from the theory of economic growth). These ratios are regarded as the theoretical counterparts of detrended and deseasonalized output y, consumption c, and investment i.

Two different specifications for TFP are considered. Under the first specification, θ ($\equiv \log \Theta$) is white noise with standard deviation $\sigma_\theta = 1\%$. The performance of the model is disappointing. The variability of aggregate output is too weak ($\sigma_y = 1.78\%$), although hours worked fluctuate quite a lot ($\sigma_L = 1.34\%$). Since capital evolves smoothly and the productivity shocks are not autocorrelated, there is almost no autocorrelation in aggregate output movements ($\rho_y^1 = 0.03$). This latter observation suggests how to improve the model's performance: by assuming autocorrelated productivity shocks. Accordingly, the second specification assumes $\theta_t = 0.9\theta_{t-1} + \vartheta_t$, where ϑ is white noise with $\sigma_\vartheta = 1\%$ (hence $\rho_\theta^1 = 0.9$ and $\sigma_\theta = 2.29\%$). Now King *et al.* (1988) obtain more variability and high persistence in aggregate output ($\sigma_y = 4.26\%, \rho_y^1 = 0.93$). Since consumption is relatively smooth ($\sigma_c = 2.73\%$), investment is very volatile ($\sigma_i = 9.82\%$). The standard deviation of hours worked equals $\sigma_L = 2.04\%$. This calibration exercise supports Prescott's (1986: 21) contention that '[T]he match between theory and observation is excellent'.

---

impulse dynamics' (Cogley and Nason 1995: 493). (Box 5.2 briefly reviews the discussion of the role of productivity shocks in RBC models.) Second, since the capital stock grows relatively smoothly, the most important endogenous source of variability in aggregate output is employment fluctuations. Since full employment is assumed, a sizable wage elasticity of the supply of labour is required. Most economists agree that the long-run wage elasticity of labour supply is low, due to counteracting income and substitution effects (see Pencavel 1986). This does not imply that the short-run elasticity, which is relevant to variations in employment at business cycle frequency, is low as well, for transitory variations in the real wage rate have a small impact on lifetime

....

Box 5.2   Productivity shocks

RBC theorists justify their reliance on productivity shocks with the observation that measured TFP fluctuates markedly. This is shown by means of *growth accounting.* Assume that production is Cobb–Douglas: $Y_t = \Theta_t K_t^{1-\alpha} L_t^\alpha$. Then $\Delta\theta_t = \Delta y_t - (1-\alpha)\Delta k_t - \alpha\Delta l_t$ (where lower-case letters denote logarithms): TFP growth is the portion of output growth which is not explained by growth in the tangible factors of production. With time series for $y_t, k_t,$ and l_t and an estimate for α, a time series for $\Delta\theta_t$ can be constructed. This procedure goes back to Solow (1957), $\Delta\theta_t$ is therefore called the *Solow residual.* Proceeding this way, Prescott (1986: 15) finds that 'the process on the technology parameter is highly persistent with the standard deviation of change being about 0.90'. This lends support to the way technology enters the RBC models. In fact, modern RBC models do not specify the process for TFP *ad hoc*, but use estimates of actual TFP numbers.

Several objections to this approach have been raised, however. First, variations in measured TFP may be due to labour hoarding and measurement error. Second, the RBC theory is unspecific about what these productivity shocks are ('Why don't we read about them in the Wall Street Journal?'). Oil price shocks have been suggested as a good example. But Kim and Loungani (1992: 186) find that 'the inclusion of energy price shocks leads to only a modest reduction in the RBC model's reliance on unobserved technology shocks'. Third, if one interprets TFP shocks more literally as variations in technological capabilities, adverse productivity shocks are hard to explain, and the probability of an adverse shock is 37 per cent with a TFP process obtained from conventional growth accounting (Burnside *et al.* 1996: 867). Fourth, technological shocks to different sectors of the economy should to a large extent average out, so that the impact on the aggregate economy is weak. Fifth, output movements of a given sector in different countries should be more closely correlated than movements of different sectors in a given country. Actually, the opposite is true. Sixth, given that variations in TFP are the only source of shocks to the economy, the correlation between TFP and aggregate output should be very high. But empirical estimates generally range below one-half. Prescott (1986: 12), for instance, reports a value of 0.34. Seventh, since the RBC model contains only weak propagation mechanisms, 'output dynamics are essentially the same as impulse dynamics' (Cogley and Nason 1995: 493). Since productivity is highly autocorrelated (recall that King *et al.* 1988 assume $\rho_\theta^1 = 0.9$, which is in line with Prescott's 1986 estimate), productivity growth is close to a random walk. So output growth too is close to a random walk in the RBC model. Empirically, by contrast, the autocorrelation of productivity growth at lag one is about 0.3 and significantly positive (Cogley and Nason 1995: 494). Eighth and relatedly, since the output dynamics are essentially the same as the impulse dynamics and the impulse dynamics are random, only a small portion of future output movements should be forecastable. Empirically, however, a sizeable portion of future output is forecastable (Rotemberg and Woodford 1996). These criticisms do not deny the importance of productivity shocks, but they cast doubt on the all-importance assigned to them by the RBC theory.

....

income (i.e. a small income effect), but a potentially significant substitution effect. It is conceivable that households shift leisure from period to period in response to price signals, enjoying more leisure in recessions, when real wages are low, than in expansions, when real wages are high. New classical

---

Box 5.3 The Intertemporal substitution hypothesis

New classical economics and the RBC theory stress the procyclicality of the real wage rate and assert that the supply of labour is strongly positively related to transitory movements in the real wage rate. In a classical paper, Lucas and Rapping (1969), using annual US data for the period 1930–65, estimate that (while a permanent change in the real wage rate leaves labour supply practically unchanged) a transitory 1 per cent increase in the real wage rate causes a 1.40 per cent increase in the supply of labour. Two objections can be made. First, empirically, the procyclicality of real wages is not very pronounced, so that the pecuniary incentives to substitute intertemporally are weak. Second, 'as much as three quarters of the variation in total hours of employment takes the form of movements in and out of the labor force rather than adjustments in average hours of work' (Cho and Cooley 1994: 411). So what the intertemporal substitution hypothesis claims is not so much that everyone chooses to work somewhat less in recessions, when wages are low, but that some choose not to work at all: there are sizable variations in voluntary unemployment. One piece of evidence against this view is studies of self-reported happiness: unemployed people usually report themselves as significantly less happy than employed people do (Clark and Oswald 1994). This may be considered as inconclusive because of the problems of measuring and comparing individual happiness and because a third factor may cause both unemployment and unhappiness. Yet, there is also Lucas-Rapping type econometric evidence that casts doubt on the intertemporal substitution hypothesis. Altonji (1982: 794) obtains a negative labour supply elasticity of −1.89 per cent for the US for the period 1931–76 using a different treatment of expectations. Also, Ham (1986) demonstrates that people who become unemployed tend to be off their labour supply curves, working less than they would want to.

---

economists and RBC theorists assert the validity of this *intertemporal substitution hypothesis*: 'leisure in one period is an excellent substitute for leisure in other, nearby periods' (Lucas 1977: 225). But empirical investigations raise severe doubts (see Box 5.3).

5.4 Extensions to the Basic RBC Model

From the mid-1980s to the mid-1990s, the RBC theory was the most active field of research in business cycle theory. (Since then, new classical-style monetary models have come back to the fore.) In this section, we review some of the most prominent extensions to the basic RBC model. The first part of the section is concerned with extensions to the basic RBC model which address the relationship between productivity, wages, and hours worked. The second part is concerned with other variants of the basic RBC model.

Productivity, wages, and work hours

According to Christiano and Eichenbaum (1992: 430), 'the single most salient shortcoming of existing RBC models' is that the predicted correlation between productivity (or wages) and hours worked is much too large, 'well in excess of 0.9, whereas the actual correlation is much closer to zero'. Despite this high correlation, which others criticize, the predicted volatility of hours worked relative to GNP is too low. That is, the optimizing agents inhabiting the basic RBC model supply labour too inelastically. The RBC model would yield more precise numerical predictions if hours worked responded more sensitively to wage rate changes, so that a realistic degree of variability in hours worked could be obtained with a realistic value for the correlation between wages and hours. This is not an easy task. We have seen that the wage elasticity of labour supply is already high in standard calibrations (equal to 4 in King *et al.*'s 1988 model, whereas it is close to zero empirically, see Boxes 5.1 and 5.3). So it is implausible to aim at a higher wage elasticity of labour supply by increasing the substitutability of labour for leisure along the intensive margin, that is, changes in the hours worked by employed workers. Accordingly, RBC theorists often emphasize substitution along the extensive margin, that is, movements into and out of the labour force, which is in line with the observation that this accounts for most of the variation in hours worked (see Box 5.3).

Kydland and Prescott (1982) assume that preferences are nonseparable: the harder people work today, the higher they value leisure tomorrow. Clearly, this raises the wage elasticity of labour supply, since the incentives to rest in recessions after having worked hard in expansions are magnified, but the effect of this enhanced substitution along the intensive margin is not important numerically (Rouwenhorst 1991). Hansen (1985) proposes a way of generating an infinite wage elasticity of labour supply, which is frequently used in subsequent RBC papers. He assumes that utility is logarithmic: $u(C, 1 - L) = \log C + v \log (1 - L)$. Labour is indivisible. So agents work either full time ($L = \bar{L}$, where $\bar{L}$ is given and $0 < \bar{L} < 1$) or not at all ($L = 0$). All workers receive the same wage rate, but only a fraction η of them, drawn at random from the total population of workers, has to work. The expected utility of a worker thus equals $Eu = \log C + \eta v \log (1 - \bar{L})$. Average hours worked per hired worker are $L = \eta \bar{L}$. Substituting $\eta = L/\bar{L}$ into the expected utility function yields

$$Eu = \log C + v \frac{\log (1 - \bar{L})}{\bar{L}} L.$$

The trick is that, even though utility is a strictly concave function of leisure $1 - L$, expected utility is linear in L because L enters the expression for

87

expected utility only through the employment probability $L/\bar{L}$. As a result, hours of leisure in different periods are perfect substitutes and the elasticity of leisure in different periods and the wage elasticity of the supply of labour are infinite. Hansen's (1985) calibration demonstrates that in his RBC model with indivisible labour, the variability of hours worked is considerably larger than in the basic RBC model. Similarly, Cho and Cooley (1994) assume that there is a fixed cost associated with each working day. So households adjust their supply of labour in response to wage rate changes along both the intensive margin and the extensive margin. Cho and Cooley demonstrate that this helps to explain a high labour supply elasticity and improves the match between simulated and observed business cycle data. Benhabib *et al.* (1991) introduce a choice between home production and market production into the basic RBC model. When the wage rate rises, agents substitute labour for leisure and for home production. This increases the predicted volatility of hours worked and reduces the predicted correlation between wages and GNP. Christiano and Eichenbaum (1992) introduce government expenditure shocks. Additional government expenditure draws resources from the private sector. This makes agents feel poorer and enjoy less leisure, since leisure is a normal good. Hence, government expenditure shocks induce movements along firms' downward-sloping labour demand curve and, therefore, reduce the positive correlation between wages and hours. Bencivenga (1992) introduces preference shocks that explain additional variability in hours worked. Following Merz (1995), search unemployment has been introduced to RBC models. In booms, when wages are high, search activity is high and unemployed people quickly move into the labour force. In recessions, the opposite situation prevails. The papers mentioned so far argue that, for various reasons, the supply of labour is more volatile than in the basic RBC model. Cho and Cooley (1995) take a different route in order to come up with stronger variations in employment, which emphasizes the volatility of the demand for labour. They incorporate nominal wage stickiness and monetary shocks into the basic RBC model. Like government shocks, monetary shocks induce movements along a given labour demand curve, thereby reducing the predicted correlation between wages and hours. Boldrin and Horvath (1995) argue that standard RBC models overstate the correlation between productivity and wages because they neglect implicit contracts between employers and workers. If workers are more risk-averse than employers and are unable to insure against income risk in the insurance market, the contractual wage rate involves an insurance component: to smooth income, employers pay wages above the marginal productivity of labour in recessions and wages below the marginal productivity of labour in booms. Boldrin and Horvath demonstrate that including implicit contracts in an otherwise standard RBC model makes real wages less volatile and almost acyclical.

Other extensions

Many other extensions to the basic RBC model are discussed in the literature. Kydland and Prescott (1982) assume that investments over several periods of time ('time to build') are necessary in order to complete an investment project (as in the over-investment theory). This increases the amount of persistence predicted by the model, but the effect is not important numerically (Rouwenhorst 1991). Long and Plosser (1983) consider a multi-sector RBC model. The advantage of the multisectoral structure is that it allows for more complex dynamics than the basic RBC model. Unlike in most other RBC models, cyclical movements in Frisch's sense may occur. However, it becomes more difficult to explain aggregate fluctuations because independent shocks to different sectors average out to a large extent at the economy-wide level (see Box 5.2). Benhabib and Nishimura (1985) show analytically that endogenous cycles can emerge in a two-sector variant of the basic RBC model. King and Plosser (1984) explain the correlation between aggregate output and money in an RBC model with reverse causation (cf. Box 3.1). Money is modelled as a produced intermediate good which facilitates market transactions. When productivity shocks raise real aggregate production, the financial sector adjusts to the increased demand for money. Hence, aggregate production and money move together, with the former causing the latter movement. Backus *et al.* (1994) explain the countercyclicality of the trade balance with an open economy version of the basic RBC model. The intuition behind their explanation is that in response to a positive productivity shock, investment rises sharply, so that the sum of consumption and investment rises by more than aggregate production, and net exports fall. The model is also successful at explaining the negative relation between net exports and the terms of trade. The model displays two important anomalies, however. First, contrary to the data, it predicts that the correlation of consumption levels across countries is greater than the correlation of aggregate output levels (the 'quantity anomaly'). This is because when productivity is low at home and high abroad, domestic citizens sustain consumption levels by increasing net exports. Second, the predicted volatility of the terms of trade is too low (the 'price anomaly'). In Cho and Cooley's (1995) monetary RBC model mentioned above, unlike in the King–Plosser (1984) model, money has an impact on the real economy because of nominal wage stickiness. Besides helping to explain variable work hours, this model represents a conceptual departure from the original RBC approach because it breaks with the original attempt to model business fluctuations as a pure supply-side phenomenon. Cho and Cooley show that monetary shocks (i.e. demand shocks) of a realistic magnitude are sufficient to explain observed output movements. They emphasize, however, that the Dunlop–Tarshis critique (Box 2.3) then applies: as monetary shocks induce movements along a given labour demand function, the predicted correlation between output and real wages is strongly negative. Burnside and Eichenbaum (1996), and King and Rebelo (1999) stress the importance of varying degrees of capacity utilization. In the basic RBC model, capital $K_{t+1} = (1 - \delta)K_t + \Theta_t F(K_t, L_t) - C_t$ is a predetermined variable, so the short-run elasticity of the supply of capital is zero. With variable capacity utilization, the supply of capital becomes elastic. This has a direct positive impact on the variability of aggregate output. This direct effect is amplified because the marginal productivity of labour and, therefore, equilibrium employment move in the same direction as capacity utilization. Farmer and Guo (1994), and Carlstrom and Fuerst (1997) introduce sunspots and financial constraints to the RBC model, topics we address in the following chapter.

A final remark on aggregate supply and aggregate demand

New classical economics and the RBC theory have had an outstanding methodological impact on the science of macroeconomics. Macroeconomic theorizing conforms to different standards now after Lucas's (1972), and Kydland and Prescott's (1982) papers. It seems fair to say, however, that their impact on our understanding of the mechanisms generating business fluctuations has not been comparably profound. Chari (1998: 181), a strong advocate of the new methods of macroeconomic theorizing, contends that '[N]either paper's substantive message has been accepted by the profession at large'. The reason why the RBC theory's impact on our understanding of business fluctuations is limited is that, whereas Keynesian theory failed to take adequate account of aggregate supply, the RBC theory inadequately plays down the role of aggregate demand. The attempt to explain business fluctuations with a complete neglect of the demand side, with at best a minor role to play for shifts in the demand for consumption, investment, and net exports, appears to stretch the importance of the supply side too far.

....

5.5   Summary

....

1. The RBC theory explains business cycles by means of models with perfect markets and rational expectations. Observed business fluctuations are regarded as the efficient outcome of the interaction between agents' maximizing behaviour.

2. Monetarism brought the supply side, which had been pushed to the background in Keynesian economics, back to the fore. The RBC theory ignores the demand side altogether and offers a pure supply-side explanation for business fluctuations.
3. The RBC theory aims at explaining observed business fluctuations not only qualitatively, but also numerically. Calibrated RBC models generate time series for output, consumption, and investment whose statistical properties mimic the statistical moments of observed time series closely.
4. A serious drawback of the RBC approach is that much of the variability and persistence generated by the calibrated models is due to exogenous productivity shocks. And the very notion of large economy-wide productivity shocks is debatable.
5. In the basic RBC model, hours are not volatile enough even though the predicted correlation between hours and real wages is too high. One strand of the literature aims at getting the correlations between productivity and wages, on the one hand, and hours worked, on the other hand, right. The required high wage elasticity of labour supply can be achieved in extended RBC models with labour indivisibilities, home production, government expenditure shocks, or preference shocks. An alternative explanation for the volatility of hours worked is based on nominal wage stickiness.
6. Other extensions to the basic RBC model are concerned with time to build, multisectoral dynamics, money, and the international economy.

Further Reading

The classic RBC papers are Kydland and Prescott (1982), and Long and Plosser (1983). Prescott (1986) provides an authoritative survey from an RBC theorist's point of view. A critical assessment from a new Keynesian perspective is in Mankiw (1989). Stadler (1994) gives an impartial account of the merits and weaknesses of the RBC theory. A very recent survey is in King and Rebelo (1999).

References

Altonji, J. (1982). 'The Intertemporal Substitution Model of Labor Market Fluctuations: An Empirical Analysis'. *Review of Economic Studies*, 47: 783–824.

Backus, D. K., Kehoe, P. J. and Kydland, F. E. (1994). 'Dynamics of the Trade Balance and the Terms of Trade: The J-Curve?' *American Economic Review*, 84: 84–103.

Bencivenga, V. R. (1992). 'An Econometric Study of Hours and Output Variation with Preference Shocks'. *International Economic Review*, 33: 449–71.

Benhabib, J. and Nishimura, K. (1985). 'Competitive Equilibrium Cycles'. *Journal of Economic Theory*, 35: 284–306.

—— Rogerson, R., and Wright, R. (1991). 'Homework in Macroeconomics: Household Production and Aggregate Fluctuations'. *Journal of Political Economy*, 99: 1166–87.

Boldrin, M. and Horvath, M. (1995). 'Labor Contracts and Business Cycles'. *Journal of Political Economy*, 103: 972–1004.

Burnside, C. and Eichenbaum, M. (1996). 'Factor Hoarding and the Propagation of Business Cycle Shocks'. *American Economic Review*, 86: 1154–74.

—— —— and Rebelo, S. T. (1996). 'Sectoral Solow Residuals'. *European Economic Review*, 40: 861–9.

Carlstrom, C. and Fuerst, T. (1997). 'Agency Costs, Net Worth, and Business Fluctuations: A Computable General Equilibrium Analysis'. *American Economic Review*, 87: 893–910.

Chari, V. V. (1998). 'Nobel Laureate Robert E. Lucas, Jr.: Architect of Modern Macroeconomics'. *Journal of Economic Perspectives*, 12: 171–86.

Cho, J.-O. and Cooley, T. F. (1994). 'Employment and Hours Over the Business Cycle'. *Journal of Economic Dynamics and Control*, 18: 411–32.

—— —— (1995). 'The Business Cycle with Nominal Contracts'. *Economic Theory*, 6: 13–33.

Christiano, L. J. and Eichenbaum, M. (1992). 'Current Real-Business-Cycle Theories and Aggregate Labor-Market Fluctuations'. *American Economic Review*, 82: 430–50.

Clark, A. E. and Oswald, A. J. (1994). 'Unhappiness and Unemployment'. *Economic Journal*, 104: 648–59.

Cogley, T. and Nason, J. M. (1995). 'Output Dynamics in Real-Business-Cycle Models'. *American Economic Review*, 85: 492–511.

Farmer, R. E. A. and Guo, J.-T. (1994). 'Real Business Cycles and the Animal Spirits Hypothesis'. *Journal of Economic Theory*, 63: 42–72.

Ham, J. C. (1986). 'Testing Whether Unemployment Represents Intertemporal Labour Supply Behaviour'. *Review of Economic Studies*, 53: 559–78.

Hansen, G. (1985). 'Indivisible Labor and the Business Cycle'. *Journal of Monetary Economics*, 16: 309–28.

Kim, I.-M. and Loungani, P. (1992). 'The Role of Energy in Real Business Cycle Models'. *Journal of Monetary Economics*, 29: 173–89.

King, R. G. and Plosser, C. I. (1984). 'Money, Credit, and Prices in a Real Business Cycle'. *American Economic Review*, 74: 363–80.

—— —— and Rebelo, S. T. (1988). 'Production, Growth and Business Cycles, I. The Basic Neoclassical Model'. *Journal of Monetary Economics*, 21: 195–232.

—— and Rebelo, S. T. (1999). 'Resuscitating Real Business Cycles', in J. B. Taylor and M. Woodford (eds), *Handbook of Macroeconomics*. Amsterdam: North-Holland, pp. 927–1007.

Kydland, F. and Prescott, E. C. (1982). 'Time to Build and Aggregate Fluctuations'. *Econometrica*, 50: 1345–70.

Long, J. B. and Plosser, C. I. (1983). 'Real Business Cycles'. *Journal of Political Economy*, 91: 39–69.

Lucas, R. E., Jr (1972). 'Expectations and the Neutrality of Money'. *Journal of Economic Theory*, 4: 103–24.

—— (1977). 'Understanding Business Cycles', in K. Brunner and A. Meltzer (eds), *Stabilization of the Domestic and International Economy*. Amsterdam: North-Holland, pp. 7–29.

—— (1988). 'On the Mechanics of Economic Development'. *Journal of Monetary Economics*, 22: 3–42.

—— and Prescott, E. C. (1971). 'Investment under Uncertainty'. *Econometrica*, 39: 659–81.

—— and Rapping, L. A. (1969). 'Real Wages, Employment and Inflation'. *Journal of Political Economy*, 77: 721–54.

Mankiw, N. G. (1989). 'Real Business Cycles: A New Keynesian Perspective'. *Journal of Economic Perspectives*, 3: 79–90.

McCallum, B. T. and Nelson, E. (1999). 'An Optimizing IS–LM Specification for Monetary Policy and Business Cycle Analysis'. *Journal of Money, Credit and Banking*, 31: 296–316.

Merz, M. (1995). 'Search in the Labor Market and the Real Business Cycle'. *Journal of Monetary Economics*, 36: 269–300.

Pencavel, J. (1986). 'Labor Supply of Men: A Survey', in O. Ashenfelter and R. Layard (eds), *Handbook of Labor Economics*, vol. 1. Amsterdam: North-Holland, pp. 3–102.

Prescott, E. S. (1986). 'Theory Ahead of Business Cycle Measurement'. *Federal Reserve Bank of Minneapolis Quarterly Review*, 9–22.

Rotemberg, J. J. and Woodford, M. (1996). 'Real-Business-Cycle Models and the Forecastable Movements in Output, Hours, and Consumption'. *American Economic Review*, 86: 71–89.

Rouwenhorst, K. G. (1991). 'Time to Build and Aggregate Fluctuations. A Reconsideration'. *Journal of Monetary Economics*, 27: 241–54.

Solow, R. M. (1956). 'A Contribution to the Theory of Economic Growth'. *Quarterly Journal of Economics*, 70: 65–94.

—— (1957). 'Technical Change and the Aggregate Production Function'. *Review of Economics and Statistics*, 39: 312–20.

Stadler, G. W. (1994). 'Real Business Cycles'. *Journal of Economic Literature*, 32: 1750–83.

Exercises

5.1 In the simplest RBC model of Section 5.2 with θ_t white noise, compute:

$$\sigma_{\tilde{y}}^2 = \frac{1}{1 - (1 - \alpha)^2} \sigma_\theta^2.$$

How high is $\sigma_{\tilde{y}}^2/\sigma_\theta^2$ for $\alpha = 2/3$? Are the productivity shocks amplified strongly?

5.2 The Neoclassical growth model (based on Solow 1956). Assume technology is non-stochastic and labour supply inelastic in the model of Section 5.3: $\Theta_t = 1$, $u = u(C_t)$, and $L_t = L$ for all t. Show that

$$u'(C_t) = \beta[1 - \delta - \partial F(K_{t+1}, L)/\partial K_{t+1}]u'(C_{t+1}).$$

Characterize the behaviour of the model by means of a phase diagram in the K–C space.

5 Real Business Cycles

5.3 Human capital accumulation (based on Lucas 1988). Ignore physical capital and assume the homogeneous consumption good is produced using human capital alone:

$$C_t = (x_t H_t)^\alpha,$$

where H_t is total human capital, x_t is the fraction of human capital used in production, and $0 < \alpha < 1$. Human capital accumulation is governed by the education technology

$$H_{t+1} = \mu(1 - x_t)H_t, \quad \mu > 0.$$

The utility function is isoelastic: $u(C_t) = (C_t^{1-\sigma} - 1)/(1 - \sigma)$ with $\sigma > 0$. There is no uncertainty. The maximization problem that yields the optimal growth path is:

$$\max_{\{C_\tau\}_{\tau=t}^\infty} : \sum_{\tau=t}^\infty \beta^{\tau-t} \frac{C_\tau^{1-\sigma} - 1}{1 - \sigma}$$

$$\text{s.t.} : H_{t+1} = \mu(H_t - C_t^{1/\alpha}).$$

Show that on the optimal growth path, consumption growth is constant and given by

$$C_t/C_{t-1} = (\beta\mu)^{1/[\sigma+(1-\alpha)/\alpha]}$$

(provided that this is greater than one), human capital growth is given by

$$H_t/H_{t-1} = (C_t/C_{t-1})^{1/\alpha},$$

and

$$x_t = 1 - (\beta\mu)^{\alpha/[\sigma+(1-\alpha)/\alpha]}/\mu$$

is constant.

5.4 Consider the market equilibrium of the economy described in the previous problem. Since a capital market does not exist, consumption equals $C_t = \pi_t + W_t x_t H_t$, where W_t is the wage rate for human capital in production and π_t is profit income. W_t is the marginal product of human capital in production and π_t is taken as given. Argue the following: First, the accumulation constraint can be written as

$$H_{t+1} = \mu[H_t - (C_t - \pi_t)/W_t].$$

Second, utility maximization implies

$$C_t/C_{t-1} = \beta\mu(W_t/W_{t-1})^{1/\sigma}.$$

Third, together with the assumption that human capital is rewarded according to its marginal productivity, it follows that consumption growth and x_t take on the same values as in Exercise 5.3, so that the equilibrium growth path is efficient.

5.5 Macroeconomics without the LM curve (based on McCallum and Nelson 1999). Recall the model without an LM curve introduced in Section 4.3. We have now seen that intertemporal utility maximization gives rise to a positive relationship between the expected growth rate of consumption and the real interest rate. Based on this insight, one can modify the IS curve (4.19) as follows:

$$y_t = -\sigma(i_t - E_t \Delta p_{t+1}) + E_t y_{t+1} + \epsilon_t.$$

Does this affect the results derived in Section 4.3?

6
...

NEW KEYNESIAN
ECONOMICS

6.1 Introduction

New Keynesian economics covers a disparate range of papers that have appeared since the late 1970s and that aim to prove Keynesian-style propositions within models which conform to the postulates of rational expectations and optimizing behaviour. Loosely following Mankiw and Romer (1991: 3), new Keynesian economics can be divided into three broad categories concerned with real rigidities, nominal rigidities, and aggregate demand externalities, respectively. Such models are the subject of this chapter.

In Section 6.2, we present a real business cycle (RBC)-style model in which the interplay of real rigidities in the markets for credit and labour causes fluctuations. Section 6.3 examines similar ideas in a monetarist-style model (which is un-new Keynesian in that it is not based on maximizing behaviour and rational expectations). Section 6.4 investigates the effectiveness of monetary policy under rational expectations and staggered wage setting. In Section 6.5, a model with aggregate demand externalities is examined. Section 6.6 concludes.

6.2 A Real Business Cycle Model with Balance Sheet Effects

Introduction

Greenwald and Nobel Laureate Stiglitz (1993a: 26) propose explaining business cycles as the outcome of the interplay between imperfections (real rigidities) in financial markets and in the labour market. The *financial market imperfection* consists of firms' using standard debt contracts to raise funds. As debt contracts specify fixed repayment obligations, firms are exposed to the risk of going bankrupt. As a result, the level of investment depends on firms' *net worth*, the difference between their assets and liabilities. This is because firms' willingness to incur debt and lenders' willingness to supply funds increases as firms' net worth rises, since net worth is a hedge against bankruptcy and both firms and lenders aim to avoid bankruptcy. (Fisher (1933) was the first to emphasize the importance of balance sheets for firm behaviour. The main idea of his debt deflation theory is that, given standard debt contracts, deflation hurts firms by raising their indebtedness in real terms.) The level of investment, in turn, affects the marginal product of labour and, therefore, the demand for labour. The theory assumes that *labour market imperfections*, such as efficiency wages or union wage setting, prevent the real wage rate from adjusting in such a way as to keep employment constant (the discussion of the intertemporal substitution hypothesis in Box 5.3 suggests that labour market imperfections are required in order to explain significant employment variations in supply-side models). So shocks which affect firms' profits and net worth lead to variations in investment, employment, and aggregate production. Since firms' balance sheet position is a state variable, these fluctuations naturally feature persistence. The strong emphasis of credit and corporate profits is in line with the observations that credit and profits are strongly procyclical and that profits are very volatile (see Box 1.4). In the present section, we develop a novel real business cycle model with maximizing behaviour and rational expectations in order to formalize these ideas. The main ideas are adopted from Greenwald and Stiglitz (1993b). The model is closely related to the computable RBC model with exogenous labour supply, linear utility, and full depreciation expounded in Section 5.3.

Credit contracts versus state-contingent claims

In the RBC model of Section 5.3, it was assumed (implicitly) that the interest rate is state-contingent: when capital K_{t+1} is transferred from households to firms at time t, the interest rate $r_{t+1} = \Theta_{t+1} \partial F(K_{t+1}, L_{t+1}) / \partial K_{t+1}$ is not yet known because there is uncertainty about the level of TFP Θ_{t+1}. This state-contingency implies the absence of bankruptcy risk: the factors of production are rewarded according to their marginal productivities, so that firms make zero profit with certainty (see equation (5.8)). Alternatively, we could have assumed that households trade (state-contingent) Arrow securities (see Arrow 1964). In this case, the Modigliani–Miller theorem would hold and corporate

....

Box 6.1 The importance of standard debt contracts

A debt contract specifies a fixed repayment obligation and, therefore, creates a bankruptcy risk (in the absence of a complete set of Arrow securities) that would not be present if state-contingent claims were used for financing investment. This raises the question of whether it is sensible to assume that firms rely on debt for financing their investment. Empirically, debt is the major source of external corporate finance, as emphasized by Mayer (1988). According to Brealey and Myers (1996: Section 14.4), internally generated cash covers about three-quarters of US non-financial corporations' capital requirements and the major source of external finance is debt. Similarly, Mishkin (1998: ch. 9) reports that bonds and loans account for 90 per cent of the external funds raised by US nonfinancial businesses. A sizeable indexed bonds market, where repayments are contingent on specific characteristics of the economy (like the economy-wide level of TFP or the rate of inflation), simply does not exist (Fischer 1977a). Stocks are similar to state-contingent claims in that dividend payments are high in booms and low in recessions. But the stock market is surprisingly unimportant as a source of corporate finance. Usually, stock issues cover less than 5 per cent of firms' capital requirements (see Brealey and Myers 1996: section 14.4 and Mishkin 1998: ch. 9). The economics of information provides explanations for the predominance of debt: Greenwald and Stiglitz (1993a) point out that if firm owners have private information about the profitability of their firms, 'auctioning off shares in the firm is no different from auctioning off dollar bills' (Greenwald and Stiglitz 1993a: 27) held in one's back pocket, because there is an adverse selection of overvalued low-profit firms. Gale and Hellwig (1985) develop a model with costly monitoring in which standard debt is the optimal financial instrument. In reality, debt contracts usually contain restrictive covenants, which aim at overcoming informational problems: '[D]ebt contracts are typically extremely complicated legal documents that place substantial restrictions on the behavior of the borrower' (Mishkin 1998: 199).

....

finance would be irrelevant (see, e.g. Sargent 1979: section VII.3). As noticed above, the crucial financial imperfection assumed here consists of firms' using standard debt contracts to finance their investment projects. The fact that the interest rate r_{t+1} is determined before productivity Θ_{t+1} is observed brings the risk of going bust back to the fore: if Θ_{t+1} is low and the negotiated interest rate r_{t+1} is high, firms are unable to meet their repayment obligations. The assumption that debt is the only admissible financial instrument is motivated by the empirical observation that debt is the dominant source of external corporate finance (see Box 6.1).

Model

Consider a closed economy with a single homogeneous final good Y_t. In what follows, the final good is the numeraire good. The final good can be consumed or invested: $Y_t = C_t + I_t$. Capital depreciates fully at the end of each period.

So the capital stock at t equals I_{t-1}. L_t denotes labour. The productivity of labour L_t depends multiplicatively on workers' effort e_t. The production process is described by the neoclassical production function:

$$Y_t = \Theta_t F(I_{t-1}, e_t L_t).$$

TFP Θ_t is independently and identically distributed. It is assumed that the minimum possible level of TFP (the lower bound of the support of Θ), denoted $\underline{\Theta}$, is strictly positive: $\underline{\Theta} > 0$. The marginal productivities are positive but decreasing ($\partial F/\partial x > 0 > \partial^2 F/\partial x^2$ for $x = I_{t-1}, e_t L_t$) with $\partial F/\partial x = \infty$ for $x = 0$ and $\partial F/\partial x = 0$ for $x = \infty$ ($x = I_{t-1}, e_t L_t$). Increases in investment raise the marginal productivity of labour:

$$\frac{\partial^2 F}{\partial I_{t-1} \partial (e_t L_t)} > 0.$$

Importantly, we assume that the production function F is *strictly* concave:

$$\frac{\partial^2 F}{\partial I_{t-1}^2} \frac{\partial^2 F}{\partial (e_t L_t)^2} > \left[\frac{\partial^2 F}{\partial I_{t-1} \partial (e_t L_t)} \right]^2.$$

Strict concavity of F implies decreasing returns to scale. As will be seen below, this assumption ensures an interior solution for firms' optimal investment decision.

The economy is inhabited by two kinds of agents: workers and entrepreneurs. In equilibrium, unemployment among workers will prevail because of efficiency wages. The total number of workers is denoted by $\bar{L}$ (>0). Each worker is endowed with one unit of labour per period, which he supplies inelastically in the labour market. Employed workers' effort is either e^* (>0) ('work') or zero ('shirk'). Effort is only imperfectly observable: the exogenous and constant probability that a shirker is caught shirking, denoted q, is less than one ($0 < q < 1$). Employed workers are paid the going wage rate W_t unless they are caught shirking, in which case they do not receive any wage payment. If there is unemployment, the L_t ($<\bar{L}$) workers who get a job are drawn randomly from the total of all workers. This is a drastically simplified version of Shapiro and Stiglitz's (1984) work-or-shirk model. Let D_t denote a worker's consumption at t and γ his discount factor ($0 < \gamma < 1$). B_{t+1} denotes the funds lent out at time t and, hence, falling due at time $t+1$. R_{t+1} is the associated interest factor (i.e. one plus the interest rate). Notice that the standard debt contract determines R_{t+1} at time t. So there is no uncertainty about R_{t+1} as of time t. X_t is a dummy variable that equals one if the worker receives the wage payment W_t at t and zero otherwise. Workers are risk neutral. They maximize expected utility

$$E_t \left[\sum_{\tau=t}^{\infty} \gamma^{\tau-t}(D_\tau - e_\tau) \right], \tag{6.1}$$

subject to the budget constraint

$$B_{t+1} = R_t B_t + X_t W_t - D_t, \tag{6.2}$$

with an appropriate choice of consumption $\{D_\tau\}_{\tau=t}^{\infty}$ and effort $\{e_\tau\}_{\tau=t}^{\infty}$.

There is a continuum of unit length of entrepreneurs. Each entrepreneur owns one firm, which has access to the production technology described above. Entrepreneurs have no labour endowment. The assumptions that production is characterized by decreasing returns to scale and that the number of production units is fixed can be justified by assuming that production displays constant returns to scale in capital, labour, and managerial know-how and that entrepreneurs are the sole suppliers of managerial know-how, which they use in their own firms. Their utility depends on consumption C_t alone. As with the workers, expected utility

$$E_t \left(\sum_{\tau=t}^{\infty} \beta^{\tau-t} C_\tau \right)$$

is linear in consumption. The entrepreneurs are assumed to be more 'impatient' than the workers in that their discount factor β is smaller than the consumers' discount factor $\gamma : 0 < \beta < \gamma$. This assumption, borrowed from Carlstrom and Fuerst (1997), will ensure that, in equilibrium, firms do not accumulate so much equity that bankruptcy considerations cease to play a role. Given the interest factor R_t and the wage rate W_t, the entrepreneurs choose employment L_t, investment I_t, and consumption C_t so as to maximize expected utility. Let π_t^* denote (indirect) profit $Y_t - W_t L_t$ given that employment L_t is chosen optimally, and let A_t denote the entrepreneurs' assets available for consumption or internal finance at time t, that is, their net worth. Then the entrepreneurs' budget constraint is

$$A_{t+1} = \pi_{t+1}^* - R_{t+1}(C_t + I_t - A_t).$$

Here, $C_t + I_t - A_t$ is the amount of debt incurred at time t and $R_{t+1}(C_t + I_t - A_t)$ is the ensuing repayment obligation at time $t + 1$. At time $t + 1$, assets available for consumption or internal finance A_{t+1} are given by current operating profit π_{t+1}^* minus debt repayment. $A_{t+1} < 0$ signifies that current profit is insufficient to service the debt. In this case, the firm is declared bankrupt. It is assumed that firms, though they are risk neutral according to the usual definition (utility is linear in consumption), are *strictly bankruptcy-averse*: they act in such a way that A_t never becomes negative. (Gale 1983 makes this very assumption in a quantity rationing model.) The assumption that firms act in a bankruptcy-averse manner is non-standard. It is borrowed from Greenwald and Stiglitz (1993b). There is some empirical evidence that supports the notion of bankruptcy-averse firm behaviour. Gilson (1989) finds that managers' risk of being fired increases significantly when the firms they run are in financial distress and that they are unlikely to find employment in a comparable position elsewhere after having been fired (see Box 6.2). 'To avoid these costs, managers will rationally favor investment and financing policies that reduce the probability of financial distress. They will choose more conservative levels of debt for their firms' (Gilson 1989: 241). Moreover, the resulting positive link between net worth and credit also generally occurs in models with financial market imperfections and non-bankruptcy-averse firms. In a subsequent paragraph, we demonstrate that in the model considered here the assumption that firms are bankruptcy-averse can be replaced with the assumption that banks are bankruptcy-averse and ration credit to firms without altering the results. So the notion of bankruptcy-averse firms can be regarded as one simple way of modelling the more general positive link between net worth and credit.

Before proceeding, let us briefly compare this model to Greenwald and Stiglitz's (1993b) model. Greenwald and Stiglitz (1993b) consider firm-specific shocks instead of aggregate shocks and allow for lower degrees of bankruptcy aversion, so that bankruptcies occur in equilibrium. In these respects, their model is more attractive than the one presented here. However, the model presented here has some advantages over that of Greenwald and Stiglitz (1993b).

Box 6.2   Bankruptcy-averse firm behaviour

Gilson (1989) investigates management turnover in the worst-performing exchange-listed US firms during the period 1979–84 (381 firms in total). His major finding is that management changes are much more frequent in firms that default on their debt than in other firms: 0.52 management changes per defaulting firm per year on average, compared to 0.19 in the other, similarly unprofitable, firms in Gilson's sample and 0.12 in a random sample (Gilson 1989: 247–8). Moreover, Gilson points out that departed managers generally do not find a comparable position elsewhere: none of the departed managers entered a comparable position in another exchange-listed firm within the subsequent three-year period covered by the study (Gilson 1989: 255). So managers have strong incentives to avoid bankruptcy.

First, in their model, labour is the only factor of production and the risk of going bankrupt has a direct impact on labour demand, whereas here bankruptcy affects the investment decision, which in turn affects employment via the marginal productivity of labour, which is more appealing. Second, households' work-or-shirk choice is explicitly modelled. Greenwald and Stiglitz (1993b: section IV) assert the validity of a 'no shirking constraint' à la Shapiro and Stiglitz (1984), but it is well known that the Shapiro–Stiglitz analysis is very hard to apply in settings with discrete time and uncertainty. Third, firms' retention behaviour is endogenous. Greenwald and Stiglitz specify an exogenous relation between retentions and profits. Fourth, no approximations are required; the model's qualitative dynamic behaviour can be characterized analytically whereas in Greenwald and Stiglitz (1993b: 94) approximations are required. Fifth, expectations are fully rational. In Greenwald and Stiglitz (1993b: 86) price expectations are not fully rational. Sixth, the model is constructed in such a way that the assumption that firms are bankruptcy-averse can be replaced with the more appealing assumption that bankruptcy-averse banks ration credit.

Factor prices

We now turn to the characterization of the general equilibrium. First of all, it is shown that the necessary optimality conditions from the workers' utility maximization problem alone determine the equilibrium interest factor and the equilibrium wage rate and that both the interest factor and the wage rate are constants. The value function $V(B_t)$ for the households' utility maximization problem obeys

$$V(B_t) = \max_{D_t, e_t}\{D_t - e_t + \gamma E_t[V(B_{t+1})]\},$$

subject to (6.2). For an interior optimum with $D_t > 0$, it follows that $1 = \gamma E_t[V'(B_{t+1})]$ and $V'(B_t) = \gamma R_t E_t[V'(B_{t+1})]$. Hence, $V'(B_t) = R_t$, $E_t[V'(B_{t+1})] = R_{t+1}$, and $R_{t+1} = \gamma^{-1}$ (where use is made of the fact that R_{t+1} is known with certainty at t). The interest factor $R_{t+1} \equiv \gamma^{-1}$ makes workers indifferent between spending one unit of income on consumption at t (which yields one unit of utility) and saving the unit of income (which yields R_{t+1} dollars and, hence, $\gamma R_{t+1} = 1$ units of utility one period later).

$$R_{t+1} = \gamma^{-1}$$

is the equilibrium interest factor, for there is no supply of funds if R_{t+1} is smaller and excess supply if R_{t+1} is bigger. Thus, as asserted above, the interest factor is constant. Turning to the determination of the equilibrium wage rate, consider an employed worker's work-or-shirk decision. Given $R_{t+1} = \gamma^{-1}$, the worker is indifferent between spending and saving his current wage income W_t. Since, according to the utility function (6.1), W_t units of consumption at time t yield W_t units of instantaneous utility, it follows that the wage payment W_t contributes W_t units to expected intertemporal utility. The contribution of working to intertemporal utility is thus $W_t - e^*$, while the contribution of the expected income as a shirker is $(1 - q)W_t$. Use is made of the assumption that shirking today has no influence on the future income prospects, since the employed workers are drawn randomly from the total population of workers. Thus, effort equals

$$e_t = \begin{cases} e^*, & \text{if } W_t \geq W^*, \\ 0, & \text{if } W_t < W^*, \end{cases}$$

where $W^* \equiv e^*/q$ is the wage rate that makes workers indifferent between working and shirking and where it is assumed that workers do not shirk when they are indifferent between shirking and not shirking. W^* is called the efficiency wage. The supply curve of labour in efficiency units $e_t L_t$ is rectangular: $e_t L_t = e_t \bar{L} = 0$ for $W_t < W^*$, since $e_t = 0$; $e_t L_t = e^* \bar{L}$ for $W_t \geq W^*$. Throughout this chapter, we assume that $\bar{L}$ is larger than the firms' demand for labour (derived below), so that the economy operates at the horizontal portion of the labour supply curve. Then, there is equilibrium unemployment and firms pay the wage rate W^*:

$$W_t = W^*.$$

Given that the supply of labour is sufficiently large, the imperfect observability of workers' effort induces complete real wage stickiness and equilibrium unemployment. (Alternatively, real wage rigidity could be introduced via union wage setting. We do not pursue this approach in the present text.)

Profit maximization

We now turn to the entrepreneurs' profit-maximization problem. It is somewhat tedious to derive the relevant properties of the indirect profit function. The formulas become much simpler if one focuses on the Cobb–Douglas special case of the model with $Y_t = \Theta_t I_{t-1}^{\eta(1-\alpha)} (e_t L_t)^\alpha$ ($0 < \alpha < 1, 0 < \eta < 1$), where decreasing returns to scale is implied by $\eta(1 - \alpha) + \alpha < 1$. If one prefers to do so, one can restrict attention to the Cobb–Douglas special case.

Entrepreneurs maximize their expected intertemporal utility subject to the constraint that the probability of bankruptcy is zero with an appropriate choice of employment L_t, investment I_t, and consumption C_t, taking as given the interest factor γ^{-1}, the wage rate W^*, the induced effort e^*, and the capital stock installed in the previous period I_{t-1}. The employment level enters this maximization problem only through its impact on current profit:

$$\pi_t \equiv \Theta_t F(I_{t-1}, e^* L_t) - W^* L_t.$$

So, independently of the investment and consumption decisions, L_t is chosen (after Θ_t has been observed) so as to maximize profit π_t:

$$\frac{\partial \pi_t}{\partial L_t} = \Theta_t e^* \frac{\partial F(I_{t-1}, e^* L_t)}{\partial (e^* L_t)} - W^* = 0.$$

Since the marginal productivity of labour falls from plus infinity to zero as employment rises from zero to infinity, a unique solution $L_t = L(\Theta_t, I_{t-1})$ exists and the sufficient optimality condition is satisfied. Since the marginal product of labour increases with TFP and with the capital stock, $L(\Theta_t, I_{t-1})$ increases with both arguments:

$$\frac{\partial L}{\partial \Theta_t} = -\frac{\partial F / \partial (e^* L_t)}{\Theta e^* \partial^2 F / \partial (e^* L_t)^2} > 0,$$

$$\frac{\partial L}{\partial I_{t-1}} = -\frac{\partial^2 F / [\partial I_{t-1} \partial (e^* L_t)]}{e^* \partial^2 F / \partial (e^* L_t)^2} > 0. \tag{6.3}$$

With the Cobb–Douglas production function, the profit-maximizing employment level is given by $e^* L_t = (\Theta_t \alpha e^* / W^*)^{1/(1-\alpha)} I_{t-1}^{\eta}$, and it is obvious that the partial derivatives with respect to Θ_t and I_{t-1} are positive. As mentioned above, we assume that $L_t < \bar{L}$, so that the wage stickiness implied by the work-or-shirk decision leads to equilibrium unemployment.

Evaluating the profit function π_t at the optimal employment level $L(\Theta_t, I_{t-1})$ yields the indirect profit function:

$$\pi^*(\Theta_t, I_{t-1}) \equiv \Theta_t F[I_{t-1}, e^* L(\Theta_t, I_{t-1})] - W^* L(\Theta_t, I_{t-1}).$$

For future reference, let us derive some important properties of the indirect profit function π^*. Obviously, $\pi^*(\Theta_t, 0) = 0$. Differentiating $\pi^*(\Theta_t, I_{t-1})$ with respect to I_{t-1} yields

$$\frac{\partial \pi^*}{\partial I_{t-1}} = \Theta_t \frac{\partial F}{\partial I_{t-1}} + \left[\Theta_t e^* \frac{\partial F}{\partial (e^* L_t)} - W^* \right] \frac{\partial L}{\partial I_{t-1}} = \Theta_t \frac{\partial F}{\partial I_{t-1}} > 0. \tag{6.4}$$

This envelope result says that changes in investment affect indirect profit only through their direct impact on the capital stock. There is no indirect effect through induced changes in employment because the effect of employment on profit is zero in equilibrium. Since $\partial F(0, e^* L_t)/\partial I_{t-1} = \infty$,

$$\frac{\partial \pi^*(\Theta_t, 0)}{\partial I_{t-1}} = \Theta_t \frac{\partial F(0, e^* L_t)}{\partial I_{t-1}} = \infty,$$

for all Θ_t. Furthermore, since $\partial F(\infty, e^* L_t)/\partial I_{t-1} = 0$,

$$\frac{\partial \pi^*(\Theta_t, \infty)}{\partial I_{t-1}} = \Theta_t \frac{\partial F(\infty, e^* L_t)}{\partial I_{t-1}} = 0,$$

for all Θ_t. Differentiating equation (6.4) with respect to I_{t-1}, we have

$$\frac{1}{\Theta_t} \frac{\partial^2 \pi^*}{\partial I_{t-1}^2} = \frac{\partial^2 F}{\partial I_{t-1}^2} + e^* \frac{\partial^2 F}{\partial I_{t-1} \partial (e^* L_t)} \frac{\partial L}{\partial I_{t-1}}.$$

After rearranging terms and substituting for $\partial L/\partial I_{t-1}$ from equation (6.3), it becomes evident that the strict concavity of the production function F implies strict concavity of the indirect profit function π^* in investment I_{t-1}:

$$\frac{1}{\Theta_t} \frac{\partial^2 \pi^*}{\partial I_{t-1}^2} = \frac{1}{\partial^2 F/\partial (e^* L_t)^2} \left\{ \frac{\partial^2 F}{\partial I_{t-1}^2} \frac{\partial^2 F}{\partial (e^* L_t)^2} - \left[\frac{\partial^2 F}{\partial I_{t-1} \partial (e^* L_t)} \right]^2 \right\} < 0.$$

The strict concavity of the indirect profit function is essential because, as will be seen below, it ensures an interior optimum investment level. Increases in Θ_t raise π^*:

$$\frac{\partial \pi^*}{\partial \Theta_t} = F + \left[\Theta_t e^* \frac{\partial F}{\partial (e^* L_t)} - W^* \right] \frac{\partial L}{\partial \Theta_t} = F > 0.$$

This is another envelope result. The effect of an increase in TFP Θ_t is to increase output proportionally, given the optimal employment level. There is no indirect effect through the induced change in the optimal level of employment because, at the optimum, changes in L_t do not affect profit. Differentiating $\partial \pi^*/\partial \Theta_t$ with respect to I_{t-1} shows that increases in Θ_t raise the marginal profit of investment:

$$\frac{\partial^2 \pi^*}{\partial \Theta_t \partial I_{t-1}} = \frac{\partial F}{\partial I_{t-1}} + e^* \frac{\partial F}{\partial (e^* L_t)} \frac{\partial L}{\partial I_{t-1}} > 0.$$

In sum, for all Θ_t, indirect profit $\pi^*(\Theta_t, I_{t-1})$ is an increasing and strictly concave function of investment I_{t-1} with $\pi^*(\Theta_t, 0) = 0$. For all Θ_t, the derivative of indirect profit with respect to investment $\partial \pi^*/\partial I_{t-1}$ falls from infinity to zero as I_{t-1} goes from zero to infinity. Increases in TFP Θ_t raise both indirect profit π^* and the derivative of indirect profit with respect to investment $\partial \pi^*/\partial I_{t-1}$. All these properties of the indirect profit function are evident in the Cobb–Douglas special case, where $\pi_t^* = \kappa \Theta_t^{1/(1-\alpha)} I_{t-1}^{\eta}$ with $\kappa \equiv (1-\alpha)(\alpha e^*/W^*)^{\alpha/(1-\alpha)}$.

Investment and consumption

We now turn to the entrepreneurs' investment and consumption behaviour. The investment decision determines the behaviour of aggregate employment $L(\Theta_t, I_{t-1})$ and aggregate production $Y_t = \Theta_t F[I_{t-1}, e^*L(\Theta_t, I_{t-1})]$ over time. Given $R_t = \gamma^{-1}$, $W_t = W^*$, and the indirect profit function $\pi^*(\Theta_t, I_{t-1})$, the maximization problem at time t is:

$$\max_{\{C_\tau, I_\tau\}_{\tau=t}^{\infty}} : E_t \left(\sum_{\tau=t}^{\infty} \beta^{\tau-t} C_\tau \right), \tag{6.5}$$

$$\text{s.t.} : A_{t+1} = \pi^*(\Theta_{t+1}, I_t) - \gamma^{-1}(I_t + C_t - A_t), \tag{6.6}$$

$$\gamma \pi^*(\underline{\Theta}, I_t) - (I_t + C_t - A_t) \geq 0, \tag{6.7}$$

$$C_t \geq 0. \tag{6.8}$$

Use is made of the fact that indirect profit increases with TFP, so that non-negative wealth A_{t+1} in the case of minimum TFP $\underline{\Theta}$ is necessary and sufficient for the absence of bankruptcy risk. Contrary to the previous chapter, the non-negativity constraint on consumption (6.8) will prove essential, so we must not focus on an interior solution. An initial important observation is that, due to the entrepreneurs' relative 'impatience', the no-bankruptcy-risk constraint (6.7) is always binding in equilibrium. Suppose that this is not the case. Then entrepreneurs could borrow an additional unit of income, spend it on consumption, and increase current utility by one unit. By assumption, this would not lead to a positive bankruptcy risk. To repay the additional debt, they could reduce consumption one period later by γ^{-1} units, which would reduce discounted utility by $\beta \gamma^{-1}$ units. The net change in intertemporal utility $1 - \beta \gamma^{-1}$ would be positive because $\beta < \gamma$. So, the original consumption profile cannot be optimal. Intuitively, since entrepreneurs are more impatient (have a lower discount factor) than workers, they always extend their borrowing to the point where the no-bankruptcy-risk constraint becomes binding. The Bellman equation for problem (6.5)–(6.8) is

$$V(A_t) = \max_{C_t, I_t}\{C_t + \beta E_t[V(A_{t+1})]\},$$

subject to (6.6)–(6.8). Let μ_t and λ_t denote the Lagrange multipliers on constraints (6.7) and (6.8), respectively. Then, as necessary optimality conditions, we obtain:

$$1 = \mu_t + \lambda_t + \beta \gamma^{-1} E_t[V'(A_{t+1})],$$
(6.9)

$$\mu_t \left[\gamma \frac{\partial \pi^*(\Theta, I_t)}{\partial I_t} - 1 \right] + \beta E_t \left\{ V'(A_{t+1}) \left[\frac{\partial \pi^*(\Theta_{t+1}, I_t)}{\partial I_t} - \gamma^{-1} \right] \right\} = 0,$$
(6.10)

$$V'(A_t) = \mu_t + \beta \gamma^{-1} E_t[V'(A_{t+1})].$$
(6.11)

At the optimum, μ_t is the impact of an additional unit of net worth A_t on contemporaneous utility, λ_t is the shadow value of a relaxation of the non-negativity constraint on consumption by one unit, and $V'(A_{t+1})$ is the impact of an additional unit of net worth at $t + 1$ on intertemporal utility from time $t + 1$ onwards. Equation (6.9) is the condition for an optimal consumption level C_t. The left-hand side gives the marginal utility of consumption, which is unity. The right-hand side is the marginal cost of an additional unit of consumption, which is made up of three components. First, in the no-bankruptcy-risk constraint (6.7), a one unit increase in C_t acts like a one unit decrease in A_t, which has a shadow cost of μ_t. Second, it makes the constraint (6.8) more stringent, which costs λ_t. Third, the one unit decrease in A_t reduces next-period net worth A_{t+1} by γ^{-1} units (principal plus interest), each of which is worth $\beta E_t[V'(A_{t+1})]$ from today's point of view. Equation (6.10) is the condition for an optimal investment level I_t. An increase in I_t by one unit acts like a change in current net worth A_t by the first term in square brackets. It changes tomorrow's net worth A_{t+1} by the second term in square brackets. Multiplying these quantities by the respective valuations μ_t and $V'(A_{t+1})$, taking expectations, and discounting yields the impact on utility. At the margin, a change in investment must not affect utility. According to (6.11), the effect of additional net worth A_t on intertemporal utility $V(A_t)$ is made up of two components. First, a one unit increase in current net worth relaxes constraint (6.7) by one unit, which raises current utility by μ_t units. Second, from (6.6), it increases next-period net worth A_{t+1} by γ^{-1} units (principal plus interest), each of which is worth $\beta E_t[V'(A_{t+1})]$ from today's point of view.

Equations (6.9) and (6.11) imply

$$V'(A_t) = 1 - \lambda_t.$$
(6.12)

From (6.9) and (6.12), it follows that $\mu_t = 1 - \lambda_t - \beta \gamma^{-1} + \beta \gamma^{-1} E_t \lambda_{t+1}$. Using the latter equation and (6.12) in order to eliminate $V'(A_t)$ and μ_t from

(6.10), we obtain

$$(1 - \lambda_t) \left[\frac{\partial \pi^*(\Theta, I_t)}{\partial I_t} - \gamma^{-1} \right]$$
$$+ \beta \gamma^{-1} E_t \left\{ (1 - \lambda_{t+1}) \left[\frac{\partial \pi^*(\Theta_{t+1}, I_t)}{\partial I_t} - \frac{\partial \pi^*(\Theta, I_t)}{\partial I_t} \right] \right\} = 0. \quad (6.13)$$

The first term in the sum is the impact of a change in investment on current utility via current consumption. The second term in the sum is the indirect impact on intertemporal utility via next-period net worth.

We have to distinguish two cases, according to whether the non-negativity constraint on consumption (6.8) is binding or not. Suppose, first, that it is not binding: $C_t > 0$ and $\lambda_t = 0$. From (6.12), we know that the Lagrange multiplier $\lambda_{t+1} = 1 - V'(A_{t+1})$ depends on the value of next-period net worth A_{t+1} alone. As (6.7) is binding in equilibrium, we have $C_t = \gamma \pi^*(\Theta, I_t) - I_t + A_t$. From (6.6), it follows that next-period net worth is determined by investment I_t and productivity Θ_{t+1} alone: $A_{t+1} = \pi^*(\Theta_{t+1}, I_t) - \pi^*(\Theta, I_t)$. So we can write $\lambda_{t+1} = \lambda(I_t, \Theta_{t+1})$, and for a given I_t, λ_{t+1} is independently and identically distributed. Given $\lambda_t = 0$ and given that the distribution of $\lambda_{t+1} = \lambda(I_t, \Theta_{t+1})$ conditional on I_t is time-invariant, equation (6.13) determines a time-invariant solution $I_t = I^*$. Assuming $\lambda(I_t, \Theta_{t+1})$ is continuous in I_t, the existence of a solution is implied by the fact that $\partial \pi^*(\Theta_{t+1}, I_t)/\partial I_t$ falls from infinity to zero as I_t goes from zero to infinity, for all Θ_{t+1}, which implies that the left-hand side of (6.13) falls from infinity to $-\gamma^{-1}$ as I_t goes from zero to infinity (see Fig. 6.1). I^* is assumed unique. In the second case, the non-negativity constraint on consumption (6.8) is binding: $C_t = 0$ and

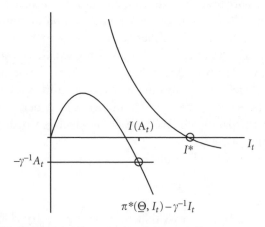

Fig. 6.1 Equilibrium investment.

$\lambda_t > 0$. Investment I_t is determined as a function $I(A_t)$ of current net worth A_t by the requirement that the constraint (6.7) holds with equality for $C_t = 0$:

$$\gamma \pi^*[\Theta, I(A_t)] - I(A_t) + A_t = 0. \tag{6.14}$$

That is, entrepreneurs refrain from consumption and choose the maximum level of investment consistent with the absence of bankruptcy risk. The optimal investment choice is illustrated in Fig. 6.1. The absence of bankruptcy risk requires that the curve $\pi^*(\Theta, I_t) - \gamma^{-1}I_t$ lies above the horizontal line at height $-\gamma^{-1}A_t$. If this is the case at I^*, then I^* is optimal. Otherwise, investment $I(A_t)$ is the abscissa value of the intersection of $\pi^*(\Theta, I_t)$ and the horizontal line at height $-\gamma^{-1}A_t$.

Suppose the constraint (6.7) is satisfied for $C_t = 0$, $A_t = 0$, and $I_t = I^*$: $\pi^*(\Theta, I^*) - \gamma^{-1}I^* \geq 0$. Then the constraint is never binding. For all t, investment equals $I_t = I^*$, consumption is $C_t = \gamma \pi^*(\Theta, I^*) - I^* + A_t$, and aggregate output is independently and identically distributed: $Y_t = \Theta_t F[I^*, e^* L(\Theta_t, I^*)]$. Investment is independent of financial considerations, and the model's dynamics look pretty much like the dynamics of the RBC model with linear utility and full depreciation considered in Section 5.3. In order for financial considerations to play a role, we thus assume that if $C_t = 0$ and $A_t = 0$, the constraint (6.7) is violated for $I = I^*$: $\pi^*(\Theta, I^*) - \gamma^{-1}I^* < 0$. In terms of Fig. 6.1, the curve $\pi^*(\Theta, I_t) - \gamma^{-1}I_t$ intersects the abscissa to the left of I^*. Then, there exists a positive value $\bar{A}$ such that for $C_t = 0$ and $I_t = I^*$, the constraint (6.7) is satisfied if $A_t \geq \bar{A}$ and is violated if $A_t < \bar{A}$. $\bar{A}$ satisfies

$$\pi^*(\Theta, I^*) - \gamma^{-1}I^* = -\gamma^{-1}\bar{A}.$$

In Fig. 6.1, $A_t = \bar{A}$ is such that the horizontal line at height $-\gamma^{-1}A_t$ intersects the curve $\pi^*(\Theta, I_t) - \gamma^{-1}I_t$ at $I_t = I^*$. It follows that

$$I_t = I^*, \tag{6.15}$$

$$C_t = \gamma \pi^*(\Theta, I^*) - I^* + A_t, \tag{6.16}$$

$$Y_{t+1} = \Theta_{t+1} F[I^*, e^* L(\Theta_{t+1}, I^*)], \tag{6.17}$$

for $A_t \geq \bar{A}$, and

$$I_t = I(A_t), \tag{6.18}$$

$$C_t = 0, \tag{6.19}$$

$$Y_{t+1} = \Theta_{t+1} F[I(A_t), e^* L(\Theta_{t+1}, I(A_t))], \tag{6.20}$$

for $A_t < \bar{A}$.

For future reference, three properties of the function $I(A_t)$ are important. All three results can be deduced from Fig. 6.1. First, $I(0) > 0$. Even with zero net worth ($A_t = 0$), some investment is possible without incurring a positive bankruptcy risk. This follows from the observation that $I(0)$, the abscissa intercept of the curve $\pi^*(\underline{\Theta}, I_t) - \gamma^{-1}I_t$, is strictly positive. Second, an increase in net worth A_t, by shifting the horizontal line at height $-\gamma^{-1}A_t$ downward and its intersection with the curve $\pi^*(\underline{\Theta}, I_t) - \gamma^{-1}I_t$ to the right in Fig. 6.1, raises the maximum investment level consistent with the absence of bankruptcy risk:

$$I'(A_t) = -\frac{\gamma^{-1}}{\partial\pi^*(\underline{\Theta}, I_t)/\partial I_t - \gamma^{-1}} > 0.$$

Third, $I(A_t)$ is continuous.

Notice that in order to give a complete characterization of the optimal investment decision, we would have to determine the multiplier function $\lambda(I_t, \Theta_{t+1})$ explicitly. (In view of (6.12), that is equivalent to finding the value function $V(A_t)$, which is the problem of the simultaneous determination of the choice variables and the value function encountered in Section 5.3.) To this end, we would have to insert the investment function ($I_t = I(A_t)$ for $A_t < \bar{A}$ and $I_t = I^*$ for $A_t \geq \bar{A}$, where both $\bar{A}$ and I^* depend on λ_{t+1}) into (6.13) and solve the resulting difference equation in λ_t. This is a difficult task. Fortunately, it is obsolete for the qualitative characterization of the equilibrium, so we refrain from an explicit consideration.

Dynamics

With (6.7), (6.15), and (6.18) we can rewrite the difference equation for net worth (6.6) as

$$A_{t+1} \equiv \Psi(\Theta_{t+1}, A_t) = \begin{cases} \pi^*(\Theta_{t+1}, I^*) - \pi^*(\underline{\Theta}, I^*), & \text{for } A_t \geq \bar{A}, \\ \pi^*[\Theta_{t+1}, I(A_t)] - \pi^*[\underline{\Theta}, I(A_t)], & \text{for } A_t < \bar{A}. \end{cases}$$
(6.21)

Once the behaviour of A_t is inferred from equation (6.21), the behaviour of investment I_t, consumption C_t, and aggregate production Y_t is determined by equations (6.15)–(6.17) or (6.18)–(6.20), depending on whether $A_t \geq \bar{A}$ or $A_t < \bar{A}$, respectively. Since the difference equation (6.21) is nonlinear, the methods described in Chapter 1 cannot be applied. To get a feel for what the net worth dynamics look like, we first investigate the 'deterministic dynamics' which arise when profit expectations are fulfilled. Let Θ^* be the productivity level for which profit expectations are fulfilled, given investment

I^*: $\pi^*(\Theta^*, I^*) = E_t[\pi^*(\Theta_{t+1}, I^*)]$. The deterministic dynamics obey

$$A_{t+1} \equiv \Psi(\Theta^*, A_t) = \begin{cases} \pi^*(\Theta^*, I^*) - \pi^*(\underline{\Theta}, I^*), & \text{for } A_t \geq \bar{A}, \\ \pi^*[\Theta^*, I(A_t)] - \pi^*[\underline{\Theta}, I(A_t)], & \text{for } A_t < \bar{A}. \end{cases}$$

$$(6.22)$$

Given our knowledge of the shapes of the indirect profit function $\pi^*(\Theta_{t+1}, I_t)$ and the function $I(A_t)$, we can infer the shape of the function $\Psi(\Theta^*, A_t)$ (see Fig. 6.2). Since $I(0)$ is positive, we have $\Psi(\Theta^*, 0) > 0$. For $A_t < \bar{A}$, $\Psi(\Theta^*, A_t)$ increases with A:

$$\frac{\partial \Psi}{\partial A_t} = \left[\frac{\partial \pi^*(\Theta^*, I_t)}{\partial I_t} - \frac{\partial \pi^*(\underline{\Theta}, I_t)}{\partial I_t} \right] I'(A_t) > 0.$$

This follows from $\partial^2 \pi^*/(\partial I_t \, \partial \Theta_{t+1}) > 0$ and $I'(A_t) > 0$. Since $I(\bar{A}) = I^*$, $\Psi(\Theta^*, A_t)$ is continuous. The fact that $\Psi(\Theta^*, I^*) = \pi^*(\Theta^*, I^*) - \pi^*(\underline{\Theta}, I^*)$ is flat for $A_t > \bar{A}$ implies that a steady state A^* (with $A^* = \Psi(\Theta^*, A^*)$) exists. Clearly, the steady state is in the non-finance-constrained region: $A^* > \bar{A}$. Otherwise, the entrepreneurs would realize zero consumption in the steady state (and for $A_t < A^*$). They could raise intertemporal utility by investing $I_t = I(0)$ and consuming $C_t = \gamma \pi^*[\underline{\Theta}, I(0)] - I(0) + A_t = A_t = \pi^*[\Theta_t, I(0)] - \pi^*[\underline{\Theta}, I(0)]$ for all t. We can thus characterize the deterministic net-worth dynamics as follows (see Fig. 6.2): if A_t is greater than $\bar{A}$, the economy jumps to its steady state A^*. If $A_t < \bar{A}$, the economy converges to the steady state A^*.

Next, consider the usual impulse-response thought experiment. Suppose that the economy is at its steady state and that a one-off shock $\Theta_t \neq \Theta^*$ occurs.

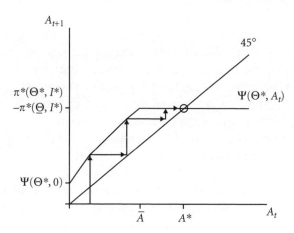

Fig. 6.2 Net-worth dynamics.

If the shock is positive or sufficiently small in absolute value, the economy stays in the $A_t > \bar{A}$ region. Consumption C_t moves one-to-one with the additional output generated by the productivity shock, and investment $I_t = I^*$ remains constant. Employment $L(\Theta_t, I^*)$ fluctuates because the productivity shock alters the marginal productivity of labour. From time $t + 1$ onwards, the economy is back at its steady state. If the shock is negative and sufficiently large in absolute value, the economy enters the $A_t < \bar{A}$ regime, where investment is positively correlated with net worth. Here, investment $I(A_t)$ fluctuates. Both productivity shocks and the variations in investment contribute to variability in employment $L[\Theta_t, I(A_t)]$. The impact of the shock on output is amplified because of procyclical investment and employment. It takes time until the economy is back at the steady state. If the economy is continually subject to productivity shocks, investment fluctuates whenever the economy is in the finance-constrained region. The output and investment movements feature a certain degree of persistence since the economy recovers only gradually from sufficiently strong adverse productivity shocks. This is consistent with the observation of short contractions and long expansions (see Box 1.1).

Following standard RBC methodology, Carlstrom and Fuerst (1997) calibrate a model similar to the one presented here. They show that with auto-correlated productivity shocks the presence of financial constraints helps to explain hump shapes in the impulse-response function for aggregate output.

Credit rationing

In this section, we give up the assumption that firms act in a strictly bankruptcy-averse manner. We assume instead that banks are strictly bankruptcy-averse. They ensure solvency under all contingencies by rationing credit in an appropriate fashion. The assumption that every bank plans its investments 'so as to be able to meet its deposit obligations in each period, even under the worst possible set of outcomes' is borrowed from Bernanke and Gertler's (1987: 96) banking model. Actually, for fear of financial instability, the banking industry is among the most heavily regulated sectors of the economy. So, with regard to banks, the assumption of strict bankruptcy aversion, either voluntary or enforced by regulation, is more appealing than with regard to firms. Greenwald and Stiglitz (1993a: 31) contend that 'with risk averse banks, the same kinds of factors which affect firm behavior—changes in risk perception and changes in net worth, affecting the willingness to bear risk—affect bank behavior, too'. In the specific model examined here, the two alternative assumptions—firms are strictly bankruptcy-averse or banks are strictly bankruptcy-averse—are interchangeable: prices and quantities take on the same values in the model with credit rationing as in the model with bankruptcy-averse firms.

Suppose all funds are intermediated, costlessly, by banks. There is free entry into banking. Banks' net worth is zero. As before, standard debt contracts are the only financial instrument. Banks receive funds from households and lend them to entrepreneurs at the interest factor R_{t+1}. The level of credit granted to entrepreneurs is $C_t + I_t - A_t$. Contractual repayment is $R_{t+1}(C_t + I_t - A_t)$ and actual repayment is $\min\{R_{t+1}(C_t + I_t - A_t), \pi^*(\Theta_{t+1}, I_t)\}$. So firms' net worth obeys

$$A_{t+1} = \max\{0, \pi_{t+1}^* - R_{t+1}(C_t + I_t - A_t)\}. \tag{6.23}$$

Our goal is to prove that equilibrium prices and quantities are exactly the same as in the model with bankruptcy-averse firms. The same arguments as above can be used to show that the wage rate is W^*, the interest factor paid to the workers is γ^{-1}, $L(\Theta_t, I_{t-1})$ gives the demand for labour, and $\pi_{t+1}^* = \pi^*(\Theta_{t+1}, I_t)$. To show that the equilibrium allocation is the same as in the model with bankruptcy-averse firms, it remains to show that the interest factor charged to firms R_{t+1} is γ^{-1} and that entrepreneurs' consumption C_t and investment I_t are the same as above. The proof is in two steps. In the following, let $\{C_\tau, I_\tau\}_{\tau=t}^\infty$ denote the sequence of consumption and investment levels which solves the bankruptcy-averse firms' expected-utility maximization problem (6.5)–(6.8). First, we demonstrate that there does not exist a consumption–investment sequence, consistent with the absence of bankruptcy risk for banks, which yields a higher expected utility for the firms than $\{C_\tau, I_\tau\}_{\tau=t}^\infty$ does. Second, we show that the bankruptcy-averse banks can induce the firms to choose $\{C_\tau, I_\tau\}_{\tau=t}^\infty$ by appropriately rationing credit. We know from the model with bankruptcy-averse firms that with $\{C_\tau, I_\tau\}_{\tau=t}^\infty$ firms are always able to repay their debts. So banks make zero profit with certainty—there is no bankruptcy risk (and no opportunity to accumulate bank capital). Since no feasible consumption–investment sequence is preferred to $\{C_\tau, I_\tau\}_{\tau=t}^\infty$ and $\{C_\tau, I_\tau\}_{\tau=t}^\infty$ is feasible, competition in banking ensures that it is realized in equilibrium.

Step 1   To lend $C_t + I_t - A_t$ to firms, banks have to borrow the same amount of funds from the households, which entails the repayment obligation $\gamma^{-1}(C_t + I_t - A_t)$. The absence of a positive bankruptcy risk for banks requires that the repayments received from the firms are sufficient in order to meet this repayment obligation under all circumstances:

$$\min\{R_{t+1}(C_t + I_t - A_t), \pi^*(\Theta_{t+1}, I_t)\} \geq \gamma^{-1}(C_t + I_t - A_t)$$

for all Θ_{t+1}. This implies $R_{t+1} \geq \gamma^{-1}$ and

$$\pi^*(\underline{\Theta}, I_t) \geq \gamma^{-1}(C_t + I_t - A_t). \tag{6.24}$$

We can use these two inequalities and $\pi^*_{t+1} = \pi^*(\Theta_{t+1}, I_t)$ to rewrite (6.23) as

$$A_{t+1} \leq \max\{0, \pi^*(\Theta_{t+1}, I_t) - \gamma^{-1}(C_t + I_t - A_t)\}$$
$$= \pi^*(\Theta_{t+1}, I_t) - \gamma^{-1}(C_t + I_t - A_t). \tag{6.25}$$

The equilibrium consumption–investment sequence has to satisfy equations (6.24) and (6.25). Since (6.24) is equivalent to (6.7) and (6.25) puts a more stringent restriction on the evolution of A_{t+1} than (6.6), there cannot exist a consumption–investment sequence with $C_t \geq 0$ for all t which yields a higher expected value of intertemporal utility $E_t(\sum_{\tau=t}^{\infty} \beta^{\tau-t} C_\tau)$ than $\{C_\tau, I_\tau\}_{\tau=t}^{\infty}$.

Step 2   It remains to show that banks can induce firms to choose the sequence $\{C_\tau, I_\tau\}_{\tau=t}^{\infty}$ that solves (6.5)–(6.8) by charging the interest factor γ^{-1} and appropriately rationing credit. Let Z_t denote the credit ceiling set by the banks. Firms are restricted to choose C_t and I_t such that $C_t + I_t - A_t \leq Z_t$. If firms demand credit in excess of Z_t, they are credit rationed. This is Type 1 credit rationing. (Type 2 credit rationing prevails when among observationally identical individuals some are denied credit, while others are not. Cf. Blanchard and Fischer (1989: 479). Also see Exercises 6.3 and 6.4.) Mishkin (1998: 249) emphasizes the empirical relevance of this type of credit rationing: 'Since more borrowers repay their loans if the loan amounts are small, financial institutions ration credit by providing borrowers with loans smaller than they seek.' Suppose banks set the credit ceiling

$$Z_t = \gamma \pi^*(\underline{\Theta}, I_t).$$

Notice that the maximum level of credit depends on how much firms choose to invest: the higher the investment I_t, the higher the credit ceiling Z_t. It is thus assumed that banks have the capability of enforcing restrictive covenants which oblige firms to in fact invest a given amount I_t. (This is essential because there is a time consistency problem: once firms have received credit, they would want to consume more and invest less. See Exercise 6.2.) In view of the widespread use of restrictive covenants in debt contracts noted in Box 6.1, this is a plausible assumption. The fact that $C_t + I_t - A_t \leq Z_t = \gamma \pi^*(\underline{\Theta}, I_t)$

implies

$$A_{t+1} = \max\{0, \pi^*(\Theta_{t+1}, I_t) - \gamma^{-1}(I_t + C_t - A_t)\}$$
$$= \pi^*(\Theta_{t+1}, I_t) - \gamma^{-1}(I_t + C_t - A_t).$$

Entrepreneurs maximize expected intertemporal utility subject to this condition, the constraint that the level of credit cannot exceed Z_t, and the non-negativity constraint for consumption:

$$\max_{\{C_\tau, I_\tau\}_{\tau=t}^\infty} : E_t \left(\sum_{\tau=t}^\infty \beta^{\tau-t} C_\tau \right),$$

$$\text{s.t.} : A_{t+1} = \pi^*(\Theta_{t+1}, I_t) - \gamma^{-1}(I_t + C_t - A_t),$$
$$\pi^*(\underline{\Theta}, I_t) - \gamma^{-1}(I_t + C_t - A_t) \geq 0,$$
$$C_t \geq 0.$$

This is exactly the problem (6.5)–(6.8), which proves that the risk neutral entrepreneurs choose $\{C_\tau, I_\tau\}_{\tau=t}^\infty$.

We have proved that strictly bankruptcy-averse banks induce risk neutral entrepreneurs to consume and invest as if the latter were themselves strictly bankruptcy-averse by appropriately rationing credit. A cautionary remark is in order. The model presented neglects many of the functions banks perform, such as risk diversification, liquidity transformation, maturity transformation, monitoring, screening, consumption smoothing, etc. (cf. Bhattacharya and Thakor 1993). It shows, however, that the way a bankruptcy-averse banking system handles aggregate economic shocks is very similar to the way bankruptcy-averse firms deal with these disturbances.

Summary

In this section, we have developed a prototype new Keynesian model with rational expectations and maximizing behaviour that is concerned with the role of firms' balance sheets in business cycles. Following Greenwald and Stiglitz's (1993b) suggestion, this model explains business fluctuations as the result of the interplay between financial market imperfections and labour market imperfections. Firms and suppliers of finance have a strong interest in firms not going bankrupt. The financial market is incomplete: debt is the only financial instrument. Since firms' net worth is a hedge against the risk of bankruptcy, firms' investment demand increases with their net worth. Because of efficiency wages (union wage setting would serve the same purpose), the ensuing fluctuations in the demand for labour cause variations in employ-ment and unemployment. So shocks to firms' net worth lead to fluctuations in employment. Since net worth is a state variable, these fluctuations are char-acterized by a certain degree of persistence. The model presented in order to formalize the interplay between imperfections in the financial markets and in the labour market is special; the mechanisms at work are much more general.

6.3 Digression: A Monetarist Model with Balance Sheet Effects

Introduction

Greenwald and Stiglitz (1993b: 103) remark that their model 'seems to attribute all the sources of output variability to the supply side rather than the demand side [...] in accord with standard real business cycle doctrine'. This observation holds true for the model presented in the previous section as well. Despite the label 'new Keynesian economics', the model is un-Keynesian if one agrees with Tobin that the distinguishing characteristic of Keynesian economics is the principle of aggregate demand (cf. Section 2.1). In this sec-tion, we present a model with balance sheet effects that assigns an important role to the economy's demand side. The model is a slightly modified and extended version of the monetarist model introduced in Section 3.2. As such, it is un-new Keynesian in that it does not assume maximizing behaviour and rational expectations. That is why this section is called a digression in the title.

Model

The monetarist model expounded in Section 3.2 is modified in two respects. The crucial new assumption is that balance sheet effects are at work: an increase in past profits leads to higher net worth in the business sector, improves firms' access to financial capital, and, therefore, raises the demand for investment. To keep the model tractable, a second slight change is neces-sary: inflation expectations depend not on observed inflation, but on current money growth. As in Section 3.2, the model applies to the closed as well as to the open economy. Here is the monetarist model with balance sheet effects:

$$y_t = \delta(s_t + p_t^* - p_t) + \psi\pi_{t-1} - \sigma r_t + \epsilon_t, \tag{6.26}$$

$$m_t - p_t = \phi y_t - i_t/\lambda, \tag{6.27}$$

6.3 Digression: A Monetarist Model with Balance Sheet Effects

$$i_t = r_t + \Delta p_{t+1}|_t^e, \tag{6.28}$$

$$\Delta p_{t+1}|_t^e = \Delta m_t, \tag{6.29}$$

$$\delta = 0 \text{ or } \delta > 0, \ i_t = i^* + \Delta s_{t+1}|_t^e, \tag{6.30}$$

$$r^* = i_t^* - \Delta p_{t+1}^*|_t^e, \tag{6.31}$$

$$\bar{s}_t \equiv p_t - p_t^*, \tag{6.32}$$

$$\Delta(s_{t+1} - \bar{s}_{t+1})|_t^e = -\theta(s_t - \bar{s}_t), \tag{6.33}$$

$$\gamma y_t = -(w_t - p_t), \tag{6.34}$$

$$\pi_t = \iota(p_t - w_t) + \kappa y_t, \tag{6.35}$$

$$w_t = p_t|_{t-1}^e, \tag{6.36}$$

$$\Delta p_t|_{t-1}^e = \Delta m_{t-1}. \tag{6.37}$$

Equation (6.26) is the IS curve. Increases in lagged profits π_{t-1} raise investment and aggregate demand (ψ is a positive constant). One explanation for this positive dependence of investment on lagged profits is balance sheet effects: lagged profits are conducive to credit availability because they provide a hedge against bankruptcy. In the previous section, this has been modelled with explicit microfoundations. The *ad hoc* specification in equation (6.26) assumes, rather than proves, the presence of balance sheet effects. Zarnowitz (1999: 76) mentions two other explanations for the positive relation between investment and lagged profit: 'rising profits from past and current operations are probably the main source of expectations of higher profits on investments already underway [... and] recorded profitability serves as the decisive indicator of the appropriateness of past investment decisions and has reputational effects on the access to credit for external financing'. The random variable ϵ_t reflects random changes in autonomous expenditure. It is assumed that ϵ_t follows a random walk. Government expenditure is ignored. Equations (6.27) and (6.28) are the LM curve and the Fisher equation, respectively. According to equation (6.29), inflation expectations are given by the current money growth rate. Since the rate of inflation converges to the money growth rate in the absence of shocks, expectational errors do not grow large. With $\delta = 0$, one obtains the closed economy model. In the open economy, where $\delta > 0$, uncovered interest parity holds (equation (6.30)). According to equation (6.31), the foreign real interest rate is constant. Formulas (6.32) and (6.33) state that the spot exchange rate s_t is expected to regress towards the exchange rate $\bar{s}_t$ that is consistent with PPP. These three equations do not play a role in the determination of aggregate production in the closed economy. Equation (6.34) is the standard aggregate supply curve. According to (6.35), profit π_t depends positively on the markup of prices over wages $p_t - w_t$ and on aggregate demand y_t (ι and κ are positive constants). Equation (6.36) says that wages are set such that if inflation expectations are correct, aggregate output is at its natural rate $y_t = 0$. As in the monetarist model of Section 3.2, wages are set one period in advance. According to equation (6.37), when period-t wages w_t are set in period $t - 1$, inflation expectations are given by the most recent money growth observation Δm_{t-1}. As in Section 3.2, money growth Δm_t is assumed to follow a random walk, so that $\Delta^2 m_t$ is white noise.

In what follows, we first consider the closed economy with $\delta = 0$ and then the open economy with $\delta > 0$ and uncovered interest parity. We demonstrate that for appropriate parameter values, the model gives rise to business cycles in Frisch's sense.

Closed economy

From (6.34), (6.36), and (6.37), aggregate supply can be expressed as

$$\gamma y_t = \Delta p_t - \Delta m_{t-1}. \tag{6.38}$$

This formula holds both in the closed and in the open economy. Let $\delta = 0$ so that the IS curve (6.26) becomes $y_t = \psi \pi_{t-1} - \sigma r_t + \epsilon_t$. Inserting $r_t = i_t - \Delta m_t$ (from (6.28) and (6.29)), $i_t = \lambda(\phi y_t - m_t + p_t)$ (from (6.27)), and $\pi_t = (\iota \gamma + \kappa) y_t$ (from (6.34) and (6.35)), and letting $\Psi \equiv (\iota \gamma + \kappa)\psi$, we have

$$(1 + \sigma \lambda \phi)y_t - \Psi y_{t-1} = \sigma \lambda(m_t - p_t) + \sigma \Delta m_t + \epsilon_t. \tag{6.39}$$

This is the aggregate demand (AD) curve. It relates aggregate output y_t in a simultaneous equilibrium in the markets for goods and money inversely to the price level p_t. The money stock m_t, money growth Δm_t, lagged aggregate output y_{t-1}, and expenditure shocks ϵ_t are shift parameters of the aggregate demand curve. The process for equilibrium aggregate output is obtained by eliminating the price level from the aggregate supply and aggregate demand equations (6.38) and (6.39). To do so, take differences in (6.39), substitute $\Delta m_t - \Delta p_t = \Delta^2 m_t - \gamma y_t$ (from (6.38)) and rearrange terms:

$$y_t - \frac{1 + \sigma \lambda \phi + \Psi}{1 + \sigma \lambda(\phi + \gamma)}y_{t-1} + \frac{\Psi}{1 + \sigma \lambda(\phi + \gamma)}y_{t-2} = \frac{\sigma(1 + \lambda)\Delta^2 m_t + \Delta \epsilon_t}{1 + \sigma \lambda(\phi + \gamma)}. \tag{6.40}$$

This stochastic second-order difference equation displays business cycles if

$$\frac{4\Psi}{1 + \sigma \lambda(\phi + \gamma)} > \left[\frac{1 + \sigma \lambda \phi + \Psi}{1 + \sigma \lambda(\phi + \gamma)}\right]^2,$$

and

$$\frac{\Psi}{1 + \sigma\lambda(\phi + \gamma)} < 1.$$

These conditions can be rewritten as

$$\gamma > \frac{[\Psi - (1 + \sigma\lambda\phi)]^2}{4\sigma\lambda\Psi},$$

and

$$\gamma > \frac{\Psi - 1}{\sigma\lambda} - \phi,$$

respectively. Obviously, there is persistence. Three necessary conditions for the emergence of cycles are the presence of balance sheet effects ($\psi > 0$, hence $\Psi > 0$), a strictly positive interest elasticity of money demand ($\lambda < \infty$), and a strictly negative interest elasticity of investment ($\sigma > 0$). Given that these necessary conditions are fulfilled, business cycles in Frisch's sense tend to occur when the real wage elasticity of aggregate supply $1/\gamma$ is sufficiently small.

To explain the possible occurrence of business cycles, three pieces of information are essential. First, from the aggregate supply curve (6.38), aggregate output y_t and inflation Δp_t move in the same direction when the rate of money growth does not change ($\Delta^2 m_t = 0$). The greater γ is, the faster inflation soars as output rises. Second, aggregate production in a goods market equilibrium obeys $y_t = \Psi y_{t-1} - \sigma i_t + \sigma \Delta m_t + \epsilon_t$ (from (6.26), (6.28), (6.29), (6.34), and (6.35)). Hence,

$$\Delta y_t = \Psi \Delta y_{t-1} - \sigma \Delta i_t$$

if $\Delta^2 m_t = \Delta \epsilon_t = 0$. The balance sheet effect tends to give output movements a cumulative character. Because of the negative interest elasticity of investment, increases in the interest rate put a check on output growth. Third, from the LM equation (6.27),

$$\Delta i_t = \lambda(\phi \Delta y_t + \Delta p_t - \Delta m_t).$$

The interest rate tends to rise when output rises and when inflation exceeds money growth. Suppose the conditions for the occurrence of business cycles are satisfied and the economy is at its steady state, and consider the response of aggregate output to a one-off positive monetary shock ($\Delta^2 m_0 > 0$, $\Delta^2 m_t = 0$ for $t = 1, 2, \ldots$). Why does aggregate output oscillate in response to the shock? The monetary expansion raises output y_0, and the balance sheet effect tends to give the output movement a cumulative character. But inflation moves in the same direction as aggregate output, and the assumption that γ

is large, in that the conditions for cycles are satisfied, ensures that inflation rises quickly as aggregate output expands. From the LM equation, it follows that the interest rate rises. This increase in the interest rate is responsible for the upper turning point. After the turning point, Δy_t is negative while, by continuity, Δi_t is still positive. So both the balance sheet effect and the interest rate effect tend to accelerate the downward movement in aggregate economic activity. The economy overshoots into the $y_t < 0$ region, where $\Delta p_t < \Delta m_{t-1}$. As $\Delta y_t < 0$ and $\Delta p_t < \Delta m_t$, the interest rate now falls quickly. Eventually, this expansionary interest rate effect outweighs the balance sheet effect, and the economy reaches its lower turning point. A cumulative upswing takes its course, in which the balance sheet effect ($\Delta y_t > 0$) and the interest rate effect ($\Delta i_t < 0$) both stimulate aggregate demand. The economy does not settle down at $y_t = 0$, but overshoots into the $y_t > 0$ region. This process repeats with declining amplitudes.

Small open economy

Next, we turn to the open economy, where net exports contribute to aggregate demand ($\delta > 0$) and, because of perfect capital mobility, uncovered interest parity (equation (6.30)) holds. Following the arguments already used in Section 3.2, we first show that these international interrelations make the IS curve more interest elastic. Subtracting $\Delta \bar{s}_{t+1}|_t^e = \Delta p_{t+1}|_t^e - \Delta p^*_{t+1}|_t^e$ (from (6.32)) from the uncovered interest parity condition (6.30) and making use of the Fisher equations (6.28) and (6.31) yields uncovered interest parity in real terms:

$$\Delta(s_{t+1} - \bar{s}_{t+1})|_t^e = r_t - r^*.$$

If the domestic real interest rate is lower than the foreign real interest rate, investors have to be compensated with an expected real appreciation of the domestic currency (a decrease in the real exchange rate $s_t - \bar{s}_t \equiv s_t + p^*_t - p_t$). Inserting this into equation (6.33) gives $s_t - \bar{s}_t = -(r_t - r^*)/\theta$. From equation (6.32) and the IS expression (6.26), we have

$$y_t = \psi \pi_{t-1} - \Gamma r_t + \delta r^*/\theta + \epsilon_t,$$

with $\Gamma \equiv \delta/\theta + \sigma$. Since $\Gamma > \sigma$, the IS curve is more interest elastic than in the closed economy. This is because a rise in the real interest rate implies higher expected real depreciation of the domestic currency, which, given regressive real exchange rate expectations, leads to a current real appreciation and a decline in net exports.

6.3 Digression: A Monetarist Model with Balance Sheet Effects

The remainder of the analysis runs parallel to the closed economy scenario. The LM curve (6.27), the Fisher equation (6.28), and the expectation formation rule (6.29) imply $r_t = \lambda(\phi y_t - m_t + p_t) - \Delta m_t$. Equations (6.34) and (6.35) imply $\pi_t = (\iota\gamma + \kappa)y_t$. So the IS equation can be rewritten as

$$(1 + \Gamma\lambda\phi)y_t - \Psi y_{t-1} = \Gamma\lambda(m_t - p_t) + \Gamma\Delta m_t + \delta r^*/\theta + \epsilon_t.$$

Taking differences, substituting $\Delta m_t - \Delta p_t = \Delta^2 m_t - \gamma y_t$ (from (6.38)), and rearranging terms, one obtains

$$y_t - \frac{1 + \Gamma\lambda\phi + \Psi}{1 + \Gamma\lambda(\phi + \gamma)}y_{t-1} + \frac{\Psi}{1 + \Gamma\lambda(\phi + \gamma)}y_{t-2} = \frac{\Gamma(1 + \lambda)\Delta^2 m_t + \Delta\epsilon_t}{1 + \Gamma\lambda(\phi + \gamma)}.$$

This is equation (6.40) with σ replaced with Γ. Business cycles occur if γ is sufficiently large:

$$\gamma > \frac{[\Psi - (1 + \Gamma\lambda\phi)]^2}{4\Gamma\lambda\Psi}, \quad \gamma > \frac{\Psi - 1}{\Gamma\lambda} - \phi.$$

Necessary conditions for the emergence of business cycles are that the balance sheet effect is at work ($\psi > 0, \Psi > 0$) and that the demands for money and goods are interest elastic ($\lambda < \infty, \Gamma > 0$). Since the main effect of international trade in goods and securities is to make the IS curve more interest elastic, the mechanisms responsible for cycles are the same as in the closed economy version of the model: the balance sheet effect tends to provide output movements with a cumulative character and procyclical interest rate movements act as a stabilizer.

The monetary transmission channels

In the Keynesian IS–LM and AS–AD models (Sections 2.4 and 2.5) and in the monetarist model of Section 3.2, changes in the supply of money have an immediate impact on aggregate production through the *interest rate channel* (provided that the demand for money and investment are interest elastic): in response to expansionary monetary policy, interest rates fall and investment soars. In the open economy versions of the models, the *exchange rate channel* magnifies the effects by raising the interest elasticity of the IS curve: the domestic currency depreciates as lower interest rates make financial investments in the home country less attractive. The ensuing improvement in domestic competitiveness boosts net exports and aggregate demand. In the model considered in the present section, there is a third monetary transmission channel, the *balance sheet channel of monetary policy*: after an increase in production and profits, firms are endowed with more internal funds and, because of financial market imperfections, have better access to external finance, which is conducive to corporate investment. The theoretical literature has identified another monetary transmission channel that relies on financial market imperfections, the *bank lending channel*: suppose the central bank channels additional money to commercial banks via open market operations, say. This allows banks to increase their lending to firms without hurting reserve requirements or worsening their liquidity position. If, because of financial market imperfections, there are some firms with no other means of raising funds than bank loans, this boosts credit, investment, and aggregate demand. Moreover, the balance sheet and the bank lending channel affect not only corporate investment, but also consumers' durable goods purchases. This is because, as with firms, consumers' creditworthiness depends on their net worth (the difference between their assets and liabilities). Falling interest rates increase households' net worth and access to credit, thereby raising durable consumer goods purchases and aggregate demand.

The relative importance of the different transmission channels is an empirical question. Most economists agree that the interest elasticity of investment is relatively low. It is unlikely, therefore, that the interest rate channel

....

Box 6.3   The balance sheet channel of monetary policy

The working of the balance sheet channel of monetary policy hinges upon the impact of firms' cash flow on investment. Bernanke and Gertler (1995) review the empirical evidence on the balance sheet channel: 'empirical studies of supposedly "interest-sensitive" components of aggregate spending have in fact had great difficulty in identifying a quantitatively important effect of the neoclassical cost-of-capital variable. Indeed, the most common finding is that nonneoclassical factors—for example, "accelerator" variables such as lagged output, sales or cash flow—have the greatest impact on spending' (Bernanke and Gertler 1995: 27–8). For instance, Fazzari, Hubbard, and Petersen's (1988) prominent analysis of the investment and financing behaviour of US manufacturing firms from 1970–84 shows that cash flow has a significant influence on investment and that the strength of this influence is greater, the lower firms' net worth is. Taking dividend payments as a proxy for net worth, Fazzari, Hubbard, and Petersen (1988) report that the correlation between investment and cash flow is 0.20 for firms with a dividend–income ratio above 20 per cent and 0.92 for firms with a dividend–income ratio below 10 per cent. Regression analysis shows that a one per cent increase in the cash flow–capital ratio increases the investment–capital ratio by 0.20 per cent in the high-dividend firms and by 0.34 per cent in the low-dividend firms. Mishkin (1976) emphasizes that net worth is quantitatively important not only for firms' investment decisions, but also for households' durable goods purchases. Transitory income changes, debt holdings, and financial wealth have a significant influence on households' expenditure on durable consumer goods.

....

alone is sufficient to explain the observed correlation between money and output. In fact, empirical studies provide convincing evidence that the balance sheet channel of monetary policy makes a significant contribution to the explanation of why monetary policy is effective (see Box 6.3).

6.4 Nominal Rigidities

Introduction

New Keynesian models with balance sheet effects highlight that, if because of financial market imperfections, credit availability depends on net worth, monetary policy affects real economic activity through the balance sheet channel. Another strand of new Keynesian economics is concerned with the efficacy of monetary policy under rational expectations in the presence of nominal rigidities. Fischer (1977b) observes that the validity of the Sargent-Wallace policy ineffectiveness proposition (see Sections 4.2 and 4.3) presupposes not only rational expectations, but also wage and price flexibility. For, suppose 'economic agents contract in nominal terms for periods longer than the time it takes the monetary authority to react to changing economic circumstances' (Fischer 1977b: 191). Then activist monetary policy can play an effective role in stabilizing the aggregate economy. This is demonstrated in the present section using the Fischer (1977b) model.

Model

The Fischer (1977b) model differs from the rational expectations monetarist model expounded at the beginning of Section 4.3 (see equations (4.13)–(4.15)) in exactly one respect: wages are set not for one, but for two periods in advance. There are two equally sized groups of workers and wage setting is staggered: one group negotiates wages at even dates, the other one at odd dates. So at each date t, half the workers receive the wage rate w_t^I negotiated at $t-1$, and half receive the wage rate w_t^{II} negotiated at $t-2$. The quantity theory holds, aggregate supply depends negatively on the real wages of the two groups of workers, expectations are rational, the target output level of each group is normalized to equal zero, and the money supply rule (4.4) introduced in Section 4.2 is valid (for simplicity, with a feedback to lagged values of the money supply, but not to other variables):

$$m_t - p_t = \phi y_t, \qquad (6.41)$$

123

$$\gamma y_t = -\frac{(w_t^I - p_t) + (w_t^{II} - p_t)}{2}, \tag{6.42}$$

$$w_t^I = E_{t-1}p_t, \quad w_t^{II} = E_{t-2}p_t, \tag{6.43}$$

$$m_t = a + \sum_{j=1}^{\infty} b_j m_{t-j} + \eta_t. \tag{6.44}$$

Equilibrium

Substituting for w_t^I and w_t^{II} from equation (6.43) in (6.42), one obtains aggregate output as a function of the price surprises $p_t - E_{t-1}p_t$ and $p_t - E_{t-2}p_t$:

$$2\gamma y_t = (p_t - E_{t-1}p_t) + (p_t - E_{t-2}p_t). \tag{6.45}$$

Eliminating y_t using equation (6.41),

$$\phi[(p_t - E_{t-1}p_t) + (p_t - E_{t-2}p_t)] = 2\gamma(m_t - p_t).$$

Then, taking expectations at $t - 2$ and $t - 1$ we obtain

$$E_{t-2}p_t = E_{t-2}m_t,$$

and

$$E_{t-1}p_t = \frac{2\gamma}{\phi + 2\gamma}E_{t-1}m_t + \frac{\phi}{\phi + 2\gamma}E_{t-2}m_t,$$

respectively. Inserting these equations together with $p_t = m_t - \phi y_t$ (from (6.41)) into (6.45), output can be expressed as a function of the one-period and two-period money surprises:

$$(\phi + \gamma)y_t = \frac{\gamma}{\phi + 2\gamma}(m_t - E_{t-1}m_t) + \frac{\gamma + \phi}{\phi + 2\gamma}(m_t - E_{t-2}m_t).$$

According to the money supply rule (6.44), $m_t - E_{t-1}m_t = \eta_t$, and $m_t - E_{t-2}m_t = b_1(m_{t-1} - E_{t-2}m_{t-1}) + \eta_t = b_1\eta_{t-1} + \eta_t$. Hence,

$$y_t = \frac{\eta_t}{\phi + \gamma} + \frac{b_1\eta_{t-1}}{\phi + 2\gamma}.$$

Unlike in the rational expectations monetarist model of Section 4.3, the policy ineffectiveness proposition is not valid. The behaviour of aggregate production y_t depends on the policy parameter b_1. A Friedmanian k-percent money growth rule ($a = k, b_1 = 1$, and $b_j = 0$ for $j > 1$, hence $\Delta m_t = k + \eta_t$), for instance, leads to $y_t = \eta_t/(\phi + \gamma) + \eta_{t-1}/(\phi + 2\gamma)$. In order to minimize the variance of aggregate production, by contrast, the central bank has to set $b_1 = 0$, which nullifies the impact of lagged shocks on GNP. Then,

$$y_t = \frac{\eta_t}{\phi + \gamma}.$$

This is precisely the equation which determines aggregate production in the rational expectations monetarist model with wage setting one period in advance presented in Section 4.3. Thus, in this simple model, the central bank is capable of eliminating altogether the nominal rigidity that results from wages being set two periods, rather than only one period in advance.

Discussion

[T]here are long-lived nominal-wage commitments out there in the world.

Phelps (1990: 60)

The general lesson that can be drawn from the Fischer model is that monetary policy is effective, rational expectations notwithstanding, whenever monetary policy decisions are more frequent than wage negotiations. In this case, the central bank can, to a certain extent, eliminate the nominal rigidity caused by long-term contracting. This raises several questions.

Why do agents not make use of indexation? Indexed labour contracts in the Fischer model would make the wage rates, w_t^I and w_t^{II}, paid to the two worker groups contingent on the prevailing price level p_t. For instance, it is possible to let $w_t^I = w_t^{II} = p_t$. The target output level $y_t = 0$ is then realized for all t. (Analogously, indexation can be used to eliminate output fluctuations altogether in the model with one-period wage setting in Section 4.3: $y_t = 0$ for all t if labour contracts specify $w_t = p_t$ at $t - 1$.) Two reasons for the non-utilization of indexed contracts have been put forward in the literature. For one thing, indexation precludes the necessary adjustments in response to real (as opposed to monetary) shocks because in effect it predetermines real variables. This is not a problem in the Fischer model. But if one introduces random productivity, indexation is not necessarily conducive to output stability (see Gray 1978 and Exercises 4.4 and 6.9), as has been experienced after the first oil price shock in the mid-1970s. For another, indexation makes the economy more inflation-prone (Dornbusch and Simonsen 1983) by initiating wage–price spirals. For this reason, legal obstacles to indexation have been raised in several countries.

Even if indexation is not used, why do agents contract in nominal terms for several periods, and not for one period only? One strand of the literature (see Akerlof and Yellen 1985, and Mankiw 1985) emphasizes the physical costs of changing prices ('menu costs'). Also, if information acquisition is costly, it is not generally profitable for firms to be perfectly informed about all events that would make wage or price changes necessary. Finally, as emphasized by Okun (1981), in markets with long-lasting employer–employee or buyer–seller relationships, firms hold prices fixed when the macroeconomic data change in order not to deter employees and customers ('implicit contracts').

Why is there staggering? According to Phelps (1990: 60), the 'New Keynesian approach would be of rather limited usefulness in explaining booms and slumps in most countries if, according to the theory, all wage setting were synchronized'. Ball and Cecchetti (1988) develop a model in which firms' price setting decisions convey information to competitors. Staggering may arise as an equilibrium, with half the firms waiting for the price signals from the other half, each period.

6.5 Sunspots

Even apart from the instability due to speculation, there is the instability due to the characteristic of human nature that a large proportion of our positive activities depend on spontaneous optimism rather than on a mathematical expectation, whether moral or hedonistic or economic. Most, probably, of our decisions to do something positive, the full consequences of which will be drawn out over many days to come, can only be taken as a result of animal spirits—of a spontaneous urge to action rather than inaction, and not as the outcome of a weighted average of quantitative benefits multiplied by quantitative probabilities.

Keynes (1936/1973: 161)

Introduction

Expectations play a pivotal role in both Keynesian economics and the subsequent monetarist and new classical theories, though with a strikingly different emphasis. Keynesian economics stresses the impact of autonomous (exogenous) shifts in expectations on aggregate expenditure and, via the Keynesian multiplier, on aggregate production. New classical economics holds that the very notion of autonomous changes in expectations is flawed because expectations are rational and, therefore, endogenous. The sunspot theory shows that the Keynesian concept of autonomous shifts in expectations does have significance even if expectations are rational once one considers models in which (in contrast to all the models expounded so far) the equilibrium is

---

Box 6.4 Sunspots and economic activity

Sunspots featured prominently in the nineteenth-century business cycle theories of Herschel and Jevons. Unlike the new Keynesian economists, Herschel, Jevons, and their contemporaries did not regard sunspots as intrinsically irrelevant variables but as economic fundamentals that affect the economy through their impact on harvests. Jevons (1884) observed that the average interval between commercial crises was 10.44 years and the average interval between periods of sunspot activity 10.45 years. He concluded: 'Judging this close coincidence of results according to the theory of probabilities, it becomes highly probable that two periodic phenomena, varying so nearly in the same mean period, are connected as cause and effect' (Jevons 1884: 215, quoted from Persons 1927: 104). Cass and Shell (1983) re-introduced the term to modern economic theory.

---

not unique. To see this, suppose a model has multiple rational expectations equilibria. Then, expectations are self-fulfilling: the equilibrium that actually occurs is the one agents expect to occur. Consequently, an autonomous shift in beliefs leads to the occurrence of a different rational expectations equilibrium. This implies that any variable which serves to coordinate expectations has an impact on the selection of the equilibrium outcome, no matter whether it affects the economic fundamentals (intrinsic uncertainty) or not (extrinsic uncertainty). Suppose, for instance, that agents use sunspot activity to coordinate beliefs (Box 6.4 gives a brief overview of the role of sunspots in economic theory). Then sunspots affect real economic activity. If strong sunspot activity raises business optimism and business optimism is a self-fulfilling prophecy, then strong sunspot activity causes high economic activity.

In this section, we develop a model in which there are multiple equilibria with differing levels of aggregate production due to demand externalities. Expectations about the level of aggregate demand, which may be coordinated by sunspot activity, determine which of the multiple equilibria occurs. The model is static. It provides microfoundations for the income expenditure analysis of Section 2.2 and rationalizes the Keynesian notion of animal spirits-driven fluctuations in investment.

Model

The model has a simple two-period structure. In period one, competitive firms produce a homogeneous output good Y using labour L only, according to the usual neoclassical production function $Y = F(L)$. The output good is used for consumption C or investment $I : Y = C + I$. The economy is inhabited by two kinds of agents, consumers and investors. In period one,

127

consumers supply $\bar{L}$ (>0) units of labour. Full employment is $\bar{Y} \equiv F(\bar{L})$. The consumers own the firms, so their aggregate income in period one is Y. They consume the final good in period one and a set of differentiated products j in period two. The inclusion of differentiated consumer goods is essential because it enables us to model imperfect competition. Letting $R(j)$ denote the quantity consumed of differentiated good j and n the total number of goods (determined endogenously below), consumers' utility is $u = C^c \int_0^n R(j)^{1-c}dj$ ($0 < c < 1$). Consumers maximize u subject to the budget constraint $\int_0^n P(j)R(j)dj = (1+r)(Y-C)$, where $P(j)$ is the price of good j, r is the interest rate, and the homogeneous output good is the numeraire. Investors dispose of no wealth in period one. They have the ability to produce one unit of any differentiated good j from one unit of output invested in period one provided that they incur a fixed cost of F (>0) units of output. Aggregate investment, therefore, equals

$$I = nF + \int_0^n R(j)dj. \tag{6.46}$$

Because of the fixed cost, the differentiated consumption goods are supplied by monopolists in period two. As monopolistic competitors, the investors make positive profit gross of the fixed cost $\pi(j) \equiv P(j)R(j) - (1+r)R(j)$. *Ex ante* every investor is capable of producing any good. So the number of goods n is determined by the requirement that the monopoly profits $\pi(j)$ are just sufficient to cover the fixed cost $F : \pi(j) = (1+r)F$.

Equilibrium

Let λ denote the Lagrange multiplier on the budget constraint in the consumers' utility maximization problem. The necessary optimality conditions are

$$cu/C = \lambda(1+r), \tag{6.47}$$

$$(1-c)C^c R(j)^{-c} = \lambda P(j). \tag{6.48}$$

Multiplying with $R(j)$ and integrating over j in (6.48) and using the budget constraint yields $(1-c)u = \lambda(1+r)(Y-C)$. Together with (6.47), one obtains a Keynesian consumption function with zero autonomous consumption ($C = cY$) and, using $Y = C + I$, a Keynesian multiplier formula:

$$Y = \frac{I}{1-c} \tag{6.49}$$

(cf. Section 2.2). Choosing any pair of goods j and j', (6.48) gives $[R(j)/R(j')]^{-c} = P(j)/P(j')$. Substituting for $R(j')$ in the budget equation $\int_0^n P(j')R(j')dj' = (1+r)(Y-C)$, solving for $R(j)$, and inserting $Y - C = (1-c)Y$ yields the demand function for good j:

$$R(j) = \frac{P(j)^{-1/c}}{\int_0^n P(j')^{-(1-c)/c}dj'}(1+r)(1-c)Y. \qquad (6.50)$$

The elasticity of demand for the differentiated products is a constant: $[dR(j)/dP(j)][P(j)/R(j)] = -1/c$.

Let Y^e denote the level of aggregate demand Y investors expect to prevail in period one. Since each investor is small relative to the aggregate economy, the investors take Y^e as given. Moreover, following Keynesian tradition, it is assumed that Y^e *is exogenous*.

For instance, expectations may be conditioned on sunspot activity: if the number of sunspots is $\epsilon \cdot 100\%$ of the maximum number of sunspots, then expected aggregate demand equals $\epsilon \cdot 100\%$ of aggregate production at full employment: $Y^e = \bar{Y}\epsilon$. More realistically, changes in Y^e reflect autonomous changes in business optimism ('animal spirits'). Investors maximize expected profit $\pi(j) \equiv P(j)R(j) - (1+r)R(j)$ given the demand functions (6.50) and given the aggregate demand expectations $Y = Y^e$. Investors' optimal pricing and investment behaviour is described by:

$$P(j) = (1+r)/(1-c),$$
$$R(j) = (1-c)^2 Y^e/n.$$

The former equation follows from the monopoly pricing rule $[P(j) - (1+r)]/P(j) = -[dP(j)/dR(j)][R(j)/P(j)] = c$. The latter is obtained by substituting $P(j)$ into equation (6.50) with $Y = Y^e$. (We ignore the usual time consistency problem that a monopolist would want to maximize revenue, not profit, once production costs are sunk.) The resulting monopoly profit gross of the fixed cost is $\pi(j) = c(1-c)(1+r)Y^e/n$. Inserting this into the free entry condition $\pi(j) = (1+r)F$ and solving for n yields

$$n = c(1-c)Y^e/F.$$

The higher expected aggregate demand Y^e relative to the fixed cost of investment F is, the higher is the equilibrium number of differentiated consumption goods.

Equilibrium aggregate investment is obtained by inserting $nF = c(1-c)Y^e$ and $nR(j) = (1-c)^2 Y^e$ into equation (6.46):

$$I = (1-c)Y^e.$$

The higher expected aggregate demand is, the higher investment I is. Substituting for I from this equation in the multiplier formula (6.49), we have:

$$Y = Y^e.$$

This equation looks familiar: aggregate output Y equals expected aggregate output Y^e. As in the new classical model and in the RBC model, expectations are rational. This result is surprising, however. In the new classical model and the RBC model, it is *assumed* that expectations are rational, and this assumption is used to determine the equilibria of the models. Here, it has been assumed that expectations are exogenous, and it turns out that, nonetheless, expectations *are* rational. Expectations are self-fulfilling, and the rational expectations hypothesis does not suffice to select a unique equilibrium. If expectations are conditioned on sunspot activity in the manner described above, equilibrium aggregate output depends on sunspots (extrinsic uncertainty matters): $Y = \bar{Y}\epsilon$.

Aggregate demand externalities and stabilization policies

The reason why, for given output expectations, aggregate production does not rise if the economy is in a state of less than full employment (i.e. Say's law fails to hold) is the presence of *aggregate demand externalities*, also called *thick markets externalities*. Suppose starting from the profit-maximizing output level, a single entrepreneur increases his investment spending. Since he is small relative to the aggregate economy, aggregate demand is unaffected. Consequently, the increase in production leads to a violation of the conditions for profit maximization. Only if all entrepreneurs increase investment spending simultaneously, do aggregate demand and aggregate production rise. In other words, since one producer's supply creates the other producers' demand, aggregate demand is a public good, and the provision of this public good poses a severe coordination problem in a complex economy with decentralized decision making. (Technological externalities between producers can lead to a similar coordination problem, see Exercise 6.10.) If people rely on sunspots to coordinate their expectations, then sunspots matter, despite the clear inefficiency associated with less than full employment. An important implication for the effectiveness of stabilization policies is that attempts to stimulate the economy are successful, even if they leave the economic fundamentals unaffected, if they bring about a coordinated switch to more optimistic expectations.

Criticisms of sunspot theories

The standard framework for analysing the macroeconomic impact of sunspots is Azariadis's (1981) seminal monetary overlapping generations model. We have chosen to approach the problem starting from a different direction because we regard aggregate demand externalities as the most relevant application of the sunspot theory in the field of business cycles, as it rehabilitates Keynes's position that autonomous shifts in expectations have a potentially important impact on aggregate demand and output. In our simple static model, sunspots govern the selection of one among several possible static rational expectations equilibria. By contrast, Azariadis type models are explicitly dynamic and offer additional insights that cannot be gained from our simple model. For one thing, prices and quantities potentially show a very different dynamic behaviour in a sunspot equilibrium than along a perfect foresight path. For another, it can be shown that in nonlinear dynamic models there is a close connection between the existence of endogenous cycles and the existence of sunspot equilibria (Azariadis and Guesnerie 1986).

Sunspot theories have been criticized on three grounds (see Woodford 1987). First, because of their reliance on multiple equilibria, sunspot theories offer no definite predictions. In particular, it is impossible to predict the effects of policy measures, because comparative statics exercises are meaningless in the presence of multiple equilibria. Proponents of the sunspot approach answer that sunspot models do have definite implications, for instance, for the co-movements of macroeconomic variables. Farmer and Guo (1994) analyse an extension to the basic RBC model expounded in Section 5.3 which incorporates monopolistic competition of the kind encountered in our sunspot model. They show that multiple convergent perfect foresight growth paths (indeterminacy) may exist and that recurrent sunspot-induced jumps from one convergent path to another are consistent with rational expectations (an example of sunspot equilibria which look very different from perfect foresight equilibria). Farmer and Guo then demonstrate that sunspot equilibria in a calibrated version of their model match the second moments of observed US time series data with the same degree of precision as standard RBC models with productivity shocks. In this sense, their sunspot model has the same predictive power as a standard RBC model. As for the unpredictability of policy effects—maybe that is the sad truth.

Second, there are innumerable sources of extrinsic uncertainty. So it is questionable that agents agree on one specific random event which coordinates their expectations. This criticism has led to a different interpretation of the theory. Consider a random shock (intrinsic uncertainty) that has a small impact on the economy in the absence of extrinsic uncertainty. Suppose that, in addition, this economic variable serves as a means of coordinating expectations. Then, the economy responds more strongly to the random shock than justified by market fundamentals alone. Under this interpretation, the sunspot theory offers an explanation for potentially strong over-response to small disturbances to the economic fundamentals.

Third, and most fundamentally, that sunspots matter presupposes some sort of market imperfection. For instance, Balasko (1984) shows that sunspot equilibria cannot exist in Azariadis's (1981) model if there are complete markets for state-contingent securities. So the emergence of sunspot equilibria requires a specific form of market incompleteness. Similarly, full employment is achieved in the sunspot model presented above if the demand coordination problem is solved by writing contracts which specify the investment level $I = (1 - c)\bar{Y}/n$ for each entrepreneur. Here, the proponents' answer is that the argument that sunspots do not matter in the absence of market imperfections is a serious challenge in theory, but has little practical importance because market imperfections abound in reality.

6.6 Summary

1. New Keynesian economics is concerned with real rigidities, nominal rigidities, and aggregate demand externalities in models that conform to the new classical postulates of rational expectations and maximizing behaviour.
2. The use of standard debt contracts makes bankruptcy a matter of concern. As a result, firms' demands for investment and labour are functions of their balance sheet position. In conjunction with real rigidities in the labour market, this explains fluctuations in employment and aggregate output despite inelastic labour supply.
3. Investment depends on lagged profits because past profits contribute to firms' net worth and firms' net worth is a determinant of their demand for investment. Business cycles à la Frisch can be explained in a monetarist-style model with investment dependent on lagged profits.
4. Monetary policy is effective even if the interest elasticity of investment is low because of the balance sheet channel of monetary policy: a reduction in the interest rate makes debt service less burdensome. This

improvement in firms' balance sheet position raises the demand for, and the availability of, credit and boosts equilibrium investment.

5. Rational expectations notwithstanding, the policy ineffectiveness proposition is not valid in the presence of nominal rigidities. If, after a shock, the monetary authority is able to react before nominal contracts expire, it has the power to stabilize the economy.

6. One producer's supply creates other producers' demand. Because of this aggregate demand externality, multiple rational expectations equilibria may exist. Equilibrium selection can then be governed by extrinsic random events such as sunspot activity. In such a situation, stabilization policy is effective, even if it does not affect economic fundamentals, if it leads to increased business optimism.

Further Reading

Mankiw and Romer (1991) is a collection of prominent new Keynesian articles. The authoritative papers on the role of balance sheets in business cycle models with firm microfoundations are Bernanke and Gertler (1989), and Greenwald and Stiglitz (1993b). A simplified version of the model presented in Section 6.2 is in Arnold (2002). Arnold (2000) presents a model with microfoundations which explains business cycles in Frisch's sense as a result of debt deflation à la Fisher. Gertler (1988) provides a brilliant survey on the role of financial market imperfections in macroeconomics and Hubbard (1998) reviews the huge empirical literature on capital market imperfections and investment initiated by Fazzari et al. (1988). Taylor's (1980) classic paper offers a different approach to nominal rigidity due to long-term contracts, where wages are constrained to be constant over the lifetimes of the contracts. Ball et al. (1988) survey the literature. On the working of the balance sheet channel of monetary policy, see Bernanke and Gertler (1995). The classics of the sunspot theory are Azariadis (1981), and Cass and Shell (1983). The authoritative textbook treatment is in Farmer (1993: section 9). The role of aggregate demand externalities has been pioneered by P. Diamond (1982) and Weitzman (1982) (see also Holländer 1988). Cooper and John (1988) provide an informative survey. Interesting applications of the sunspot approach include bank runs (D. Diamond and Dybvig 1983) and currency crises (Sachs et al. 1996).

References

Akerlof, G. and Yellen, J. (1985). 'A Near-Rational Model of the Business Cycle with Wage and Price Inertia'. *Quarterly Journal of Economics*, 100: 823–38.

Arnold, L. G. (2000). 'A Model of Debt Deflation and the Phillips Curve: Implications for Business Cycles and the Balance Sheet Channel of Monetary Policy'. *Jahrbücher für Nationalökonomie und Statistik*, 220: 385–99.

—— (2002). 'Financial Market Imperfections, Labour Market Imperfections, and Business Fluctuations'. *Scandinavian Journal of Economics*, 104: 105–24.

Arrow, K. J. (1964). 'The Role of Securities in the Optimal Allocation of Risk Bearing'. *Review of Economic Studies*, 31: 91–6.

Azariadis, C. (1981). 'Self-Fulfilling Prophecies'. *Journal of Economic Theory*, 25: 380–96.

—— and Guesnerie, R. (1986). 'Sunspots and Cycles'. *Review of Economic Studies*, 53: 725–37.

Balasko, Y. (1984). 'Extrinsic Uncertainty Revisited'. *Journal of Economic Theory*, 31: 203–10.

Ball, L. and Cecchetti, S. G. (1988). 'Imperfect Information and Staggered Price Setting'. *American Economic Review*, 78: 999–1018.

—— Mankiw, N. G., and Romer, D. (1988). 'The New Keynesian Economics and the Output-Inflation Tradeoff'. *Brookings Papers on Economic Activity*, 1–65.

Bernanke, B. S. and Gertler, M. (1987). 'Banking and macroeconomic equilibrium', in W. A. Barnett and K. J. Singleton (eds), *New Approaches to Monetary Economics: Proceedings of the 2nd International Symposium in Economic Theory and Econometrics*. Cambridge: Cambridge University Press, pp. 89–111.

—— —— (1989). 'Agency Costs, Net Worth, and Business Fluctuations'. *American Economic Review*, 79: 14–31.

—— —— (1995). 'Inside the Black Box: The Credit Channel of Monetary Transmission'. *Journal of Economic Perspectives*, 9: 27–48.

Bhattacharya, S. and Thakor, A. V. (1993). 'Contemporary Banking Theory'. *Journal of Financial Intermediation*, 3: 2–50.

Blanchard, O. J. and Fischer, S. (1989). *Lectures on Macroeconomics*. Cambridge, MA: MIT Press.

Brealey, R. A. and Myers, S. C. (1996). *Principles of Corporate Finance*. New York: McGraw-Hill.

Bryant, J. (1983). 'A Simple Rational-Expectations Keynes-Type Model'. *Quarterly Journal of Economics*, 98: 525–8.

Carlstrom, C. and Fuerst, T. (1997). 'Agency Costs, Net Worth, and Business Fluctuations: A Computable General Equilibrium Analysis'. *American Economic Review*, 87: 893–910.

Cass, D. and Shell, K. (1983). 'Do Sunspots Matter?' *Journal of Political Economy*, 91: 193–227.

Cooper, R. W. and John, A. (1988). 'Coordinating Coordination Failures in Keynesian Models'. *Quarterly Journal of Economics*, 103: 441–63.

Diamond, D. W. and Dybvig, P. H. (1983). 'Bank Runs, Deposit Insurance, and Liquidity'. *Journal of Political Economy*, 91: 401–19.

Diamond, P. A. (1982). 'Aggregate Demand Management in Search Equilibrium'. *Journal of Political Economy*, 90: 881–94.

Dornbusch, R. and Simonsen, M. H. (1983). *Inflation, Debt, and Indexation*. Cambridge: MIT Press.

Farmer, R. E. A. (1993). *The Macroeconomics of Self-Fulfilling Prophecies*. Cambridge: MIT Press.

—— and Guo, J.-T. (1994). 'Real Business Cycles and the Animal Spirits Hypothesis'. *Journal of Economic Theory*, 63: 42–72.

Fazzari, S. M., Hubbard, R. G., and Petersen, B. C. (1988). 'Financing Constraints and Corporate Investment'. *Brookings Papers on Economic Activity 1*, 141–95.

Fischer, S. (1977*a*). 'On the Nonexistence of Privately Issued Index Bonds in the U.S. Capital Market', in E. Lundberg (ed.), *Inflation Theory and Anti-Inflation Policy*. Boulder: Westview Press, pp. 502–18.

—— (1977*b*). 'Long Term Contracts, Rational Expectations and the Optimal Money Supply'. *Journal of Political Economy*, 85: 191–206.

Fisher, I. (1933). 'The Debt-Deflation Theory of Great Depressions'. *Econometrica*, 1: 337–57.

Gale, D. (1983). 'Competitive Models with Keynesian Features'. *Economic Journal*, 93: 17–33.

—— and Hellwig, M. (1985). 'Incentive-Compatible Debt Contracts I: The One-Period Problem'. *Review of Economic Studies*, 52: 647–64.

Gertler, M. (1988). 'Financial Structure and Aggregate Economic Activity: An Overview'. *Journal of Money, Credit and Banking*, 20: 559–88.

Gilson, S. C. (1989). 'Management Turnover and Financial Distress'. *Journal of Financial Economics*, 25: 241–62.

Gray, J. A. (1978). 'On Indexation and Contract Length'. *Journal of Political Economy*, 86: 1–18.

Greenwald, B. and Stiglitz, J. E. (1993*a*). 'New and Old Keynesians'. *Journal of Economic Perspectives*, 7: 23–44.

—— and Stiglitz, J. E. (1993*b*). 'Financial Market Imperfections and Business Cycles'. *Quarterly Journal of Economics*, 108: 77–114.

Holländer, H. (1988). 'Increasing Returns and the Foundations of Unemployment Theory: A Note'. *Economic Journal*, 98: 165–71.

Hubbard, R. G. (1998). 'Capital-Market Imperfections and Investment'. *Journal of Economic Literature*, 36: 193–225.

Jevons, W. S. (1884). *Investigations in Currency and Finance*. London: Macmillan.

Keynes, J. M. (1st edn 1936/cited edn 1973). *The General Theory of Employment, Interest and Money*. London: Macmillan.

Mankiw, N. G. (1985). 'Small Menu Costs and Large Business Cycles'. *Quarterly Journal of Economics*, 100: 529–37.

—— and Romer, D. (1991). *New Keynesian Economics, Vols. 1 and 2*. Cambridge: Cambridge University Press.

Mayer, C. (1988). 'New Issues in Corporate Finance'. *European Economic Review*, 32: 1167–89.

Mishkin, F. S. (1976). 'Illiquidity, Consumer Durable Expenditure, and Monetary Policy'. *American Economic Review*, 66: 642–54.

—— (1998). *The Economics of Money, Banking, and Financial Markets*, 5th edn. Reading: Addison-Wesley.

Okun, A. M. (1981). *Prices and Quantities. A Macroeconomic Analysis*. Washington: Brookings Institution.

Persons, W. M. (1927). 'Theories of Business Fluctuations: I. A Classification of the Theories'. *Quarterly Journal of Economics*, 41: 94–128.

Phelps, E. S. (1990). *Seven Schools of Macroeconomic Thought*. Oxford: Clarendon Press.

Sachs, J., Tornell, A., and Velasco, A. (1996). 'The Mexican Peso Crisis: Sudden Death or Death Foretold?' *Journal of International Economics*, 41: 265–83.

Sargent, T. J. (1979). *Macroeconomic Theory*. New York: Academic Press.

Shapiro, C. and Stiglitz, J. E. (1984). 'Equilibrium Unemployment as a Worker Discipline Device'. *American Economic Review*, 74: 433–44.

Stiglitz, J. E. and Weiss, A. (1981). 'Credit Rationing in Markets with Imperfect Information'. *American Economic Review*, 71: 393–410.

Taylor, J. B. (1980). 'Aggregate Dynamics and Staggered Contracts'. *Journal of Political Economy*, 88: 1–24.

Weitzman, M. L. (1982). 'Increasing Returns and the Foundations of Unemployment Theory'. *Economic Journal*, 92: 787–804.

Woodford, M. (1987). 'Three Questions about Sunspot Equilibria as an Explanation of Economic Fluctuations'. *American Economic Review*, 77: 93–8.

Zarnowitz, V. (1999). 'Theory and History Behind Business Cycles: Are the 1990s the Onset of a Golden Age?' *Journal of Economic Perspectives*, 13: 69–90.

Exercises

6.1 Consider the Cobb–Douglas example in Section 6.2. Suppose the production of the homogeneous output good is characterized by constant returns to scale: $Y = \Theta K^{1-\alpha}(e^*L)^\alpha$ with $0 < \alpha < 1$. Furthermore, let the technology that transforms investment I_{t-1} into capital be described by $K_t = I_{t-1}^\eta$ with $0 < \eta < 1$. Show: The indirect profit function is exactly the same as in the main text. This highlights that we need decreasing returns to scale somewhere, but not necessarily in the production of the homogeneous final good.

6.2 Consider the model with bankruptcy-averse banks introduced in Section 6.2. Suppose banks set the credit ceiling Z_t which is independent of investment I_t (and other variables under the control of the entrepreneurs); that is, they do not make use of restrictive covenants. In the main text, we have claimed that the equilibrium allocation of the model with bankruptcy-averse banks cannot be achieved this way. To show this, assume that banks charge the interest factor γ^{-1} and set Z_t such that the firms are able to repay under all circumstances. Argue: the entrepreneurs borrow up to the credit ceiling Z_t. Show that the optimal investment level I_t solves

$$\beta E_t \left[\frac{\partial \pi^*(\Theta_{t+1}, I_t)}{\partial I_t} \right] = 1,$$

and is less than I^* even if $A_t > \bar{A}$.

6.3 Type 2 credit rationing (Stiglitz and Weiss 1981). Stiglitz and Weiss show that in a credit market with asymmetric information about the riskiness of investment projects, there is adverse selection in that at a given interest rate r only the riskiest investors apply for credit. Increases in r aggravate this adverse selection problem: low-risk investors cease to demand capital, and the average riskiness of the pool of applicants increases. As a result, the average return to lending ρ can be inversely related to the interest rate charged to borrowers r. This is because those investors who repay their loans repay more, but the probability of repayment shrinks as the average riskiness of the pool of applicants rises. Suppose ρ is a hump-shaped function $\rho(r)$ of r with its maximum at r^*. Suppose further that full employment prevails ($Y = \bar{Y}$), that the propensity to save depends positively on the deposit rate ($S = s(\rho)\bar{Y}$ with $s' > 0$), and that the demand for investment capital depends negatively on the borrowing rate ($I = I(r)$ with $I' < 0$). Construct the function $s[\rho(r)]\bar{Y}$ graphically. Argue that credit is rationed if $I(r^*) > s[\rho(r^*)]\bar{Y}$. Explain why the interest rate r fails to bring about credit market clearing.

6.4 Describe Keynesian unemployment and type 2 credit rationing using the terms excess supply and excess demand in the capital market. Is it possible (given flexible prices and wages) that Keynesian unemployment and type 2 credit rationing prevail simultaneously?

6.5 Zarnowitz's (1999) profit accelerator. Zarnowitz (1999: 74) holds that 'profitability is likely to be determined more by the *change* than by the *level* of total economic activity'. Accordingly, suppose $\pi_t = \kappa \Delta y_t$. Further, let aggregate demand be given by $y_t = \psi \pi_{t-1} + \epsilon_t$, where ϵ_t is white noise. Show:

$$y_t - \kappa\psi y_{t-1} + \kappa\psi y_{t-2} = \epsilon_t.$$

Characterize the range of parameters for which business cycles occur.

6.6 Consider the following model:

$$y_t = \tfrac{1}{25}(s_t + p_t^* - p_t) + 2\pi_{t-1} - \tfrac{1}{5}r_t,$$

$$m_t - p_t = 2y_t - \tfrac{2}{5}i_t,$$

$$i_t = r_t + \Delta p_{t+1}|_t^e,$$

$$\Delta p_{t+1}|_t^e = \Delta m_t,$$

$$i_t = i^* + \Delta s_{t+1}|_t^e,$$

$$r^* = i_t^* - \Delta p_{t+1}^*|_t^e,$$

$$\bar{s}_t \equiv p_t - p_t^*,$$

$$\Delta(s_{t+1} - \bar{s}_{t+1})|_t^e = -\tfrac{1}{5}(s_t - \bar{s}_t),$$

$$\tfrac{3}{2}y_t = -(w_t - p_t),$$

$$\pi_t = \tfrac{2}{3}(p_t - w_t) + y_t,$$

$$w_t = p_t|_{t-1}^e,$$

$$\Delta p_t|_{t-1}^e = \Delta m_{t-1},$$

where Δm_t follows a random walk. Show:

$$y_t - \tfrac{14}{9} y_{t-1} + \tfrac{8}{9} y_{t-2} = \tfrac{14}{45} \Delta^2 m_t.$$

Does the model display business cycles in Frisch's sense? Assume $y_{-2} = y_{-1} = 0$, $\Delta^2 m_0 = 45/14$, and $\Delta^2 m_t = 0$ for $t = 1, \ldots, 15$. Compute y_t for $t = 1, \ldots, 15$.

6.7 In the Fischer (1977b) model of Section 6.4, show that the output variance is

$$\sigma_y^2 = \left[\frac{1}{(\phi + \gamma)^2} + \left(\frac{b_1}{\phi + 2\gamma} \right)^2 \right] \sigma_\eta^2.$$

(Hint: use the definition of the variance $\sigma_y^2 \equiv E(y_t^2)$ and the fact that the monetary shocks are independent ($E(\eta_t \eta_{t-1}) = 0$).)

6.8 The Fischer (1977b) model with velocity shocks. Consider the following model:

$$m_t - p_t + v_t = \phi y_t,$$

$$\gamma y_t = -\frac{(w_t^I - p_t) + (w_t^{II} - p_t)}{2},$$

$$w_t^I = E_{t-1} p_t, \quad w_t^{II} = E_{t-2} p_t,$$

$$v_t = \rho v_{t-1} + \nu_t,$$

$$m_t = \sum_{j=1}^{\infty} b_j v_{t-j}.$$

Velocity v_t follows an autoregressive stochastic process: $0 < \rho < 1$. Show: Aggregate production is given by

$$y_t = \frac{v_t}{\phi + \gamma} + \frac{(b_1 + \rho) v_{t-1}}{\phi + 2\gamma}.$$

Which money supply rule minimizes the output variance?

6.9 Indexation (based on Gray 1978). Consider the following model:

$$m_t - p_t = \phi y_t,$$

$$\gamma y_t = -(w_t - p_t) + \theta_t,$$

$$w_t = \lambda p_t + (1 - \lambda)E_{t-1}(p_t + \theta_t).$$

Productivity θ_t is random and affects aggregate supply. Wages are set one period in advance with a target employment level which corresponds to $y_t = 0$ (i.e. $w_t = p_t + \theta_t$). Indexation is possible: period-t wages w_t can be made contingent on the realized price level p_t (w_t cannot be specified contingent on θ_t, however). λ indicates the degree of indexation used ($0 \leq \lambda \leq 1$). Show: equilibrium output is

$$y_t = \frac{\lambda}{\lambda\phi + \gamma}(m_t - E_{t-1}m_t) + \frac{1 - \lambda}{\lambda\phi + \gamma}(\theta_t - E_{t-1}\theta_t).$$

Under what circumstances does output stabilization imply full indexation ($\lambda = 1$)? Under what conditions should indexation not be used at all ($\lambda = 0$)?

6.10 Bryant's (1983) coordination failure model. Consider an economy inhabited by N identical agents i. Each agent i works either full time ($L_i = \bar{L}$) or not at all ($L_i = 0$). Aggregate production equals $Y = \min\{L_i\}_{i=1}^{N}$ and agents get equal shares Y/N of aggregate production. Let μ (>0) denote the disutility associated with full-time work. Then agent i's utility is $Y/N - \mu$ ($0 < \mu < \bar{L}/N$). Show: both $Y = \bar{L}$ and $Y = 0$ are expectational equilibria.

LESSONS ABOUT BUSINESS CYCLES

'I don't want to get into a religious argument with you, [...] but I wonder if you people aren't a bit too—well, strong, on the virtues of analysis. I mean, once you've taken it all apart, fine, I'll be the first to applaud your industry. But other than a lot of bits and pieces lying about, what have *you* said?'

Roger Mexico, in Pynchon's *Gravity's Rainbow*

'Why is it that the cyclical movement goes on and on and never comes to an end' (Haberler 1937/1941: 83)? In this final chapter, we summarize the lessons about business cycles that can be drawn from the theories expounded. For each of the five schools of thought, we pose three questions. How is aggregate production determined at a given point in time? Are monetary and fiscal policies effective? What are the sources of business cycle dynamics?

Keynesian economics emphasizes the central role of aggregate demand in the determination of aggregate production. This is elucidated by the *income expenditure analysis*, which shows that if consumption depends on aggregate income alone and investment is predetermined, equilibrium aggregate output is determined on the economy's demand side alone (by the condition for an equilibrium in the market for goods). It depends positively on investment, autonomous consumption, the propensity to consume, net exports, and government expenditure, and negatively on taxes. While fiscal policy is effective, money does not matter because investment does not respond to falling interest rates. The principle of acceleration states that investment depends positively on the change in aggregate production one period earlier, because rising demand makes additional capacities necessary, raises business optimism, etc. The multiplier accelerator model demonstrates that the interplay between the Keynesian consumption function and the principle of acceleration is sufficient to explain business cycles in Frisch's sense. The principle of acceleration gives upward and downward movements a cumulative element, and it explains the turning points of aggregate economic activity: as output growth slows down in the expansion, the level of investment starts to fall, thereby precipitating the upper turning point; and vice versa for the lower turning point. The pre-Keynesian over-investment theory provides alternative explanations for the turning points. In the Keynesian aggregate supply–aggregate demand (*AS–AD*) *model*, the demand for investment is interest elastic and the nominal wage rate is fixed. The equilibrium price–output combination is determined (see Fig. 7.1) by the point of intersection of the downward-sloping AD curve (simultaneous equilibrium in the markets for goods and money, intersection of IS and LM) and the upward-sloping AS curve (the profit-maximizing output level for varying price levels, given the nominal wage rate). In the closed economy, both fiscal and monetary policies are effective because they raise aggregate demand at any price level (the equilibrium moves from point A to point B in Fig. 7.1). In the open economy with flexible exchange rates and international capital mobility, monetary policy is more effective and fiscal policy is less effective than in the closed economy. This is due to the exchange rate channel of monetary transmission: expansionary monetary policy leads to a fall in the interest rate, a depreciation of the domestic currency, and, therefore, a surge in net exports, whereas additional public expenditure increases the interest rate and the price of the domestic currency so that net exports fall.

Monetarism brings the economy's supply side back to the fore. Nominal wages are set one period in advance. Wage setters have a real wage target or a target employment level, which may be full employment or may be characterized by the prevalence of structural unemployment. The corresponding output level is called the natural rate of output. Wages are set such that if expectations are fulfilled, the target wage or employment level is realized.

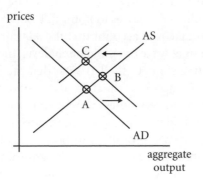

Fig. 7.1 The AS–AD model.

Inflation expectations are adaptive. Taken together, one obtains the accelerationist Phillips curve: aggregate production exceeds the natural rate of output if and only if inflation accelerates; and the higher the increase in inflation, the higher aggregate production is. In terms of Fig. 7.1, lagged inflation is a shift parameter of the AS curve. Steadily rising rates of money growth and inflation are required in order to bring about the shifts in the AD curve necessary for keeping equilibrium aggregate output below the natural rate. Monetarists are sceptical about policymakers' ability to stabilize the economy. The long and variable data lags, recognition lags, legislative lags, implementation lags, and effectiveness lags imply low accuracy of demand policies. The average rates of employment and production are independent of aggregate demand anyway. So monetarists advocate a laissez-faire policy: no cyclical changes in government expenditure and monetary policy that aims at a stable and predictable economic environment. The interplay of the quantity theory of money (or, more generally, an AD sector with a sufficiently low interest elasticity of money demand) and the accelerationist Phillips curve gives rise to business cycles. In expansions, rising inflation puts a check on output growth. As inflation continues to rise after the upper turning point, the downward movement has a cumulative character. When output has fallen below the natural rate, inflation falls, thereby reducing the speed with which output shrinks. After the lower turning point, output growth gains momentum because inflation continues to decelerate.

New classical economics introduces rational expectations into macroeconomics. The rational expectations assumption has important implications for policy effectiveness. To see this, substitute rational expectations for adaptive expectations in the monetarist model with wage setting one period in advance. Since wages are predetermined, there continues to be an upward-sloping AS curve. Suppose point A in Fig. 7.1 represents a situation where people's rational expectations are fulfilled. Then the central bank decides to increase the supply of money, so that the AD curve shifts to the right. With adaptive expectations, the equilibrium moves to point B. Under rational expectations, however, wage setters take into account that the AD curve shifts outward. In order to achieve the target wage or employment level, they raise wages in such a way that the AS curve shifts to the left such that the intersection with the new AD curve (point C) occurs at the natural rate of output. More generally, the new classical policy ineffectiveness proposition states that policies which raise aggregate demand do not have any output effects under rational expectations. Since politicians are prompted to boost inflation in vain attempts to raise aggregate output before elections, the government should delegate the responsibility for monetary policy to an independent central bank that is committed to ensuring price stability. Basic new classical models do not yield interesting business cycle dynamics. In Fig. 7.1, a positive price surprise shifts the equilibrium from A to B, but one period later the new equilibrium at C is reached. Formally, as, by definition, price surprises are unpredictable, aggregate production fluctuates randomly. When augmented by capital stock dynamics, costs of adjusting the labour force, or inventories, new classical models feature persistence.

Monetarism brought the supply side back to the fore. The *RBC theory* views business cycle fluctuations as a *pure* supply-side phenomenon. The economy is continually at full employment. Full employment aggregate production fluctuates in response to productivity shocks for three reasons: first, productivity shocks have a direct impact on aggregate output; second, they evoke procyclical movements in the real wage rate and labour supply; third, they are propagated via the capital stock. In the AS–AD diagram, the AS curve is vertical. Monetary and fiscal policies, which influence aggregate demand, cause fluctuations in the price level, but do not affect aggregate production. So the demand sector is ignored from the outset in most RBC models. The RBC theory does not aim at explaining cyclical movements in Frisch's sense. Rather, its goal is to show that in the presence of highly autocorrelated and sufficiently pronounced exogenous variations in TFP, calibrated models match observed business cycles not only qualitatively, but numerically, in that they predict realistic values for the second moments (autocorrelations, cross-correlations, and variances) of important macroeconomic variables.

New Keynesian economics comprises a diverse body of theory that aims at establishing Keynesian-style propositions in economic models that conform to the new classical modelling standards. Three important strands of new Keynesian economics are concerned with the roles of firms' balance sheets in business cycles, with nominal rigidities, and with extrinsic uncertainty (such as sunspot activity) and aggregate demand externalities in rational expectations models. *Balance sheet effects* can be studied either with rational or with adaptive expectations. In the rational expectations models, the crucial ingredients are financial market imperfections and labour market imperfections. Since standard debt is the only financial instrument, firms face fixed repayment obligations, so that bankruptcy is a matter of concern. The amount of internal and external finance firms dispose of is an increasing function of their net worth. So shocks which affect firms' profits and net worth cause fluctuations in investment and, hence, labour demand. Because of real wage rigidity, changes in employment and production obtain even if the supply of labour is inelastic. Like the RBC theory, this is a pure supply-side explanation for economic fluctuations (the AS curve is vertical) and does not give rise to business cycles in Frisch's sense. Such cycles can occur in an adaptive expectations model with investment dependent on lagged profits. The positive dependence of output on profits gives output movements a cumulative moment. Output and inflation move in the same direction. As a result, increasing money market pressure leads to rising interest rates during expansions, and vice versa for recessions. These procyclical interest rate movements bring about the turning points of aggregate economic activity. The balance sheet effects of monetary policy explain why monetary policy is effective even if the interest elasticity of investment is low. *Nominal wage rigidity* explains why monetary policy is effective even if expectations are rational when contracts fix nominal variables for periods longer than the time it takes the monetary authority to change the money supply. Consider an unanticipated increase in the supply of money in Fig. 7.1 which shifts the economy from the original equilibrium position at A to B. Under rational expectations and wage flexibility (i.e. in the new classical model), nominal wages adjust in the following period such that the AS curve moves to the left and the economy jumps from B to C. With nominal wage rigidity, wages cannot adjust instantaneously, so it takes time to move to the new equilibrium at C. Monetary policy can accelerate the movement from B to C by appropriately shifting the AD curve. The *sunspot theory* shows that, due to aggregate demand externalities, the notion of autonomous shifts in the demand for investment does not lose its significance if expectations are rational. Since investors are small relative to the aggregate economy, they take aggregate demand as given. As a consequence, any uniformly expected level of aggregate demand is self-fulfilling. The sunspot theory implies that stabilization policies may be successful even if economic fundamentals are unaffected, if an overall increase in business optimism is achieved.

In the early 1970s, after the 'monetarist revolution' most economists believed that aggregate production is determined jointly by aggregate demand (the Keynesian AD curve) and aggregate supply (the monetarist accelerationist Phillips curve). This view is still held by many economists, which is, according to De Long (2000), a 'Triumph of Monetarism'. For instance, Mankiw (1990: 1645–6) contends that 'the textbook IS–LM model, augmented by the Phillips curve, continues to provide the best way to interpret discussions of economic policy in the press and among policy makers'. However, others advocate the more recent, academically influential, pure supply-side explanations and reject the AS–AD approach. For instance, King (1993: 68) holds that 'the IS–LM model, as traditionally constructed and currently used, is a hazardous base on which to build positive theories of business fluctuations and to undertake policy analysis'. It seems fair to say that the proponents of the AS–AD approach have to take into account the impact of forward-looking expectations in evaluating the effectiveness of stabilization policies and that supply-side theorists have to recognize that aggregate demand effects are more important in reality than in their models. The purpose of this book is to equip the reader with a comprehensive overview of the different theories developed to explain business cycles, so that he can collect the grains of truth contained in each of the theories in order to understand observed business cycles movements and evaluate the potential consequences of contemplated policy measures.

References

De Long, J. B. (2000). 'The Triumph of Monetarism?' *Journal of Economic Perspectives*, 14: 83–94.

Haberler, G. (1st edn 1937/cited edn 1941). *Prosperity and Depression*. Geneva: League of Nations.

King, R. G. (1993). 'Will the New Keynesian Macroeconomics Resurrect the IS–LM Model?' *Journal of Economic Perspectives*, 7: 67–82.

Mankiw, N. G. (1990). 'A Quick Refresher Course in Macroeconomics'. *Journal of Economic Literature*, 28: 1645–60.

....

Stochastic Second-order Difference Equations

....

This appendix analyses stochastic linear second-order difference equations. To begin with, we explain the definitions and the behaviour of the sine and cosine functions. Then it is shown that under appropriate parameter combinations the solution to a non-stochastic second-order difference equation displays damped sinusoidal oscillations. Finally, it is demonstrated that the solution to a stochastic second-order difference equation which displays damped oscillations in the absence of shocks exhibits variability, persistence, and reversion in the presence of recurrent shocks.

Trigonometric functions

The *sine* and *cosine* functions are defined by

$$\sin' x = \cos x, \ \cos' x = -\sin x, \ \sin 0 = 0, \ \cos 0 = 1.$$

A first important result is

$$\sin^2 x + \cos^2 x = 1, \tag{A1.1}$$

for all x. Differentiating the left-hand side of (A1.1) with respect to x gives $2(\sin x \cos x - \cos x \sin x) = 0$. Hence, $\sin^2 x + \cos^2 x = a$ for some constant a. Setting $x = 0$ yields $a = 1$, which proves (A1.1).

Next, consider two differentiable functions $f(x)$ and $g(x)$ satisfying

$$f'(x) = g(x), g'(x) = -f(x). \tag{A1.2}$$

By definition, these requirements are fulfilled by $f(x) = \sin x$ and $g(x) = \cos(x)$. But there are further examples, such as $f(x) = \cos(-x)$ and $g(x) = \sin(-x)$, and $f(x) = \sin(x + y)$ and $g(x) = \cos(x + y)$, where y is an

147

Appendix 1

arbitrary real number. Consider the functions

$$\sin xg(x) - \cos xf(x),$$
$$\sin xf(x) + \cos xg(x).$$

Differentiating with respect to x and using (A1.2) yields $\cos xg(x) - \sin xf(x) + \sin xf(x) - \cos xg(x) = 0$ and $\cos xf(x) + \sin xg(x) - \sin xg(x) - \cos xf(x) = 0$, respectively. Hence, there exist two real numbers a and b such that

$$\sin xg(x) - \cos xf(x) = a,$$
$$\sin xf(x) + \cos xg(x) = b.$$

Multiply the former equation by $\sin x$ and the latter by $\cos x$ and add. Then multiply the former by $\cos x$ and the latter by $\sin x$ and subtract the former from the latter. Using (A1.1), one obtains

$$g(x) = a \sin x + b \cos x, \tag{A1.3}$$
$$f(x) = b \sin x - a \cos x. \tag{A1.4}$$

(A1.3) and (A1.4) can be used to prove

$$\sin(-x) = -\sin x, \cos(-x) = \cos x. \tag{A1.5}$$

To do so, let $f(x) = \cos(-x)$ and $g(x) = \sin(-x)$, which, we know, satisfy (A1.2). Then (A1.3) and (A1.4) become

$$\sin(-x) = a \sin x + b \cos x,$$
$$\cos(-x) = b \sin x - a \cos x.$$

Setting $x = 0$ yields $b = 0$ and $a = -1$. Inserting this into the equations above proves (A1.5).

Next, we derive the addition formulas

$$\cos(x + y) = \cos x \cos y - \sin x \sin y,$$
$$\sin(x + y) = \sin x \cos y + \sin y \cos x, \tag{A1.6}$$

from (A1.3) and (A1.4). Let $f(x) = \sin(x+y)$ and $g(x) = \cos(x+y)$, where y is an arbitrary real number. Then,

$$\cos(x + y) = a \sin x + b \cos x,$$
$$\sin(x + y) = b \sin x - a \cos x.$$

Setting $x = 0$ yields $b = \cos y$ and $a = -\sin y$, which yields (A1.6) upon substitution into the above pair of equations.

Since $\sin^2 x + \cos^2 x = 1$, the sine and cosine curves range between -1 and $+1$. They display harmonic oscillations: there exists a real number π such that

$$\sin 0 = 0, \cos 0 = 1, \tag{A1.7}$$

$$\sin(\pi/2) = 1, \cos(\pi/2) = 0, \tag{A1.8}$$

$$\sin \pi = 0, \cos \pi = -1, \tag{A1.9}$$

$$\sin(3\pi/2) = -1, \cos(3\pi/2) = 0, \tag{A1.10}$$

$$\sin(2\pi) = 0, \cos(2\pi) = 1, \tag{A1.11}$$

$$\sin(x + 2\pi) = \sin x, \cos(x + 2\pi) = \cos x. \tag{A1.12}$$

(A1.7): This holds true by the definitions of sine and cosine.

(A1.8): At the origin, the sine curve is upward-sloping ($\sin' 0 = \cos 0 = 1$). So the cosine curve is downward-sloping for x small: $\cos' x = -\sin' x < 0$. There exists an x ($ > 0$) such that $\sin x = 1$ (and $\cos x = 0$). Suppose this is not the case. Then $\cos x = \sin' x > 0$ for all x. $\sin x < 1$ and $\sin' x > 0$ imply that $\sin x$ converges to a constant $a > 0$. But this implies that $\cos' x = -\sin' x$ converges to $-a < 0$. This contradicts $\cos x > 0$ for all x. The smallest value x such that $\cos x = 0$ is denoted by $\pi/2$.

(A1.9): This follows from the addition formula for the cosine function: $\cos \pi = \cos(\pi/2 + \pi/2) = \cos(\pi/2)\cos(\pi/2) - \sin(\pi/2)\sin(\pi/2) = -1$. From $\sin^2 x + \cos^2 x = 1$, it follows that $\sin \pi = 0$.

(A1.10): Similarly, $\sin(3\pi/2) = \sin(\pi + \pi/2) = \sin \pi \cos(\pi/2) + \sin(\pi/2)\cos \pi = -1$ and $\cos(3\pi/2) = 0$.

(A1.11): $\cos(2\pi) = \cos(\pi + \pi) = \cos \pi \cos \pi - \sin \pi \sin \pi = 1$ and $\sin(2\pi) = 0$.

(A1.12): $\sin(x + 2\pi) = \sin x \cos(2\pi) + \sin(2\pi)\cos x = \sin x$ and $\cos(x + 2\pi) = \cos x \cos(2\pi) - \sin x \sin(2\pi) = \cos x$. The sine and cosine functions take on the same value every 2π periods.

Finally, we prove *DeMoivre's theorem*:

$$(\cos \omega \pm i \sin \omega)^t = \cos \omega t \pm i \sin \omega t$$

($i \equiv \sqrt{-1}$ denotes the imaginary unit). The proof is by induction. The validity for $t = 1$ is obvious. So it remains to show the validity for $t - 1$,

Appendix 1

that is,

$$(\cos \omega \pm i \sin \omega)^{t-1} = \cos \omega(t-1) \pm i \sin \omega(t-1),$$

entails validity for t. Multiplying both sides of the equation by $\cos \omega \pm i \sin \omega$ gives

$$(\cos \omega \pm i \sin \omega)^{t} = \cos \omega \cos \omega(t-1) - \sin \omega \sin \omega(t-1)$$
$$\pm i[\sin \omega \cos \omega(t-1) + \cos \omega \sin \omega(t-1)].$$

From the addition formulas (A1.6), $\cos \omega \cos \omega(t-1) - \sin \omega \sin \omega(t-1) = \cos \omega t$ and $\sin \omega \cos \omega(t-1) + \cos \omega \sin \omega(t-1) = \sin \omega t$. It follows that

$$(\cos \omega \pm i \sin \omega)^{t} = \cos \omega t \pm i \sin \omega t.$$

This completes the proof of DeMoivre's theorem.

Non-stochastic equations

Next, we examine second-order difference equations in the absence of stochastic disturbances:

$$y_t + a_1 y_{t-1} + a_2 y_{t-2} = 0. \tag{A1.13}$$

The first important thing to note is that if $y_{1,t}$ and $y_{2,t}$ are two particular solutions of (A1.13), then any linear combination $y_t = A_1 y_{1,t} + A_2 y_{2,t}$ of the two also satisfies (A1.13) (A_1 and A_2 are arbitrary, non-zero constants):

$$y_t + a_1 y_{t-1} + a_2 y_{t-2} = (A_1 y_{1,t} + A_2 y_{2,t}) + a_1(A_1 y_{1,t-1} + A_2 y_{2,t-1})$$
$$+ a_2(A_1 y_{1,t-2} + A_2 y_{2,t-2})$$
$$= A_1(y_{1,t} + a_1 y_{1,t-1} + a_2 y_{1,t-2})$$
$$+ A_2(y_{2,t} + a_1 y_{2,t-1} + a_2 y_{2,t-2})$$
$$= 0.$$

Suppose there exist numbers $\lambda \neq 0$ such that $y_t = \lambda^t$ are solutions to (A1.13). Then $\lambda^t + a_1 \lambda^{t-1} + a_2 \lambda^{t-2} = 0$ or, dividing by λ^{t-2} ($\neq 0$),

$$\lambda^2 + a_1 \lambda + a_2 = 0.$$

This is the *characteristic equation* of (A1.13). Its solutions,

$$\lambda_{1/2} = \frac{-a_1 \pm \sqrt{a_1^2 - 4a_2}}{2},$$

are called the *characteristic roots* of (A1.13). Assume $\Delta \equiv a_1^2 - 4a_2 < 0$. Then the characteristic roots are complex conjugates:

$$\lambda_{1/2} = \frac{-a_1 \pm i\sqrt{|\Delta|}}{2} \equiv \alpha \pm i\theta,$$

where $\alpha \equiv -a_1/2$ and $\theta \equiv \sqrt{|\Delta|}/2$. Since λ_1^t and λ_2^t are distinct solutions to (A1.13), the linear combination

$$y_t = A_1\lambda_1^t + A_2\lambda_2^t$$

also solves (A1.13). This equation is the *general solution* of (A1.13). In order for y_t to be real for all t, A_1 and A_2 must be complex numbers. Let

$$A_{1/2} \equiv \frac{A\cos e}{2} \mp i\frac{A\sin e}{2}, \tag{A1.14}$$

where A and e are real numbers. We proceed to show that the solution of (A1.13) is $y_t = A\sqrt{a_2}^t \cos(\omega t - e)$, where ω is a real number. This equation is derived in several steps, the non-self explanatory of which are explained below:

$$
\begin{aligned}
y_t &= A_1\lambda_1^t + A_2\lambda_2^t \\
&= A_1(\alpha + i\theta)^t + A_2(\alpha - i\theta)^t & \text{(A1.15)} \\
&= A_1[r(\cos\omega + i\sin\omega)]^t + A_2[r(\cos\omega - i\sin\omega)]^t & \text{(A1.16)} \\
&= r^t[A_1(\cos\omega + i\sin\omega)^t + A_2(\cos\omega - i\sin\omega)^t] \\
&= r^t[A_1(\cos\omega t + i\sin\omega t) + A_2(\cos\omega t - i\sin\omega t)] & \text{(A1.17)} \\
&= r^t[(A_1 + A_2)\cos\omega t + (A_1 - A_2)i\sin\omega t] \\
&= r^t(A\cos e \cos\omega t + A\sin e \sin\omega t) & \text{(A1.18)} \\
&= Ar^t\cos(\omega t - e) & \text{(A1.19)} \\
&= A\sqrt{a_2}^t \cos(\omega t - e).
\end{aligned}
$$

(A1.16): Let ω and r be determined by $\cos\omega \equiv \alpha/r$ and $\sin\omega \equiv \theta/r$. Then $\cos\omega/\sin\omega = \alpha/\theta$. Since, from (A1.7) and (A1.9), $\cos\omega/\sin\omega$ equals ∞ for $\omega = 0$ and $-\infty$ for $\omega = \pi$, there exists an ω and, hence, an $r = \alpha/\cos\omega$ which satisfy these equations. Substituting $\alpha = r\cos\omega$ and $\theta = r\sin\omega$ into (A1.15) gives (A1.16). Notice that $\alpha^2 + \theta^2 = r^2(\sin^2\omega + \cos^2\omega) = r^2$, hence $r = \sqrt{\alpha^2 + \theta^2}$.

(A1.17): This is the crucial step in the proof: The time argument 'wanders' into the sine and cosine terms. We obtain the equation by applying DeMoivre's theorem.

(A1.18): In this step, the imaginary unit i disappears. Use is made of the fact that $A_1 + A_2 = A \cos e$ and $(A_1 - A_2)i = (-iA \sin e)i = -i^2 A \sin e = A \sin e$, as implied by (A1.14) together with $i^2 = -1$.

(A1.19): This follows from (A1.5) and (A1.6):

$$\cos e \cos \omega t + \sin e \sin \omega t = \cos(-e) \cos \omega t - \sin(-e) \sin \omega t$$
$$= \cos(\omega t - e).$$

The period of oscillation of y_t is given by $t' - t$ where $\omega t' - e = \omega t - e + 2\pi$. It is equal to $t' - t = 2\pi/\omega$.

Random variables

Random variables are variables which take on different possible values with given probabilities. For our purposes, it is sufficient to consider continuous random variables, which can take on arbitrary real numbers y. Suppose the distribution of the variable can be described by means of the continuously differentiable distribution function $H(y)$, where $H(y)$ is the probability that the random variable takes on a value no greater than y. $H(y)$ is non-decreasing with $\lim_{y \to -\infty} H(y) = 0$ and $\lim_{y \to \infty} H(y) = 1$. The probability that the random variable falls into the interval $[y, y + dy]$ is $H(y + dy) - H(y)$. As dy goes to zero, this probability approaches $dH(y)$ and the average value of the random variable in this interval approaches y. The expectation of the random variable is obtained by 'summing' over the probability-weighted y-values:

$$Ey = \int_{-\infty}^{\infty} y \, dH(y).$$

Two random variables x and y are independent when the distribution functions $G(x)$ and $H(y)$ are independent of each other. Independent random variables satisfy $E(xy) = Ex \, Ey$:

$$E(xy) = \int_{-\infty}^{\infty} \int_{-\infty}^{\infty} xy \, dG(x) \, dH(y)$$
$$= \left[\int_{-\infty}^{\infty} x \, dG(x) \right] \left[\int_{-\infty}^{\infty} y \, dH(y) \right]$$
$$= Ex \, Ey.$$

Stochastic equations

We proceed to derive the equations concerned with the variance and autocorrelations of y_t in the presence of shocks. Since $(1 + a_1 + a_2)Ey = E\epsilon = 0$, the expectation of y_t is $Ey_t = 0$. The variance of y_t is $\sigma_y^2 \equiv Ey_t^2$, the covariance between y_t and y_{t-j} is $E(y_t y_{t-j})$, and the correlation between y_t and y_{t-j} is $\rho_j \equiv E(y_t y_{t-j})/\sigma^2$. The covariance function satisfies

$$E(y_t y_{t-j}) = E(y_{t-j} y_t) = E[y_{t-j} y_{(t-j)+j}] = E(y_t y_{t+j}).$$

Hence, $\rho_j = \rho_{-j}$. From $y_t + a_1 y_{t-1} + a_2 y_{t-2} = \epsilon_t$, we have

$$E(y_t y_{t-j}) + a_1 E(y_{t-1} y_{t-j}) + a_2 E(y_{t-2} y_{t-j}) = E(\epsilon_t y_{t-j}). \qquad \text{(A1.20)}$$

Dividing by σ^2 and making use of the fact that ϵ_t is independent of y_{t-1} and y_{t-2} and that $E(y_{t-1} y_{t-j}) = E[y_t y_{t-(j-1)}]$ and $E(y_{t-2} y_{t-j}) = E[y_t y_{t-(j-2)}]$, one obtains

$$\rho_j + a_1 \rho_{j-1} + a_2 \rho_{j-2} = 0,$$

for all $j > 0$. Setting $j = 1$ and $j = 2$, it follows that

$$\rho_1 = -\frac{a_1}{1 + a_2}, \quad \rho_2 = \frac{a_1^2}{1 + a_2} - a_2, \qquad \text{(A1.21)}$$

where use is made of the symmetry property $\rho_j = \rho_{-j}$. To calculate the variance σ^2 of y_t, set $j = 0$ in equation (A1.20) and notice that $E(\epsilon_t y_t) = \sigma_\epsilon^2$ because ϵ_t is independent of y_{t-1} and y_{t-2}:

$$\sigma^2 = \frac{1}{1 + a_1 \rho_1 + a_2 \rho_2} \sigma_\epsilon^2.$$

Substituting the expressions in (A1.21) for ρ_1 and ρ_2 yields the formula reported in the main text:

$$\sigma^2 = \frac{1 + a_2}{(1 - a_2)[(1 + a_2)^2 - a_1^2]} \sigma_\epsilon^2.$$

Further reading

In this appendix, we have followed Lang (1983: section 4.3) on trigonometric functions, Gandolfo (1996: ch. 5) on non-stochastic second-order difference equations, and Pindyck and Rubinfield (1991: section 16.2) on stochastic second-order difference equations. These sources can be consulted for related material.

Appendix 1

References

Gandolfo, G. (1996). *Economic Dynamics*, 3rd edn. Berlin: Springer.
Lang, S. (1983). *Undergraduate Analysis*. Berlin: Springer.
Pindyck, R. S. and Rubinfield, D. L. (1991). *Econometric Models and Economic Forecasts*, 3rd edn. New York: McGraw-Hill.

The Over-investment Theory

The over-investment theory represented the most prominent theory of business cycles in the pre-Keynes era. Cassel, Hayek, Robertson, Spiethoff, and Wicksell, among others, contributed to the development of the theory.

The analysis of the multiplier accelerator model in Section 2.3 proves that if the Keynesian consumption function is valid, the principle of acceleration alone is sufficient to explain both cumulative upward and downward movements as well as the turning points of aggregate economic activity. Like the multiplier accelerator model, the over-investment theory relies on the principle of acceleration to explain the upswing and the downswing: 'After the upward movement has been started, the acceleration principle explains the rapid absorption of unused factors of production' (Haberler 1937/1941: 103), and vice versa for a downturn. But it offers an independent explanation for the turning points, which is centred around a clear distinction between investment goods industries and consumption goods industries. Most attention is focused on the upper turning point. The over-investment theory emphasizes that projects do not require a one-off investment, but a stream of investment outlays spread over a considerable period of time. During the upswing, as consumption rises and factor markets become tighter, it becomes continually more difficult for firms to finance the investment outlays required to complete still unfinished projects: 'factors of production are enticed away from the higher stages of production [investment goods industries] and employed in the lower stages [consumption goods industries]. The price of labour (wages) and of other mobile means of production, which can be used in various stages and can be transferred from the higher to the lower stages, rises. This involves a rise in money cost, which affects both higher and lower stages of production. But, while in the lower stages demand has risen, this is not true of the higher stages. The collapse of the boom has begun' (Haberler 1937/1941: 50). Firms have to interrupt investment projects before the returns can be reaped. Business profits are squeezed and investment declines: 'it becomes clear that the newly initiated extensions of the structure of production cannot be completed, and the work on the new but incompleted roundabout processes must be discontinued. The investment boom collapses and a large part of the invested capital is lost' (Haberler 1937/1941: 45). Less agreement prevails among the over-investment theorists about the causes of the lower turning point. Spiethoff and Cassel contend that as wages and interest rates fall during the downswing, investment and aggregate production recover. Schumpeter emphasizes that, since the flow of technical inventions (i.e. possible innovations) is relatively smooth and (actual) investment is low, the pool of unused inventions fills up during recessions. Only a few entrepreneurs have the abilities necessary to transform the inventions into marketable innovations. But once they have taken the lead and shown up fields for profitable innovation, many have the ability to follow. Innovation activity rises sharply and initiates the cumulative upswing. Wicksell adds that the recession can be terminated via expansionary monetary policy. Hayek stresses the importance of reductions in the interest rate for the initiation of recovery. In sum, the concurrence of falling factor prices and promising investment opportunities paves the way for the recovery.

Many observers hold that the US recession of 2001 is a good example of such an over-investment cycle, initiated by excessive investment in information technology during the ten-year long expansion of 1991–2001.

Further reading

The exposition here follows Haberler's (1937/1941) brilliant account of the over-investment theory. Hansen (1964) provides an alternative treatment. The central positions of many pre-Keynesian business cycle theorists are summarized in Persons (1927).

References

Haberler, G. (1st edn 1937/cited edn 1941). *Prosperity and Depression.* Geneva: League of Nations.
Hansen, A. H. (1964). *Business Cycles and National Income* (expanded edn). New York: W.W. Norton.
Persons, W. M. (1927). 'Theories of Business Fluctuations: I. A Classification of the Theories'. *Quarterly Journal of Economics,* 41: 94–128.

Exercises

A2.1 Two-period investment projects and the principle of acceleration. Suppose that the completion of investment projects takes two periods. One project started at time $t - 1$ requires one unit of investment at $t - 1$ and κ units of investment at time t. Denote the number of projects started at time t as I_t (neglect autonomous investment, so that $I_t < 0$ is admissible). Assume all projects are completed, and let consumption equal cY_{t-1}. Then,

$$Y_t = cY_{t-1} + I_t + \kappa I_{t-1} + \epsilon_t,$$

where ϵ_t is white noise and reflects autonomous changes in aggregate expenditure. Show: If the number of investment projects started obeys the acceleration principle without a lag ($I_t = v \Delta Y_t$), then

$$Y_t - \frac{c + (\kappa - 1)v}{1 - v} Y_{t-1} + \frac{\kappa v}{1 - v} Y_{t-2} = \frac{1}{1 - v} \epsilon_t.$$

Characterize the range of parameters that give rise to business cycles.

A2.2 Two-period investment projects and changes in factor costs. The goods market condition from the previous problem remains valid. In the wage-setting process, real wages are set as an increasing function of lagged income ($W_t/P_t = \chi Y_{t-1}$), and investment starts now depend on the current real wage rate ($I_t = -v W_t/P_t$). Show:

$$Y_t - (c - v\chi) Y_{t-1} + \kappa v \chi Y_{t-2} = \epsilon_t.$$

Characterize the range of parameters that give rise to business cycles.

A Goodwinian Model

In this appendix, we present a model which emphasizes changes in the income distribution as the driving force behind cycles. The model is loosely based on Goodwin's (1967) model of growth cycles. In Goodwin's (1967) model, cycles are the outcome of the interplay between capacity effects induced by changes in the income distribution and a real wage Phillips curve. Since changes in the income distribution are likely to affect savings and, hence, capacities only very slowly, Solow (1990: 38) contends that '[P]erhaps the Goodwin growth cycle is not a model of the business cycle at all', but rather a model of longer term fluctuations. The model below does not stress capacity effects. Rather, it is assumed *ad hoc* that firms choose to expand output when profits are high, and vice versa. Another caveat is in order. Probably Goodwin's (1967) most important accomplishment was to introduce Lotka-Volterra differential equations to the economics literature. The model presented below, by contrast, uses the stochastic second-order difference equation approach to cycles. So it does not do justice to Goodwin's achievements in nonlinear dynamic economics.

Model

A closed economy is considered. The model has two essential ingredients. First, real wage pressure tends to rise as the economy expands (there is a real wage Phillips curve). Second, aggregate production tends to expand when profits are high, that is, when the real wage rate is low. Formally,

$$\Delta(w_t - p_t) = \chi y_t - \xi_t, \tag{A3.1}$$

$$\gamma \Delta y_t = \pi_t, \tag{A3.2}$$

$$\pi_t = \iota(p_t - w_t), \tag{A3.3}$$

where χ, γ, and ι are positive constants and ξ is white noise. Variations in ξ indicate autonomous changes in the degree of real wage pressure.

Equilibrium

From equation (A3.1), real wages grow or fall, depending on whether aggregate output is above or below $y = 0$, respectively (given that $\xi = 0$). From equations (A3.2) and (A3.3), $\gamma \Delta^2 y = -\iota \Delta (w - p)$. That is, output growth decreases or increases, depending on whether the real wage rate rises or falls, respectively. Taken together, it follows that

$$ y_t - \frac{2\gamma}{\gamma + \iota\chi} y_{t-1} + \frac{\gamma}{\gamma + \iota\chi} y_{t-2} = \frac{\iota}{\gamma + \iota\chi} \xi_t. \qquad (A3.4) $$

Since $\gamma/(\gamma + \iota\chi) < 1$ and

$$ 4\frac{\gamma}{\gamma + \iota\chi} > \left(\frac{2\gamma}{\gamma + \iota\chi} \right)^2 = 4\frac{\gamma}{\gamma + \iota\chi}\frac{\gamma}{\gamma + \iota\chi}, $$

business cycles occur for all χ, γ, and ι.

What is the economic explanation for the cyclical movements of aggregate production? Suppose the economy is in its steady state $y = 0$. Then a wage push shock $\xi_0 > 0$ leads to an output expansion: $y_0 > 0$. Thereafter, no wage push shocks $\xi_t \neq 0$ occur for a while ($t = 1, 2, \ldots$). $y > 0$ implies rising real wages, which in turn imply decreasing rates of output growth ($\Delta^2 y < 0$). So the expansion comes to a halt and output starts to fall. Since y is still positive, the real wage rate does not yet cease to rise. Hence, the recession gains momentum ($\Delta^2 y < 0$), and the economy does not settle down at the steady state $y = 0$, but overshoots into the $y < 0$ region. There, real wages start to decline, so that the rate of output growth, though still negative, increases ($\Delta^2 y > 0$). This explains the lower turning point. During the initial phase of the recovery, real wages continue to fall, since $y < 0$, so output growth accelerates ($\Delta^2 y > 0$). That is why the economy overshoots into the $y > 0$ region, rather than settling down at the steady state. This process repeats with declining amplitudes.

The model is un-Keynesian in that aggregate production is determined on the economy's supply side alone. That is why it is expounded separately in this appendix, although chronologically it would fit in the chapter about Keynesian economics. In order to determine the aggregate price level and the interest rate, the model can be closed with the standard demand-side equations:

$$y_t = -\sigma i_t + \mu g_t,$$
$$m_t - p_t = \phi y_t - i_t/\lambda.$$

The former equation is the IS curve, the latter the LM curve. Given an exogenous sequence of money stocks m_t and given equilibrium aggregate output y_t (determined in (A3.4)), these equations can be solved for i_t and p_t:

$$i_t = (\mu g_t - y_t)/\sigma \quad p_t = m_t - \frac{(1 + \sigma\lambda\phi)y_t - \mu g_t}{\sigma\lambda}.$$

Increases in the stock of money m_t *ceteris paribus* raise prices p_t one-for-one. Increases in government expenditure g_t raise the interest rate i_t and prices p_t. Both monetary policy and fiscal policy are ineffective.

Further reading

A very detailed exposition of Goodwin's (1967) model with many modifications and extensions is in Flaschel (1993).

References

Flaschel, P. (1993). *Macrodynamics: Income Distribution, Effective Demand and Cyclical Growth.* Frankfurt: Peter Lang.

Goodwin, R. M. (1967). 'A Growth Cycle', in C. H. Feinstein (ed.), *Socialism, Capitalism and Economic Growth.* Cambridge: Cambridge University Press, pp. 54–8.

Solow, R. M. (1990). 'Goodwin's Growth Cycle: Reminiscence and Rumination', in K. Velupillai (ed.), *Nonlinear and Multisectoral Macrodynamics: Essays in Honour of Richard Goodwin.* London: Macmillan Press, pp. 31–41.

INDEX

Index

Index